MERCEDES GILBERT

SELECTED GEMS OF POETRY,
COMEDY AND DRAMA

AUNT SARA'S WOODEN GOD

AFRICAN-AMERICAN WOMEN WRITERS, 1910–1940

HENRY LOUIS GATES, JR. *GENERAL EDITOR*

Jennifer Burton *Associate Editor*

MERCEDES GILBERT

SELECTED GEMS OF POETRY, COMEDY AND DRAMA

AUNT SARA'S WOODEN GOD

Introduction by
SUSANNE B. DIETZEL

G.K. HALL & CO.
An Imprint of Simon & Schuster Macmillan
New York

Prentice Hall International
London   Mexico City   New Delhi   Singapore   Sydney   Toronto

G. K. Hall & Co.
An Imprint of Simon & Schuster Macmillan
1633 Broadway
New York, NY 10019

Library of Congress Catalog Card Number: 96-31490

Printed in the United States of America

Printing Number
1 2 3 4 5 6 7 8 9 10

Library of Congress Cataloging-in-Publication Data

Gilbert, Mercedes.
    [Aunt Sara's wooden god]
    Aunt Sara's wooden god : Selected gems of poetry, comedy and drama
Mercedes Gilbert : introduction by Susanne Dietzel.
        p.   cm. — (African-American women writers, 1910-1949)
    ISBN 0-7838-1428-3 (alk. paper)
    1. African-American women—Literary collections. 2. Afro-Americans— Literary
collections.   I. Gilbert, Mercedes.   Selected gems of poetry, comedy and drama.
II. Title.   III. Selected gems of poetry, comedy and drama.   IV. Series.
PS3513.I4265A6 1996
818'.5209—dc20
                                                                        93-31490
                                                                            CIP

This paper meets the requirements of ANSI/NISO Z39.48.1992 (Permanence of Paper).

C O N T E N T S

GENERAL EDITORS' PREFACE

The past decade of our literary history might be thought of as the era of African-American women writers. Culminating in the awarding of the Pulitzer Prize to Toni Morrison and Rita Dove and the Nobel Prize for Literature to Toni Morrison in 1993 and characterized by the presence of several writers—Toni Morrison, Alice Walker, Maya Angelou, and the Delaney Sisters, among others—on the *New York Times* Best Seller List, the shape of the most recent period in our literary history has been determined in large part by the writings of black women.

This, of course, has not always been the case. African-American women authors have been publishing their thoughts and feelings at least since 1773, when Phillis Wheatley published her book of poems in London, thereby bringing poetry directly to bear upon the philosophical discourse over the African's "place in nature" and his or her place in the great chain of being. The scores of words published by black women in America in the nineteenth century—most of which were published in extremely limited editions and never reprinted—have been republished in new critical editions in the forty-volume *Schomburg Library of Nineteenth-Century Black Women Writers*. The critical response to that series has led to requests from scholars and students alike for a similar series, one geared to the work by black women published between 1910 and the beginning of World War Two.

African-American Women Writers, 1910–1940 is designed to bring back into print many writers who otherwise would be unknown to contemporary readers, and to increase the availability of lesser-known texts by established writers who originally published during this critical period in African-American letters. This series implicitly acts as a chronological sequel to the Schomburg series, which focused on the origins of the black female literary tradition in America.

In less than a decade, the study of African-American women's writings has grown from its promising beginnings into a firmly established field in departments of English, American Studies, and African-American Studies. A comparison of the form and function of the original series and this sequel illustrates this dramatic shift. The *Schomburg Library* was published at the cusp of focused academic investigation into the interplay between race and gender. It covered the extensive period from the publication of Phillis Wheatley's *Poems on Various Subjects, Religious and Moral* in 1773 through the "Black Women's Era" of 1890–1910, and was designed to be an inclusive series of the major early texts by black women writers. The Schomburg Library provided a historical backdrop for black women's writings of the 1970s and 1980s, including the works of writers such as Toni Morrison, Alice Walker, Maya Angelou, and Rita Dove.

African-American Women Writers, 1910–1940 continues our effort to provide a new generation of readers access to texts—historical, sociological, and literary—that have been largely "unread" for most of this century. The series bypasses works that are important both to the period and the tradition, but that are readily available, such as Zora Neale Hurston's *Their Eyes Were Watching God*, Jessie Fauset's *Plum Bun* and *There Is Confusion*, and Nella Larsen's *Quicksand and Passing*. Our goal is to provide access to a wide variety of rare texts. The series includes Fauset's two other novels, *The Chinaberry Tree: A Novel of American Life* and *Comedy: American Style*, and Hurston's short play *Color Struck*, since these are not yet widely available. It also features works by virtually unknown writers, such as *A Tiny Spark*, Christina Moody's slim volume of poetry self-published in 1910, and *Reminiscences of School Life, and Hints on Teaching*, written by Fanny Jackson Coppin in the last year of her life (1913), a multi-genre work combining an autobiographical sketch and reflections on trips to England and South Africa, complete with pedagogical advice.

Cultural studies' investment in diverse resources allows the historic scope of the *African-American Women Writers* series to be more focused than the *Schomburg Library* series, which covered works written over a 137-year period. With few exceptions, the authors included in the *African-American Women Writers* series wrote their major works between 1910 and 1940. The texts reprinted include all the works by each particular author that are not otherwise readily obtainable. As a result, two volumes contain works originally published after 1940. The Charlotte Hawkins Brown volume includes her book of etiquette published in 1941, *The Correct Thing To Do—To Say—To Wear*. One of the poetry volumes contains Maggie Pogue Johnson's *Fallen Blossoms*, published in 1951, a compilation of all her previously published and unpublished poems.

Excavational work by scholars during the past decade has been crucial to the development of *African-American Women Writers, 1910–1940*. Germinal bibliographical sources such as Ann Allen Shockley's *Afro-American Women Writers 1746–1933* and Maryemma Graham's *Database of African-American Women Writers* made the initial identification of texts possible. Other works were brought to our attention by scholars who wrote letters sharing their research. Additional texts by selected authors were then added, so that many volumes contain the complete oeuvres of particular writers. Pieces by authors without enough published work to fill an entire volume were grouped with other pieces by genre.

The two types of collections, those organized by author and those organized by genre, bring out different characteristics of black women's writings of the period. The collected works of the literary writers illustrate that many of them were experimenting with a variety of forms. Mercedes Gilbert's volume, for example, contains her 1931 collection *Selected Gems of Poetry, Comedy, and Drama, Etc.*, as well as her 1938 novel *Aunt Sarah's Wooden God*. Georgia Douglas Johnson's volume contains her plays and short stories in addition to her poetry. Sarah Lee Brown Fleming's volume combines her 1918 novel *Hope's Highway* with her 1920 collection of poetry, *Clouds and Sunshine*.

The generic volumes both bring out the formal and thematic similarities among many of the writings and highlight the striking individuality of particular writers. Most of the plays in the volume of one-acts are social dramas whose tragic endings can be clearly attributed to miscegenation and racism. Within the context of these other plays, Marita Bonner's expressionistic theatrical vision becomes all the more striking.

The volumes of *African-American Women Writers, 1910–1940* contain reproductions of more than one hundred previously published texts, including twenty-nine plays, seventeen poetry collections, twelve novels, six autobiographies, five collections of short biographical sketches, three biographies, three histories of organizations, three black histories, two anthologies, two sociological studies, a diary, and a book of etiquette. Each volume features an introduction by a contemporary scholar that provides crucial biographical data on each author and the historical and critical context of her work. In some cases, little information on the authors was available outside of the fragments of biographical data contained in the original introduction or in the text itself. In these instances, editors have documented the libraries and research centers where they tried to find information, in the hope that subsequent scholars will continue the necessary search to find the "lost" clues to the women's stories in the rich stores of papers, letters, photographs, and other primary materials scattered throughout the country that have yet to be fully catalogued.

Many of the thrilling moments that occurred during the development of this series were the result of previously fragmented pieces of these women's histories suddenly coming together, such as Adele Alexander's uncovering of an old family photograph picturing her own aunt with Addie Hunton, the author Alexander was researching. Claudia Tate's examination of Georgia Douglas Johnson's papers in the Moorland-Spingarn Research Center of Howard University resulted in the discovery of a wealth of previously unpublished work.

The slippery quality of race itself emerged during the construction of the series. One of the short novels originally intended for inclusion in the series had to be cut when the family of the author protested that the writer was not of African descent. Another case involved Louise Kennedy's sociological study *The Negro Peasant Turns Inward*. The fact that none of the available biographical material on Kennedy specifically mentioned race, combined with some coded criticism in a review in the *Crisis*, convinced editor Sheila Smith McKoy that Kennedy was probably white.

These women, taken together, began to chart the true vitality, and complexity, of the literary tradition that African-American women have generated, using a wide variety of forms. They testify to the fact that the monumental works of Hurston, Larsen, and Fauset, for example, emerged out of a larger cultural context; they were not exceptions or aberrations. Indeed, their contributions to American literature and culture, as this series makes clear, were fundamental not only to the shaping of the African-American tradition but to the American tradition as well.

Henry Louis Gates, Jr.
Jennifer Burton

PUBLISHER'S NOTE

In the *African-American Women Writers, 1910–1940* series, G. K. Hall not only is making available previously neglected works that in many cases have been long out of print, we are also, whenever possible, publishing these works in facsimiles reprinted from their original editions including, when available, reproductions of original title pages, copyright pages, and photographs.

When it was not possible for us to reproduce a complete facsimile edition of a particular work (for example, if the original exists only as a handwritten draft or is too fragile to be reproduced), we have attempted to preserve the essence of the original by resetting the work exactly as it originally appeared. Therefore, any typographical errors, strikeouts, or other anomalies reflect our efforts to give the reader a true sense of the original work.

We trust that these facsimile and reprint editions, together with the new introductory essays, will be both useful and historically enlightening to scholars and students alike.

INTRODUCTION

BY SUSANNE B. DIETZEL

Mercedes Gilbert, the author of *Selected Gems of Poetry, Comedy and Drama* and *Aunt Sara's Wooden God*, was not only a writer of fiction, poetry, and plays, but also a well-known Broadway actress, newspaper writer, composer/songwriter, and performer during the Twenties, Thirties, and Forties in New York City. During her multifaceted career of more than thirty years Gilbert composed numerous songs, managed a jazz orchestra, authored one novel, wrote poetry, took her one-woman show on the road, and provided the local black theatre with plenty of material. Little is known, however, about this multitalented woman; few of her writings have survived and her publications have been relegated to literary obscurity. The rediscovery of Mercedes Gilbert by the Afro-American Novel Project[1] and the subsequent publication of Gilbert's writings in this collection thus serve the dual purpose of reconstructing the literary heritage of African-American women and of reintroducing to both scholars and readers of African-American literature a woman who for almost thirty years actively and in various ways contributed to the production of African-American culture.

Born in 1889 in Jacksonville, Florida, Gilbert began her literary career at any early age. In her autobiographical essay Gilbert writes that "At the age of six I wrote my first poem, followed by many little verses. I recited these verses of my own authorship on any occasion that arose, these were many as my mother was an ardent worker in the church (African Methodist Episcopal)."[2] Educated at home and in private schools, Gilbert was the daughter of African-American middle-class business people, who provided their daughter with the necessary education to ensure her a successful future.[3] She graduated from Edward Waters College in Jacksonville with the intention of becoming a teacher. She taught school while in southern Florida, but reentered college to get a nursing degree. Despite her busy schedule as a schoolteacher, nursing student, and nursing superintendent, the writing of poetry and plays remained a priority in Gilbert's life. During these years she wrote and produced several plays in Florida and also worked on a book of poetry she tentatively entitled *Looking Backward*.

In 1916 Gilbert moved to New York City with the intention of becoming a city nurse. However, she soon found out that she needed more training, and instead of enrolling in yet another nursing program at a teaching hospital, she became a private nurse. It was in New York that she made acting, performing, and writing her lifetime vocation. During her early years there Gilbert began to collaborate with songwriter Chris Smith in setting her poems to music. "The Also Ran Blues," "The Decatur Street Blues," and the "Got the World in a Jug Blues" are just some of the popular songs she composed. Many of her songs were recorded by a jazz orchestra and distributed by the record label Arto Records, a company that specialized in contemporary music and featured many African-American musicians. Due to the success of her compositions, she was asked to manage a blues and jazz band for Arto. She continued to write her own songs for the vaudeville stage and also participated in various vaudeville shows with "a singing, talking, and dancing act."[4]

During this time Gilbert also got her start in the movies. She began her acting career in the "all Negro pictures" *The Call of His People* (1922) and *Secret Sorrow* (1922), produced by the Reol moving picture company. In terms of African-American film history, her most famous performance was alongside Paul Robeson—in his film debut—in Oscar Micheaux's silent movie *Body and Soul* (1924). Gilbert returned to movie acting in 1939 when she performed in the talking picture *Moon over Harlem*.

In the mid-to-late Twenties Mercedes Gilbert concentrated on becoming a stage actress. She made her stage debut in 1927 as "Mammy Dinah" in *The Lace Petticoat*, a musical comedy about "old New Orleans" in which she was one of the few black performers. Given the popularity of musical comedies with black casts in the 1920s, Mercedes Gilbert was able to maintain steady work on the New York stage.[5] In 1929 she performed in *Bomboola*, a "unique Afro-American musical comedy," and *Malinda*. Both of these musical comedies featured skits and specialty numbers, and followed an already familiar plot that chronicled the journey of a black showgirl trying to make a career in the nightclubs of Harlem. Gilbert's most steady employment came in 1930 as Zipporah, the wife of Moses, in *The Green Pastures*—a role she played for five years, both on Broadway and on tour. *The Green Pastures*, an enormously successful play based on the collection of short stories *Old Adam and His Chillun* by New Orleans writer Roark Bradford and adapted for the stage by Marc Connelly, was, like many Broadway productions of the time, extremely stereotypical in its portrayal of African Americans. Perhaps as a response to the stereotypical portrayal of black Americans and their religion, Gilbert wrote a satire appropriately entitled *In Greener Pastures*. This one-act play was performed by the Harlem YMCA in 1938.[6]

Yet Gilbert's acting and stage career extended far beyond the period of the Harlem Renaissance, continuing until her death in 1952. Though work often was hard to get, especially for black performers, Gilbert was able to maintain fairly steady employment during the Depression years. In 1935, for example, she appeared in the Broadway drama *Play, Genius, Play*. In 1936 Gilbert assumed the female lead in Langston Hughes's Broadway success *Mulatto*, which had opened the year before, after the leading actress Rose McClendon fell ill. Gilbert was extremely proud of her accomplishment in *Mulatto*: "I learned the part, which was the star role, and very long, from saturday [sic] afternoon to Monday, and played the role for one year on Broadway, and seven months on tour."[7] Gilbert's performance was lauded in the *Amsterdam News*, which wrote that she "carried on, lifting the play to the heights of art and making of the play an incisive, heart-gripping, never-to-be-forgotten contribution to the American drama."[8] During the Thirties and Forties she performed in *How Come, Lawd* (1937), a production of the Negro Theatre Guild, in Lillian

Hellman's plays *The Searching Wind* (1935) and *The Little Foxes* (1939), alongside Katherine Dunham in *Carib Song* (1945), "a musical comedy of the West Indies," and as a cast member of the all-black productions of *Lysistrata* (1946) and *Tobacco Road* (1950).

Though work on the Broadway stage seems to have kept her busy, Gilbert also pursued an independent, Off-Off Broadway career and continually expanded her artistic repertoire. In 1941 she made her debut as a performer, starring in her own "one woman theatre" where she presented her own material. Performing her own sketches was a welcome change for Gilbert, who had grown tired of playing "the too often maid parts we Negro actresses are relegated to."[9] In 1946 she revived her one-woman show and toured the United States and Canada in a performance that combined music, comedy, drama, monologues, sketches, and impersonations.

Outside of her acting, both on and Off Broadway, Mercedes Gilbert was deeply involved in service to the community. Her plays *Environment*, *In Greener Pastures*, and *Ma Johnson's Harlem Rooming House* and other sketches were performed in black neighborhood theatres such as the Harlem YMCA. Her one-woman show debuted at the St. Martin's Community Theatre in New York and then traveled to black college campuses. She also wrote a newspaper column for the Associated Negro Press; lectured to college audiences on black history; wrote and narrated "The Cavalcade of the American Negro," a recording on black history; and was active in African-American scholarly associations. In 1938, for example, she entertained the annual meeting of the Association for the Study of Negro Life and History with a dramatic reading of "The Creation."[10]

Gilbert passed away on March 1, 1952.

* * * * *

Today, silence surrounds the literary and stage career of Mercedes Gilbert. Like many female predecessors and contemporaries, Gilbert's literary and artistic contributions to African-American culture have been forgotten, obscured, and relegated to the literary margins. Even though Langston Hughes wrote a preface to *Aunt Sara's Wooden God* praising the novel as "an authentic every-day story of thousands of little families below the Mason-Dixon line," and despite her frequent presence on the Broadway stage, which led the *New York Times* to call her, in her obituary, "a well-known Negro Actress who had appeared in many Broadway productions and also on radio and television . . .,"[11] a recognition of Gilbert's overall achievement is missing from African-American literary history in general, the black female literary tradition in particular, and histories of black film and stage performers.[12]

The same holds true for her participation in the Harlem Renaissance. Her presence in 1920s movies and on the New York stage, as well as her literary activities at the time, should make her a participant—albeit a rather silent or silenced one—in this literary and cultural movement. Though she might not have participated in the salon culture of the Renaissance or submitted her work to *The Crisis* or *Opportunity* and thus made the acquaintance of Alain Locke or Jessie Fauset, the poems and monologues in *Selected Gems* were surely written during the period of the Harlem Renaissance. Though we cannot ascertain the exact writing dates of the material assembled in *Selected Gems* and none of it seems to have been previously published, it corresponds stylistically and thematically to the writings and aesthetic principles of the Renaissance. Her dialect and lyric poetry, monologues (or what she calls comedy), and the play *Environment* echo many of the themes that were central to Harlem Renaissance writers, particularly its female participants.[13] Addressing herself to an African-American audience—an audience of insiders—Mercedes Gilbert focuses on everyday African-American culture and the life of the folk, situates characters in their cultural and historical terrain, tackles the American race problem head on, and celebrates black cultural expressions as a source for "authentic" African-American art—all trademarks of the Harlem Renaissance. Her 1938 novel, *Aunt Sara's Wooden God*, similarly continues many of the themes and preoccupations central to the Harlem Renaissance.

Gilbert's writing not only successfully straddles the time frame usually allotted to the Harlem Renaissance, but also shows the influence of the literary styles and artistic concerns of the Thirties.

In continuing to write about the black folk, Mercedes Gilbert squarely fits into the literary landscape of the 1930s when a preoccupation with documenting "authentic" American culture was noticeable all across the literary spectrum.[14] Interest in the rural South and African-American history in general—as evidenced by the writers of the white Southern Renaissance, the work of the photographers of the WPA, and the sociological studies undertaken by both black and white sociologists and anthropologists, as well as the novels of Zora Neale Hurston, George Wylie Henderson, Langston Hughes, and Wallace Thurman—was very much a part of this rediscovery of an "authentic" American and African-American culture. *Aunt Sara's Wooden God* participates in this trend not only by its Southern setting, but also by its focus on the folk and its social milieu, the cultural practices that have nourished black Southerners through American history, and a careful analysis of the intricate web of Southern race relations.

A closer look at the writings collected in this volume will show that Mercedes Gilbert was not only a multitalented woman writer, performer, and actress who actively participated in the production of African-American culture, but also an astute observer of and commentator on the cultural environment in which she lived. As a writer Gilbert is primarily concerned with correcting the misrepresentations of African Americans that she encountered on the Broadway stage in particular and in the dominant culture in general, offering instead an inside and corrective view of African Americans and their expressive culture. Gilbert's writings directly challenge the tradition of (mis)representing blacks on the mainstream stage and the commodification of African-American culture during the Twenties and beyond. We can argue that her efforts at revising misrepresentations of African-American life grow directly out of her work as an actress on the New York stage where the range of roles available to her was extremely limited.[15]

Mercedes Gilbert began her stage career at an opportune time for black performers. Following a hiatus for African-American actors after the demise of the so-called Chitlin' Circus, the demand for black characters on Broadway during the Twenties increased due to a growing interest in black folk culture and music after the immense commercial success of the all-black musical revue

Shuffle Along (1921). By the mid-Twenties all-black musical comedies had become a frequent presence on Broadway and offered steady employment and a fertile training ground for many black actors and actresses. As Cary Wintz observes, "By the middle of the decade an extravagant musical production featuring black singers and dancers was one of the formulas for commercial success on Broadway."[16] Often written by white authors for a predominantly white audience, these highly successful plays may have tried to interpret the lives and culture of African Americans sympathetically, but in harking back to the (white) minstrel tradition, they did so stereotypically and often negatively, portraying African Americans as exotic, primitive, childlike, fun-loving, and simple, and as characters who shuffled, danced, and sang their way across the stage. Although these plays drew freely on the black musical tradition and highlighted selected aspects of the black experience in America, they grossly misrepresented, if not distorted and falsified, the experiences, culture, and history of African Americans. As such, these plays ultimately reinforced white hegemony and racist representations of African Americans by typecasting black actresses and actors in roles that only selectively portrayed the realities of African-American life. This underlying attitude toward African Americans and their culture is best epitomized in the *New York Times* reviewer's comments on *The Green Pastures*: "In eighteen scenes it follows the chronicle of biblical history as ignorant religious negroes of the South might conceive it in childish terms of their personal experience. . . . the fusion of all the dumb, artless hopes of an ignorant people whose simple faith sustains them."[17] While an independent black theatre was in its developing stages, roles for black performers on the mainstream stage were mostly limited to these musical comedies and the oftentimes exotic, primitivistic, and simplistic parts that reduced black subjectivity to essentialist and racist formulae. Sterling Brown sums up the portrayal of African Americans on the 1920s Broadway stage: "Broadway, for all of its growing liberal attitude, is still entrenched with the stereotype of the exotic primitive, the comic stooge and the tragic mulatto."[18]

It is these portrayals and misrepresentations that Mercedes Gilbert contests and revises in her poems, plays, novel, and possibly also in her independent performances. While much of African-American writing can be seen to engage in exactly the same revisionist project, Gilbert's revisions seem even more significant and personally relevant, given that her work on the Broadway stage forced her to portray African Americans in extremely stereotypical, patronizing, and ridiculing roles. A closer look at Gilbert's writings will show that they can be seen as direct responses to the type of shows in which she participated and the parts generally available to black actors and actresses. In fact, it can be argued that she tried to do in her fiction what she could not do in her acting—portray African Americans nonstereotypically, casting a human face on the stock characters of the Broadway stage, adding human complexity to those characters, celebrating those aspects of black speech that were often reduced to generic dialect on the stage, and recovering those cultural practices that were either reduced or discarded altogether from dominant representations. The poems, monologues, and the play collected in *Selected Gems* as well as *Aunt Sara's Wooden God* can thus be viewed as an attempt to set the slanted representations of African Americans on Broadway straight. A focus on lyric poetry, an emphasis on racial prejudice and the effects of racism on African Americans, dignified and respectful portrayals of black Southern rural life, and complex characters who possess a full humanity—complete with inner struggles, hopes, and feelings—are just some of the literary strategies and themes Gilbert employs in her revision of the misrepresentations she encountered on the stage and that pervaded American culture then and now.

* * * * *

Divided into three sections, the writings collected in *Selected Gems of Poetry, Comedy and Drama* offer insight into the wide range of Mercedes Gilbert's talents and skills as a writer. Gilbert is a versatile poet and brings together many literary influences and styles. The poems collected here reflect myriad traditional genres, styles, and themes, and range from the more personal and introspective lyrical poem to the narrative folk poem or ballad that expresses a communal sensibility. In subject matter and style,

Gilbert fits squarely into a long tradition of African-American women poets. Not unlike the poetry of her nineteenth-century predecessors, most noticeably Francis Ellen Watkins Harper, many of Gilbert's poems, both in dialect and standard English, are informed by Christian ethics and carry a strong moral message. Her poems in standard English often are uplifting, if not didactic, in style and theme. They celebrate God's providence, display faith and pride in the race, advocate perseverance and faith in Christianity in the face of adversity, give advice, and even promote temperance. Her dialect poems, on the other hand, are folk poems that proudly celebrate African-American culture, history, and language. Gilbert is at her best in comedy, where she brings to life the vibrant speech patterns and linguistic versatility of black English and adds her name to a long list of African-American storytellers, humorists, and comediennes.

Like many of her female predecessors both of the Harlem Renaissance and the nineteenth century, Gilbert only rarely addresses race and racial prejudice in her poems. When she does, however, her poems speak with a quiet sense of urgency and argue for recognition and respect. The dialect poem "That's a Fact" (36), for example, not only indicts racism for keeping black men from achieving more in their lives, but also critiques the lack of respect and recognition black soldiers received during World War I. The same ethos pervades the poem "Li'l Black Boy" (12). A poem of affirmation, "Li'l Black Boy" celebrates blackness and black subjectivity as a manifestation of God's blessing and benevolence toward African Americans, instead of seeing these qualities as the curse of Ham.

> Dey say man's made in God's image,
> When I look at you I know it's true.
> 'Cause I can see his own great spirit,
> Jes as plain 'er shinin' through. (12)

Corresponding to the Christian ethics and sense of justice that characterize many of her poems, Gilbert argues that men ought to be judged not by the color of their skin, but by the quality of their characters and the "greatness" of their hearts.

Many of her traditional poems also resemble the poetry of her contemporaries such as Georgia Douglas Johnson, Anne Spencer, and Alice Dunbar-Nelson. Gilbert's overall philosophy is best expressed in "True Worth" (11), the poem that opens *Selected Gems*. "It is only the soul,/That has 'true worth'" epitomizes her concern with the spiritual wholeness and survival of the African-American humanity. Most of her poems are quiet, sometimes personal, meditations on life and Christianity, such as "I Am So Small" (15) and "The Game of Life" (19), and what we might today call daily affirmations, such as "The Stream of Life" (21). Even though these poems seem on first reading to be about "universal," and thus "raceless," themes, they powerfully recover and affirm a black humanity and sensibility that found absolutely no expression in the dominant popular culture during that time. These poems can be read as poems of inspiration designed to model proactive ways to deal with discrimination and racism and to empower readers.

Whereas most of her poems are primarily written in traditional style and meter and in standard English, reflecting the influence of the personal nature of lyrical poetry and addressing themselves to more universal themes, the other writings assembled in *Selected Gems* proudly reflect the influence of African-American vernacular and oral culture. These poems and monologues show Mercedes Gilbert as a writer who embraces folk culture and who draws on African-American oral and literary traditions to write for and about her people. Narrative folk poems such as "How Liza Saved the Deacon" (13), "My Dear John's Place" (18), and "Amanda Jackson's Tea" (23), as well as monologues such as "I'm Glad I Ain't No Hand to Talk" (43), "Outside O' Dat We Had a Wonderful Time" (47), and "Ain't Men Deceitful?" (49), are prime examples of the stylistic and thematic versatility of the African-American storytelling tradition, a cultural practice that has nourished black Americans since their arrival in America. Many of these poems and monologues were written to be read aloud or acted out with the specific purpose of entertaining and amusing an audience.[19] Inspired by and imitating black speech patterns, particularly gossip and the day-to-day conversations or street banter of ordinary people, these poems and monologues draw on the interactive quality of much oral African-American literature and emphasize its communal sensibility and interactive function.

Focusing on love, gossip, and perseverance, these dramatized renditions of the everyday feature speakers and personae that were often absent from the Broadway stage. As such, Gilbert's folk characters defy the stereotypical portrayals of African Americans like the loose and exotic showgirl, the devout but ignorant preacher, and the self-effacing Mammy, the only character roles available to African-American actors and actresses at the time. Gilbert's personae testify to the diversity of black subjectivity and add to the portrayal of African Americans within the black literary tradition. And Gilbert's cast of characters is indeed a wide one, ranging from widowed preachers to petty widows, zealous mothers, gamblers, showgirls, and members of the black bourgeoisie. These characters are portrayed humorously, yet sympathetically, lovingly, and respectfully. Poking fun at their sometimes obnoxious and cunning behavior, Gilbert affirms blackness by celebrating black speech patterns, such as signifying, toasting, and playing the dozens.

In terms of subject matter, Gilbert also departs from the musical comedies of the period, with their shallow and predictable plots, and allows her characters to introduce a wide range of topics. Monologues such as "A Talk on Evolution" (40), "The Air Was Made for Birds" (51), and "Why Adam Ate the Apple" (42) humorously ponder epistemological, ontological, and theological questions such as the origin of the human species and the nature and origin of flying, and cast the Temptation and the Fall from Grace stories in a contemporary and innovative light. In their broad range of topics that cover both African-American life and broad philosophical themes, these monologues and poems are written in the tradition of James Weldon Johnson's folk sermon, and correspond to Langston Hughes's Simple stories, the narratives collected in Zora Neale Hurston's *Mules and Men* (1935), and Arna Bontemps and Langston Hughes's *The Book of Negro Folklore* (1958).

In her play *Environment* Gilbert leaves the terrain of folkloristic humor and moves on to social realism. The play continues

Gilbert's efforts to rewrite the portrayal of African Americans for the stage and also shows how she participated in the development of independent black theatre by writing realistic plays about Negro life. While *Environment* may not be remembered for its dialogue, plot, or dramatic potential, it is nevertheless noteworthy in its sharp departure from the musical comedies of the period. In its subject matter, setting, and tone *Environment* follows Du Bois's 1926 vision for a black theatre that demanded that black drama be "About us. . . . By us. . . . For us. . . . [and] Near us,"[20] and continues the focus on female characters introduced in the drama of black women playwrights from the Harlem Renaissance such as Georgia Douglas Johnson, Angela Weld Grimké, and Mary Burrill.[21] As a play that tries realistically to depict the lives and social conditions of the black urban working class, *Environment* also follows Wallace Thurman's drama *Harlem* (1929) and anticipates the realistic plays of the 1940s and 1950s such as Theodore Ward's *Big White Fog* (1938) and Lorraine Hansberry's *A Raisin in the Sun* (1959).

Whereas most of the plays written by black playwrights during the Twenties were folk plays set in the rural South, *Environment* introduces an urban setting.[22] This three-act play chronicles the painful descent of a Southern migrant family into urban poverty, crime, and drug addiction and their heroic efforts to escape this vicious cycle.[23] Gilbert meets Du Bois's challenge for realism head on by focusing on some of the many problems that faced recent Southern migrants to Harlem. *Environment* frankly blames the inhospitable conditions and economic situation of the urban North for the economic and moral decline of the Williams family. Instead of celebrating Harlem as an exotic place of entertainment and merriment, as many (white-authored) plays of the Twenties did, *Environment* introduces us to the seedier and far more destructive side of the "Negro capital of the world." Gilbert takes a critical look at the supposed benefits of migration and expresses extreme skepticism of Harlem and the supposed freedom and economic opportunity found there; it is migration and the false glamour of the city that leads the Williams family into decline, or as one of her characters exclaims: "It's these environments that's got him" (77). Solutions to these problems are only found in Christian perseverance, family cohesiveness, education, and a return to the South.

Environment is by far the most socially conscious and overtly critical of the texts brought together here. Whereas Gilbert's poetry, comedy, and novel only subtly hint at racism, economic disenfranchisement, and discrimination, the play openly blames these forces for the family's downfall. Yet Gilbert's social criticism does not stop here; she is equally critical of members of the black bourgeoisie and middle class who ensnare poor and unemployed blacks into their shady deals and often make them unwilling participants in criminal schemes.

The writings in *Selected Gems* serve as a good introduction to Mercedes Gilbert's literary skills, her versatility as a writer, her major themes and characters, and her moral vision. As a collection of poems and sketches, however, *Selected Gems* only provides glimpses into Gilbert's literary landscape. In her subsequent publication, the novel *Aunt Sara's Wooden God* (1938), Gilbert was able to develop in more detail the issues she had only hinted at in her poems, comedy, and play.

Published to few and mixed reviews, Gilbert's novel continues many of the themes already introduced in her previous writings.[24] Here Gilbert portrays ordinary African Americans—black Southern peasants in this case—whose urban counterparts she had already developed in her folk poetry and monologues. A sustained appreciation of black speech and humor, as well as a celebration and careful delineation of black folk culture and folkways—particularly the cultural practices and social functions of the black church but also the communal rituals that forge and maintain community—further round out the picture of African Americans and African-American life she began to paint in *Selected Gems*.

Some themes, however, are new to Gilbert's fictional universe. Like many other African-American writers before her, Gilbert draws on the stigma of miscegenation and the dramatic potential of the tragic mulatto as structuring elements for her plot. Focusing on the complicated lives of Sara Lou Carter, or Aunt Sara, as she is lovingly called by everyone in her small Georgia community, and her two sons, William and Jim, Gilbert's novel offers an in-depth portrayal of a family affected by miscegenation and the intricate workings of color prejudice and the ways in which it goes unchallenged and is perpetuated, as well as the daily racism black Southerners encounter.

In one of the few assessments of the text, Hugh Gloster has noted that as a novel about miscegenation and color prejudice, *Aunt Sara's Wooden God* "is neither bitter nor preoccupied with racial issues."[25] Though these issues form the center of the novel, they are told from a sympathetic, if not understanding, perspective. *Aunt Sara's Wooden God* is never judgmental; instead of blaming individual characters caught in a history of miscegenation and color prejudice, the novel empathetically illustrates the denial, deception, and pain caused by them. Unlike the more "angry" fictions or "social protest novels" of the Thirties and Forties, Gilbert does not paint a picture of resistance and confrontation, but rather one of quiet suffering and endurance, illustrating exactly the qualities of forgiveness, perseverance, and faith in Christianity she advocated in her poetry. *Aunt Sara's Wooden God* thus becomes a spiritual text; framed by the African-American spiritual "Down by the River Side," the novel encourages forgiveness, understanding, and sympathy for the complex and conflicted lives of the characters, who are caught in the web of Southern history and racism and the denial and deception this history engenders.

Aunt Sara's Wooden God also departs from other African-American novels usually associated with the Thirties and Forties. Unlike the fiction of Richard Wright, Richard Attaway, and Ann Petry, Gilbert's text is by no means a protest or propaganda novel. Though realistic in tone—Hugh Gloster in fact groups the novel under the rubric "folk realism"—*Aunt Sara's Wooden God* is very much a female regionalist or "local color" novel. As Langston Hughes pointed out in his Preface, *Aunt Sara's Wooden God* most closely resembles the writings of Gilbert's fellow Southerners Zora Neale Hurston and George Wylie Henderson, authors who have frequently been classified as local color or regional writers. Yet, Gilbert's novel also shares similarities with the regionalist writings of nineteenth- and early-twentieth-century white women writers such as Sarah Orne Jewett, Kate Chopin, and Mary Wilkins

Freeman. Intent on illustrating the folkways of their region or locale, these women writers, like Gilbert, emphasized the feminine virtues of domesticity, love, and a belief in Christianity.[26] In Gilbert's text, however, these virtues are rooted in concrete historical and cultural circumstances that complicate the focus on female identity usually featured in the regionalist text.

Aunt Sara's Wooden God also continues Gilbert's project of rewriting or revising hegemonic representations of African Americans. With its focus on the life-sustaining energy of the black church, *Aunt Sara's Wooden God* can be read as a revision of *The Green Pastures* and in its focus on miscegenation, as a response to Langston Hughes's play *Mulatto*. The novel was published only three years after Gilbert concluded her engagement with *The Green Pastures* and two years after she played Cora, the female lead in Hughes's highly successful play about miscegenation. If *The Green Pastures* used an imaginary black version of Christianity to illustrate and dramatize scenes from the Old Testament, *Aunt Sara's Wooden God* contests Connelly's picture of black religion by focusing on the actual practice of black Christianity among black Southerners and its function in their emotional and social lives. Furthermore, if Hughes's play radically rewrote traditional representations of the tragic mulatto theme by staging an emotional and violent confrontation between the mulatto and his white father in which the father is accidentally killed, Gilbert's novel returns to older versions of the theme and concentrates on the effects of miscegenation on a whole family as well as the conflicted nature of the tragic mulatto himself. *Aunt Sara's Wooden God* thus goes back to nineteenth-century models of the theme and offers in-depth and emotional, though at times melodramatic and sentimental, character studies of both the black mother and her biracial son, and offers a perspective on the Southern society in which they make their living.

One strategy of revision is Gilbert's focus on "authentic" folkways. Like her contemporary and fellow Floridian Zora Neale Hurston, Gilbert introduces us to a black community rich in folk culture and folklore. Gilbert also shares with Hurston a nostalgic representation of the rural South.[27] Both writers lived in the urban North, but figuratively returned to the landscapes of their youth and adolescence in their fiction. In *Aunt Sara's Wooden God* this landscape is represented as pastoral, imbued with innocence and bliss, and brings forth neighborly cooperation, Christian faith, and, of course, a rich folk culture—exactly those qualities whose loss the characters in her play *Environment* bemoan. The novel's pastoralism is reinforced by the stark contrast Gilbert establishes between the country and the city. Reminiscent of her description of New York in *Environment*, the Georgia town of Macon is represented as an almost allegorical sin city:

> The streets were filled with strangers, their dirty, sweaty overalls sticking to their bodies, as they loitered around Broad Street, filling up on White Mule, playing pool and Georgia Skin or dancing in Daddy Jenks' back room to rancorous tinpanny music. (110)

Here people are led into temptation, Christian virtues are easily abandoned in favor of more worldly pursuits, crime is inevitable, and a nourishing folk culture gives way to a debased mass culture. Gambling, drinking, and prostitution lead characters such as William, his cousin Sissy, his co-worker Slippery, the Chicago blues singer Ethel, and the gambler Sugar Kid into crime, addiction, financial ruin, and moral degeneration. Measured against Macon, the agrarian countryside does indeed appear as a site of pastoral innocence and bliss:

> Byron was beautiful with its velvet-like green grass in which nestled wild pansies and violets. The smell of young pines filled the air with a clean sweetness, as the busy farmers tilled their soil, stopping in the heat of the day to sprawl beneath the welcome shade of trees. (217)

These innocent descriptions of country life, however, are not as peaceful as they appear, for the pastoral South is also a landscape inscribed by the history of slavery, white supremacy, and racism that indelibly shapes individual characters, local customs, and race relations. Under the veneer of innocence and rural bliss are hidden the sexual exploitation of slave women and the specter of miscegenation that still cast their shadow over the countryside.

Gilbert's characters are firmly situated, if not to say trapped, within that history of slavery and miscegenation that goes back for generations; it is a history that has shaped and continues to shape the lives of the Carter family, adding complexity and drama to their otherwise "simple" lives. Aunt Sara herself is the product of a long line of black women who have borne the mulatto children of their slave masters or employers; it is, however, "a past that was filled with things she would have loved to forget" (114). This history turns the countryside into a place of deception, denial, and crime, not unlike the debauched city.

As one who has transgressed racial boundaries, Aunt Sara embodies the burdens of African-American and Southern history and has to live daily with the pain brought on by this history. The stigma of miscegenation in her small community forces Aunt Sara to lead a life of denial and deception, and in order to protect her son she never reveals to him the secret of his conception. Because she feels that William "would always walk in the middle of the road, not being able to get a firm footing on either side" (114), she elevates him to the status of her "wooden God and cornstalk Jesus." This protective worship of William produces enormous conflict for both Aunt Sara and her two sons. For example, William receives preferential treatment and monetary support and is groomed for the ministry, whereas Aunt Sara's "legitimate" son, Jim, is relegated to becoming the farmer his father was. William is portrayed as the typical tragic mulatto; torn by inner conflicts—his calling to the ministry and his love for gambling and other vices of the city—and duplicitous by nature, William wreaks havoc on every family member and even sets up his brother, Jim, for a crime. Jim, on the other hand, extends the same protective worship to his mother that she extends toward William; to shield his mother from the transgressions of her "wooden God," Jim serves a sentence on the Georgia chain gang and is only freed when the white plantation owner intervenes on his behalf.

Yet, despite its rather tragic plot, *Aunt Sara's Wooden God* is a novel that affirms African Americans and their culture. Like Gilbert's poetry and sketches, the novel testifies to and celebrates the life-sustaining energy of African-American folk culture, particularly the strength of the black community, which is held together not only by a shared history and attachment to place, but also by deep bonds of neighborly and sisterly affection, common social rituals, institutions, and cultural practices. This is manifest in the love and care Aunt Sara gives to orphans, sick and dying neighbors, friends, and her extended family, a love that they, in return, give to her. The glue that holds together this rural community of hardworking farmers is black Christianity and the black church, a cultural institution that provides the congregation with a sense of mission, vision, and community cohesiveness. It is the power of religion that enables Aunt Sara and her son Jim to go on and deal with the pain of miscegenation and unacknowledged color prejudice. It is from Christianity and the fellowship the church provides them that they draw their moral strength, so that Jim can forgive his brother for setting him up for a crime.

While character and plot development are not necessarily Gilbert's strengths as a writer, she has a keen eye for detail and an ear for black speech and dialogue. Folk customs, such as the potions the local root doctor prescribes, folk wisdom, dietary practices, prayers, and spirituals are meticulously recorded in the novel to situate her characters in an authentic environment. Gilbert is once again at her best when she adds humor to her portrayal of characters and recovers themes and dramatic structures from her earlier poems and comedies in *Selected Gems*. Characters such as Sally Ann and Martha, the constantly fighting and bickering members of the Church Aid Society, for example, add comic relief to this otherwise tragic and melodramatic story. Humor is also an integral part of her portrayal of the black church, which adds to the fullness of the church's representation and the significance she assigns to the institution. Her church and prayer scenes, apart from conveying the importance religion and religious ritual play in the life of the community, with loving humor portray exhorting preachers, a devout and responsive congregation, and the occasional church member who falls asleep during the more than two-hour service.

The same holds true for Gilbert's description of Daddy Jenks's juke joint and the singing, dancing, and gambling that goes on there. Her vivid descriptions of the card game between Daddy Jenks, William, and the Sugar Kid are extremely captivating and effectively convey the fascination the game holds for William and the other gamblers (chap. 7).

The writings of Mercedes Gilbert collected here will prove to be a worthwhile addition to the African-American literary canon in general and the black women's literary tradition in particular. The republication of her works will fill in some of the gaps in the already rich tapestry of early-to-mid-twentieth-century African-American women writers and allow for new and innovative assessments of black cultural production during that period. Gilbert's love and respect for her subjects—whether in her poetry, monologues, play, or novel—make her a powerful literary foremother of the contemporary African-American women writers who have inaugurated the rediscovery of their predecessors. A closer analysis of Gilbert's writings, as well as her career as an actress and cultural worker in New York City, will certainly shed further light on our understanding of the wide range of women's poetry from the Harlem Renaissance, our appreciation and knowledge of black humor and storytelling, and the participation of black women in the vibrant culture of New York and Harlem. *Aunt Sara's Wooden God*, when considered in the context of other black Southern writers of the period, should change our understanding of the black literary landscape of the Thirties and force us to reassess the dynamics of black female literary production in general.

NOTES

I would like to thank Maryemma Graham, David Rae Morris, and Polly Pagenhart for their helpful suggestions and criticisms, friendship, and support during the writing of this introduction. My thanks also go to the staff of the Schomburg Center for Research in Black Culture for sending me their Mercedes Gilbert materials, and the staff of the Newcomb College Center for Research on Women at Tulane University for their hospitality, generosity, and advice.

[1] During the period between 1985 and 1988 I served as a research director for the Afro-American Novel Project that began at the University of

Mississippi. Conceived by Maryemma Graham, the project recovered some 1,800 titles by little-known African-American authors. The project relocated to Northeastern University in 1989 as the Project on the History of Black Writing.

[2]Mercedes Gilbert, "Short Autobiography," n.d., n.p. Schomburg Center for Research in Black Culture, Vertical File, Part I.

[3]Her father owned a furniture business and her mother was a dressmaker ("Short Autobiography").

[4]"Short Autobiography," n.p.

[5]For a history of African-American stage actresses, see Jo A. Tanner, *Dusky Maidens: The Odyssey of the Early Black Dramatic Actress* (Westport, CT: Greenwood, 1992).

[6]This text is, to my knowledge, not available.

[7]"Short Autobiography," n.p.

[8]*The New York Amsterdam News*, 8 August 1938 (courtesy of the Schomburg Center).

[9]"Short Autobiography," n.p.

[10]*The Journal of Negro History* 24 (January 1939): 6. My biographical sketch of Mercedes Gilbert has been assembled from the following sources: Bernard Peterson, *Early Black American Playwrights and Dramatic Writers* (New York: Greenwood, 1990); Edward Mapp, *Directory of Blacks in the Performing Arts* (Metuchen, NJ: Scarecrow); Lorraine Elena Roses and Ruth Elizabeth Randolph, *Harlem Renaissance and Beyond: Literary Biographies of 100 Black Women Writers, 1900–1945* (Boston: G. K. Hall, 1990); reviews of her plays in the *New York Times*; and her short biography.

[11]*New York Times*, 6 March 1952.

[12]Only Hugh Gloster's early study *Negro Voices in American Fiction* and Joel Schraufnagel's *From Apology to Protest* mention Gilbert's novel. Hugh Gloster, *Negro Voices in American Fiction* (Chapel Hill: University of North Carolina Press, 1948), 208–9, 234–5, 241; Joel Schraufnagel, *From Apology to Protest: The Black American Novel* (DeLand, FL: Everett/Edwards, 1973), 18.

[13]For an introduction to Harlem Renaissance women poets and writers, see Maureen Honey, ed. *Shadowed Dreams: Women's Poetry of the Harlem Renaissance* (New Brunswick, NJ: Rutgers University Press, 1989), Gloria Hull, *Color, Sex, & Poetry: Three Women Writers of the Harlem Renaissance* (Bloomington: Indiana University Press, 1987), and Cheryl Wall, "Poets and Versifiers, Singers and Signifiers: Women of the Harlem Renaissance," in Kenneth Wheeler and Virginia Lee Lusser, eds.,

Women, the Arts and the 1920s in Paris and New York (New Brunswick, NJ: Transaction Books, 1982), 74–98.

[14]See Michael E. Staub, *Voices of Persuasion: Politics of Representation in 1930s America* (Cambridge: Cambridge University Press, 1994).

[15]Gilbert's stage career is no exception here. A look at the reviews of the plays in which she participated conforms to her earlier statement that black actresses on Broadway were relegated to the parts of maids. In her first Broadway appearance Gilbert performed the role of Mammy Dinah, in *Lost* she appeared as a Portuguese woman, in *Malinda* and *Bamboola* she appeared in supporting roles to the exotic showgirl, and in the Hellman plays she played the parts of maids.

[16]Cary D. Wintz, *Black Culture and the Harlem Renaissance* (Houston: Rice University Press, 1988), 94.

[17]Brooks Atkinson, "New Negro Drama of Sublime Beauty," *New York Times,* 27 February 1930, 26:1.

[18]Sterling Brown, *Negro Poetry and Drama* (Washington, DC: Associations in Negro Folk Education, 1937), 139.

[19]The monologues assembled in *Selected Gems*, according to the book's dust jacket, were broadcast on the radio and "have always amused and interested all listeners" (quoted in Roses and Randolph, 123).

[20]*Crisis* 32 (July 1926): 134.

[21]See Elizabeth Brown-Guillory, *Their Place on the Stage: Black Women Playwrights in America* (New York: Greenwood, 1988), 1–23.

[22]For a history of black theatre, see Doris E. Abramson, *Negro Playwrights in the American Theatre, 1925–1959* (New York: Columbia University Press, 1969), Loften Mitchell, *The Story of the American Negro in the Theatre* (New York: Hawthorne, 1969), Leslie C. Sanders, *The Development of Black Theatre in America* (Baton Rouge: Louisiana State University Press, 1988), and Samuel A. Hay, *African American Theatre: A Historical and Critical Analysis* (Cambridge: Cambridge University Press, 1994).

[23]Numerous bibliographies list *Environment* as a one-act play.

[24]Arthur Spingarn, for example, wrote that the "plot is good" but "the story would have been more interesting had it been better written" (*Crisis* [February 1939]: 45). The reviewer in the *Journal of Negro Education,* John Lovell, in a rather acerbic review called *Aunt Sara's Wooden God* a novel that lacks "an edge to her story: not necessarily one associated with Negroes as a race, but certainly one sharpened by the inner and outer community she has selected . . . . In spite of all the horror in which propaganda literature is held, Miss Gilbert must have a sociological, as well as a

literary, excuse if she intends to write worth-while fiction about Negroes" *(Journal of Negro Education* [January 1939]: 73–4).

[25]Gloster, 241.

[26]See Judith Fetterley and Marjorie Pryse, Introduction, in *American Women Regionalists, 1850–1910* (New York: Norton, 1992).

[27]See Hazel Carby, "The Politics of Fiction, Anthropology, and the Folk: Zora Neale Hurston," in Genevieve Fabre and Robert O'Meally, *History and Memory in African American Culture* (New York: Oxford University Press, 1994), 29–44.

SELECTED GEMS

SELECTED GEMS

OF

Poetry, Comedy and Drama

BY

MERCEDES GILBERT

BOSTON

The Christopher Publishing House
Boston, U. S. A.

[4]

TO MY FATHER, AND MOTHER.

TABLE OF CONTENTS

7

Selected Gems of Poetry, Comedy and Drama

TRUE WORTH

What are riches, that I should crave,
And cannot carry beyond the grave.

What is fame, that soon passes by,
It cannot my redemption buy.

Riches and fame, oftime at great cost,
Are hard to find, and easily lost.

They are the passing gifts of earth,
But at death, as at birth.

It is only the soul,
That has "true worth."

11

LI'L BLACK BOY

Don't you get to thinkin' honey,
Dat de Lord ain't treat you right.
Jes' 'cause yo' hair is kinky,
And yo' face is black as night.

Why de flowers dat's so pretty,
Wid dar colors all bright and gay.
Will some day get all withered,
And dar colors will fade away.

But you'se de fairest of de fair,
And de good Lord sure was right.
When he made you black outside,
'Cause inside, he's made you white.

Dar ain't no hate or malice,
In yo' eyes, dat shines so clear.
You jes' askin' as you go along,
For this old world, to treat you square.

Dey says man's made in God's image,
When I look at you, I know it's true.
'Cause I can see his own great spirit,
Jes as plain 'er shinin' through.

Don't you let this old world fool you,
You jes stay hopeful, true and mild.
Show dem you can take dere' cuffin,
And still give dem back a smile.

[10]

HOW LIZA SAVED THE DEACON

Liza Johnson took in boarders
In a little southern town,
And she put out all the scandal
That was talked for miles around.

My, but she liked Deacon Jackson
His wife had been dead a year,
Liza, she'd had three husbands
But had given them all the air.

The Deacon lived a mile from town
He called on Liza twice a day,
And it surely was a shame
The grub he could put away.

Everything was going lovely
Until one day the news got round
That a brand new city gal
Had just blown into the town.

The way Liza cried and carried on
You'd 'er thought she'd seen a mouse,
When she heard the strange gal
Was stayin' at the Deacon's house.

She vowed she'd save him from that vamp
'Fore she plum took him in,
And what she'd tell that old backslider
Sure was goin' to be a sin.

She told the Parson and his wife
And all the folks for miles around
Then she got them all together,
To run that gal right out 'er town.

But she could 'er saved herself the trouble
'Cause right there the law stepped in
And hauled that gal right down to jail
Just as quick as any thing.

It turned out to be a convict man
Dressed like a gal, tryin' to get away
And had thought the Deacon's house
About the safest place to stay.

Liza vowed she had saved the Deacon
And he ups and married her that day,
Now he wishes they had give her the convict
And put him in jail to stay.

I AM SO SMALL

I've watched the sunset's golden ray,
Paint the western skies, with colors gay,
I've stretched my arms, towards the skies,
I've tried it's greatness, and might, to realize.
I've turned away abashed, ashame.
For after all, it is so great,
I am so small.
I've seen the earth with it's mantle of snow,
On which the sun cast it's brilliant glow,
I've caught the snowflakes,
As they wafted through the air,
It filled my heart with joy and fear,
Of the majesty of God so kind,
Who sends the seasons in their time,
Who watches o'er and rules them all
He is so great,
I am so small.
I've gazed across the ocean's great expanse,
And wondered, after all what is man?
All puffed up with silly pride,
He cannot stop the ocean's roar,
Nor halt the sun, or falling snow,
I feel the need of him, who is so great.
And still withal,
Is mindful of me,
Who is so small.

DON'T NOBODY CARE

Life's battle sometimes sure are hard.
But there's no need to cry,
Nor tell your troubles, to the crowd,
That carefree passes by.
You've got to brace up and smile,
And learn to take your share.
'Cause after all you'll find this out,
Don't nobody care.

Old fate may hit you an awful blow,
But there's no need to whine,
Nor carry 'round a face that looks
Just like a distress sign.
Just put your fighting togs all on,
And laugh away your fear,
'Cause after all you'll soon find out,
Don't nobody care.

Friends may say things that will hurt,
Don't let that make you sigh.
Nor get yourself all worked up,
Trying to make them out a lie.
Just hold your head up that much higher,
'Cause true friends ain't found nowhere.
Let them know you've found out,
Don't nobody care.

DISAPPOINTMENT

We think when disappointments come
And dodge our steps and stay,
The success we had hoped for
That we have failed, but, nay.

Disappointment is to the soul,
Like refiners fire, to unfinished gold,
To purify and give us strength,
To win success, on which our heart is bent.

For were there no failures,
How could we decide the credit due to those
Who had tried, and reached success, and fame.
When others thought their efforts all in vain.

The cup of bitterness, can no man describe,
But he who has tasted the dregs inside,
True happiness is only known
To he who have suffered all alone.

When we have learned to set our aim
Above the shallow mark of gain,
And let no disappointment mar our success
God, in his own time, will do the rest.

MY DEAR JOHN'S PLACE

Hand me my specks dar, Susan,
And hand 'em here quick I say.
Dat looks jes' like brudder Green,
Headed straight dis way.
I wonder is he gonna stop,
And have a little chat.
He's stop to talk to sister Smith,
Now what you think o' dat.

Lord knows she jes' runs him down,
Ain't got no shame at all.
And he jes' lost his dear wife,
Dis last gone fall;
Here I'se a widow, for a year
Dat's jes' gone.
And I ain't seen a man yet,
Dat could take de place,
Of my dear departed John.

Give me my teeth dar, Susan;
And my side bangs, off de chiffonier.
And throw me dat brand new mourning dress,
Dat's hangin' on dat chair.
What's dat you say, Susan?
He's past wid jes' a bow.
Well, I didn't want him to stop,
I jes' can't stand dat man nohow.

He ain't nothin', but an old skinflint,
And as stingy as he can be,
I wouldn't give him a look, to save his life.
And he'd better not, make no eyes at me!
He's jes' an old hypocrite,
And I'll tell him to his face.
Dar ain't a chance, in dis wide world,
Of him 'er takin' my dear John's place.

THE GAME OF LIFE

Take all that this life has to give,
Count that day lost, that leaves for you
No lasting memory of some great joy.
Live well, love well, while you may.
With no regrets of yesterday.
Look upon the past with a smile,
Upon the future with hope.
Seek no man's friendship, if it is worth having
You will get it, if you do not, be glad,
It may have brought you sorrow, and regret.
Count your gains when you have received them,
Not before.
Play the game of life right on the square,
Win or lose, always play fair.
Seal your lips from scandal,
No one can kill you for your thoughts.
Keep your secrets, if you find that you can not,
Tell them, but remember they are no longer yours,
So don't get angry when you hear them.
Don't make friends at all, if you can not treat them
    right.
Take all that life has to give,
While you have breath,
Just live, and live, and live.

THINK BRUDDER THINK

When yo' heart am full 'ob evil,
And yo' soul is black as sin.
Turn de searchlight 'ob truth on,
And let it shine wid'in.
Put dem evil passions from you,
Lay dem way up on de shelf.
And learn to treat yo' brudder,
Jes' as you would treat yo'self.

When yo' hands, dey get all slippery.
And *yo'* am tempted fo' to steal.
Steal into yo' secret chamber,
And in de darkness kneel.
Ask de Lord, for to help you,
Make dem hands stay where dey belong.
Tell old Satan, get behind you,
And on his own way be gone.

When your angry passions rises,
And you know dar's gwine to be a squall.
Just r'member after a fight,
Dar' sometimes comes a fall.
You may think to beat yo' brudder,
But for all yo' know.
He may do de beating,
So yo' had better let him go.

THE STREAM OF LIFE

Life is like a little stream,
That flows on to the great blue sea.
On which we launch our crafts,
And drift on to eternity.

Some-times we glide by cities vast,
Some-times by meadows green.
Where peace and splendour shows around,
And happiness reigns supreme.

And then we glide by dismal forest,
Laid bare by strife and storm.
Our crafts rocked by troubled waves,
Our souls grieved and torned.

Upon the sands of idleness,
Our bows are some-times tossed.
Fate plays us funny tricks we find.
Hopes and ambitions lost.

Then high the waves of faith arise,
And float our boats again.
On our way we glide once more,
Down life's stream, again all is serene.

Until the whirl-pool claims us,
And 'round and 'round we race.
Finding no escape it seems,
From life's over-whelming pace.

Some-times we float close to shore,
And tarry for awhile.
Among the scenes of pleasure,
That delight and beguile.

Some crafts reach coves of fame,
That last for many a day.
Until the waves of destiny,
Float them on their way.

But all must move for the stream,
Flows on its way.
Whether we have failed or not,
We have our price to pay.

And as each stream, must reach its course,
In Gulf or sea some day.
Our journey too, must come to an end,
In the sea of Eternity.

AMANDA JACKSON'S TEA

It ain't no use 'er talkin'
Folks is git'in' mighty swell.
Why de difference in de Browns and Jones's
Is very hard to tell.

Dar's my friend Amanda Jackson,
What use to live in de lane.
Now is livin' in a swell apartment,
Dat for swellness is a pain.

De other evening she went an' sent out
Swell invites to a tea.
Co'se I don't know why,
But she ups and sends one of dem to me.

Well, dat day I wasn't working,
So I decided dat I'd go.
Jes' to see, what it was lak'
Dis' drinkin' tea at half past four.

You should 'er seen dem womens'
Dar was a dozen or more.
And de airs dat dey put on,
Would 'er made a fust class show.

Den Manda' sits out de tables,
De ones dat open lak' a book.
And dey started playin' cards,
I couldn't play, so I jes' looked.

Pretty soon dey all got tired,
Jes' passin' cards around.
Manda' she got tired fust,
I knows when she use to dig taters out de ground.

So she ups and rings a little bell,
A waitin' gal come'd right in.
Wid a apron on, as dressed up as could be,
Manda' said right careless, "Mary serve the tea."

And in no time de gal brung in a tray.
It looked right dainty lak' and smart.
Dar wasn't 'nough grub on it though,
To even give me a start.

When it come my turn to take a cup 'er tea,
I thought even if it killed me
I'd eat some of dem fancy little red things
Jes' to see what they could be.

So I ups and takes off four,
'Couse the odders jes' took one.
But I knowed, I could git rid of three,
'Fore de odders had half begun.

Well, it turned out to be sandwiches,
All pasted up inside with cheese and stuff.
And by the time, I had eat one,
Of dem things, I'd had 'nough.

Den I says to Manda' right out loud,
When was we gonna git something to eat,
Such as fried chicken, ham, an bread,
And dat gal jes' threw a fit.

Well, I left dat party, sorter feelin'
Dat wid Manda' and sassicity, I was done.
And though she's given, a lot of parties since.
I ain't got another invite to none.

THE VAGABOND

No, I'm not a beggar.
And did not come to ask for alms,
Although I do look seedy,
And run down at the heel
It has been many a day
Since I've tasted a regular meal.

Were I to tell you my story,
Why I am a vagabond
You would laugh at me with scorn.
You'd say my story was the old stuff
But it is as true as God above
Of that I have proof enough.

Yet it is the same old story
Of love, beneath the pale moonlight.
That was twenty years ago
She was young and fair,
With eyes that danced with sunlight
The raven's plumage for her hair.

I led her to the altar as my bride,
We were the happiest pair,
When the kiddies came,
First John, then Charles and Bess
I could have fought the world and laugh
So complete was my happiness.

My work kept me most of the time
I traveled for my firm,
And though I did not like it
She was left so much alone
It meant more money for us all
And some day our own little cozy home.

It was to have been my last trip
The thought filled my heart with delight
What should have taken hours, I finished in a night.
I bought fruit and candies for the kiddies
For her a jewel rare
My heart was singing, as to my home I drew near.

But what a sight met my eyes.
No, no it cannot be, I must be wrong
I could not believe it was my home
Burned level to the ground.
But, yes it must be, there was the smoking embers.
The firemen and the curious crowd standing around.

Where is my wife, my children? I begged
My God, why don't you speak?
They told me the story
How she left the babies, alone and locked in.
They thought the house was empty
They could not hear their voices above that awful
    din.

Of course they tried to save them
When they saw them at the window, just before the
    roof caved in.
I knew no more for days, my heart died then and
    there.
And the years that have followed
I've lived in wild despair.

Last week they found her body in the river.
I saw it in the morgue.
I got the letter that she left me
That told her story of the shame she could no longer
    bear.
I started out to find the man, who sent her there.

For years I had been a vagabond my friend
Searching for this traitor
Just to be cheated in the end.

Last night I found him
He was beyond revenge I swore would be mine.
He had gone to meet his Maker
The judge of all mankind.

But he left a message, it touched my heart somehow
And made me want to live again.
But I see tears have dimmed your eyes
I think you understand.
I do not want pity, just give me any kind of a job
And a chance to be a man.

DREAMS

What a sombre thing this life would be,
Could we not have our dreams,
Visions of rapture to beguile
With things, that are unseen.

In childhood we our ideals draw,
On the canvas of our minds.
And around it, all our hopes we build,
And paint in glowing colors quite divine.

And then as years advance,
We our childhood things lay by,
Our dreams are of fame and oftimes gain,
And great things, for which we try.

And when at last old age creeps on,
And our visions fade, as the dawn,
We dream of conquests we have made,
In days past and gone.

And when our dreaming days are over,
And we are called to face the test supreme.
I sometimes wonder, will we awake in some new
      world,
And find, that it has all been a dream.

NEVER TOO LATE

She stood upon the edge of a lofty cliff,
Amidst the sunset's golden beams.
The mountain tops around her,
At her feet, the deep ravine.

Sadly she lifted her eyes to heaven,
And a prayer her pale lips framed.
Asking God for strength, to end at last,
A life, so filled with pain.

For had not life proved a failure,
And hope long ago had died.
Ere she had decided, to end it all,
In yon fast flowing tide.

But lo' an angel whispered,
Close to the maiden's ear,
It is never too late, to begin again,
There is joy for each woe and care.

'Tis true, you have been sorely tried,
And to you, it seems that you have failed.
But that is past
And alas, can never be lived again.

The world is wide, go seek your place.
There is room, for each and all
And God above will care for you,
For he marketh the sparrows fall.

Put away the thought of failure,
To live is not to fail.
As long as life remains,
There is time to start again.

But the maiden, sadly shook her head.
I cannot go back to the life.
From which I came,
I have come here alone to die.

Wait! urged the angel softly,
A vision, you shall behold.
And she gazed upon a sea,
Of lost and tortured souls.

These are the failures of life, to live again.
The chance is gone.
But, as long as life remains,
You can always start again.

And slowly the maiden turned,
And retraced her weary way.
And started life anew,
On that eventful day.

And strange it may seem,
But true, she found a place,
Where happiness reigned,
And much useful work to do.

So have you and I, thought at times,
That we have failed.
Though we have done our best,
But could we learn to start again,
God would do the rest.

GOD'S GIFT TO MAN

Why should I this world fear,
And idly stand and pine,
For happiness, success, and fame
Had I but tried, how do I know.
What heights I might have gained.

Can the mountain tops be reached,
By simply gazing up;
While others climb with ease
And some day reach the top.
I watch them go on and on, and reach
The place for which I long.

Did not the Maker, of all things,
Create the earth and sea.
And moving things, both great and small,
And like-wise create me.
And gave into my keeping
A will that makes me free.

To do what-ere I will.
While the mountains must stand still,
As centuries pass by.
They have not the power, to move or try,
While I, who in His image, He has made.
Have power to conquer, all things He gave.

Then what excuse, have I to give,
When my life has been idly lived.
If in one place, I've stood afraid,
And have not my mission filled.
When I could have done,
 Anything! I had willed.

NOT GUILTY

It was a sultry summer morning
And a curious crowd packed in the place
The court room was jammed to the door,
When the clerk called her case.

How they stared and whispered,
When they placed her on the stand
You never would have dreamed
So small a creature, could have killed a man.

With the case they soon got started,
Just like all cases are now days
The jury box was slowly filled,
And witnesses and lawyers had their say.

Then her lawyer rose and pleaded
That she might take the stand,
And tell the court just how and why
She had taken the life of a man.

She rose and stood with her head bowed
Her face so drawn and sad,
And told of sufferings that were enough
To drive any woman mad.

HE was my husband, she said. We had two sons.
John was our oldest and baby Tim.
Well Tim was taken sick that night
And he went to bring the Doctor in for him.

All through the night I listened,
With my baby in my arms, so still he lay.
I prayed that help would come somehow
Before his last breath slipped away.

But with the dawn he lay dead
His father had not returned
Oh, my heart was sick within me
My very soul, with anguish burned.

It was mid-day when he staggered in
A drunken mad man I saw before me there
My heart turned cold at the sight of him
And I was filled with fear.

Little Tim lay dead in his bed
John stood whimpering at my knee
As his father lurched across the room
And tried to pull him away from me.

His screams seemed to arouse,
A thousand demons in that man
And before I realized what had happened
He had struck him down with his hand.

I tried to hold him back,
As he reached for a heavy chair
But before I could stop him
He had swung it high up in the air.

And then I must have gone mad, Judge
It was his life or the life of my child
I don't remember where I struck with the knife
Oh how, grief had drove me wild.

There is no more to tell, she faltered,
Tim lies buried and there sits John.
May God keep, and bless him
After I am gone.

Well, can you wonder what the end was
To that case that summer's day,
The jury was soon back in the court room
They only stayed fifteen minutes away.

The judge called for their verdict.
The foreman rose, there was not a sound,
As he said, we have reached a verdict,
The prisoner is, "Not Guilty" we have found.

LONELINESS

Have you ever felt a loneliness
That bordered on despair,
And made you fearful of something
When there was nothing there to fear.

That crept a specter of the night
With shadowy ghost of the past,
That closed you around with a wall of gloom
And held you a captive fast.

That seemed to fill your heart with dread
Of unseen nameless things
That followed you and dogged your path
Even in life's busiest dins.

That made the still cold night
As stifling as a summer's day.
As if the earth and skies had met,
In a hazy mass, to crush your life away.

When scenes of childhood seemed to pass
Like a panorama through your brain
When even God seemed miles away,
And you were afraid to pray.

THAT'S A FACT

He was jes' a little pickaninny
An' de folks all passed him by
No one stopped to love or pity
No one cared, when he'd laugh or cry.

But he jes' grew, and grew and grew.
Catchin' all the blows and scorn
Not a chance to prove his worth
Still he jes' struggled on.

And when at last manhood was reached
An' he'd try to get a show
They'd jes' look at his color
Den dey'd always answer, "No."

Den dere came a great big struggle,
Men was needed one and all
He was 'mongst de fust to answer
When he heard his country's call.

He had only known de hardships
What was dere for him to fear,
He was jes' one of de million black men
For whom no one seemed to care.

Ah, but he showed a spirit,
Dat was mighty fine an' strong,
He never shirked a duty
But jes' bravely carried on.

An' he fought a twofold battle
As did every black man at his side
Dat will echo through de ages
O'er dis country broad and wide.

Dat you cannot judge the insides
By de color of de skin
'Caise you never know the great heart
Dat oftime' beat wid in.

If you'd treat him lak you ought to
An' forget his skin is black
You'd find out dat he is a man
An' a good one, That's a fact!

YOU JES' HIT 'EM BACK

You Tom, come right in here to me
Why yo' clothes is jes' as dirty,
And as ragged as can be,
Didn't I tell yo' bout playin
Wid dem alley tramps
Turn round here what's yo' hiddin?
Dar yo'se gone and tore yo' pants.

So yo'se done been fightin'
Now ain't I tole yo' not to do dat,
An' here yo'se gone and lost yo' bran new hat,
Jes' yo' wait till your pa comes home,
He gonna beat yo' sure,
I done tole you not to fight
But if dey gives yo' de fust whack,
Don't you dare to run away,
Yo' jes' be sure to hit dem back.

HOME

Home is not a massive pile
Of wood or stone that rise
In architectural beauty
And tower towards the skies.

Nor is it a dwelling grand
Where gold is plenteous found
And fame and power rules
And spreads a golden halo round.

Home is not a cottage small
With gardens bright with cheer
Where every dainty luxury
Surround you everywhere.

Home is where love, and happiness dwells.
Encompassed by four walls
Whether it be a palace grand,
Or just a cottage small.

Where hope and faith go hand in hand,
And truth and loyalty hold sway,
Where selfishness is never found,
And peace has come to stay.

A TALK ON EVOLUTION

(*Subject*)
WHO WAS DAT FUST MONKEY'S MA?

As we all know, dis is de greatest subject of de day. I don't know who started it, but I can say dis, whoever it was, dey ain't give us no real proof, dat dey know any more 'bout it den we does.

But, we do know, dat dis world is all upset, an' gettin' worser every day.

Folks done all gone crazy, an' dey don't care what dey say.

Dey starts 'er trying to dispute, 'bout old man Adam being de fust man on de earth.

An' den dey goes on sayin' things dat is worse.

Dat we all jes' comes from monkeys. Did you ever hear dey lak's of dat?

'Couse tis true when folks gits old, dey surely do look queer, wid dere face all full of wrinkles, an' dere heads all scarse of hair.

A baby sure is cute with its immitatin' ways, and it acts jes' like a monkey, when it hops 'round and plays.

Though man don't swing from limb to limb, away up in de trees. You must admit dat he's mighty quick, when he puts his head to learnin' dem high flyin' trapezes tricks.

I'se seen some folks faces, and I declare dey looked so bad, to say dey looked lak' monkeys, sure would make dem monkeys mad.

But, all dat don't stand for nothin', 'cause dere had to be a startin' place.

Someone had to be de fust, so whar did de fust monkey come from, when he come on dis earth?

Folks sure is smart dese days, dat we'll admit, but dey's got this thing all mulled up in places it sure don't fit.

You can't finish nothin', if you never do begin. You can't go out de door, if you never ain't comed in. Dere must be a start made, to do any kind of thing.

"Now, what dey got to prove to me, where did dis monkey business begin."

Can't nobody make themselves, of such I ain't never heard, de shell as got to be cracked, fore we sees de little bird.

No matter how smart you is, you'se had a pa and ma tho' you may be smarter den dey ever was.

No matter how dey twist it, dar ain't nobody dumb, so what's I'se waitin' for dem to prove to me. "Is, where did dat fust monkey come from."

Dis old thing dat dey calls science, will jes' git you in a whirl.

Wid dem high fluttin' words, dat jes' gits your tongue all in a curl.

But folks wants facts dese days, and jus' lak' dey know dat a monkey was our pa. I'd lak' for dem prove dey know who was dat fust monkey's ma!

'Til dey does dat, I'm goin' keep right on b'lievin' 'bout Adam an' Eve, an' in dat garden way back dere.

'Cause none of us had got here den, but ain't it jes' as easy to b'lieve, as b'lievin' 'bout des monkey men?

Dey at least had a beginnin' an' it ain't half as queer, as dis here havin' monkeys sprin'in', right out de air.

Let dem have dere new fangle ideas, havin' tadpoles evolutin' into hummin' birds and such.

'Cause of dat kind of business, I ain't thinkin' much.

But let dem go right on talkin', I ain't gonna b'lieve what dey say nohow.

"Til dey prove to me, dat dey know, who was dat very fust monkey's ma."

WHY ADAM ATE THE APPLE

Fust I'm gonna tell you how come Adam to take up wid dat gal Eve.

Well, you see to start wid, little Eve was a chorus gal, and Adam saw her one night when he was sittin' in the front row. He fell for her, and fell hard. So he ups and writes her a note, askin' to take her out to Coney Island, after the show. She agreed, and dey started out to make whoopee. Well, Adam drank so much near beer, dat he got drunk, dat's dey last he remembered, 'til Eve woke him up in de subway station, by pokin' him in de ribs, with a marriage certificate. From den on de trouble started.

Adam got a job out in Long Island, keepin' a garden, and dey had a bungalow, to live in, right on de place. "Adam was some lazy, he wouldn't do a thing, but, lay 'round under de apple trees."

As for Eve, she spent all of her time, in de movies, listenin' to de talkies, and she and Adam use to have some fights, when she come home.

"Well, dar was a lot of apple trees in dat garden, but Adam didn't lak' but one. Dat was a tree dat had great big red apples on it, and every one of dem apples had a worm in it, and dey was all female worms." "So dat made Eve mad."

Eve told Adam if he dared to eat one of dem apples, she'd sue him for divorce and alimony.

One day Eve stayed in town longer den usual, the reason for dat was, she was at a bargain sale down at Gimbles. Dey had a sale on pajamas.

When she got home dar was no supper done, and Adam was some mad. Eve tried to git him to eat some apple sauce, but nothin' doin'. He started to rave, and jes' raised Cain. Eve stood it as long as she was able, den she got tired of hearin' him carry on, so she jes' grab'd de rollin' pin, and said to poor Adam, in a terrible voice. "Aw', go eat an apple."

"Adam was so excited he runned right out and grab'd one, an' started eatin' it, right off dat tree, dat he had been told to lay off." "But what else was the poor fellow to do?"

I'M GLAD I AINT NO HAND TO TALK

Well, I declare, if it aint Miss. Smith. Come right in, I sure is glad to see you. How is you feelin' dis mornin'. Now, dats to bad. I had de self same thing last winter. The doctor called it some new fangle name, I think it was newrius. But, chile, it aint a thing but de same old time rumitizm. Is that so, you met Miss. Green and dat daughter of her'n on de way up here?

Did she have de nerve to speak to you? I wouldn't think she'd have de nerve to speak to decent folks after de way she's been running after brudder White, and his wife only dead three months.

And it's jes' scanderlous de way she lets that gal Angeline go galavantin', 'round de country wid dem travelin' shows. They tells me, that Miss. Green done took up painting her face. Is you seen anything to beat of that gal's clothes? She looks jes' lak' a circus, and her dresses hardly comes up to her knees.

Last week aunt Salisberry met Angeline on the street, and you know aunt Salisberry is nearsighted. "Well, she says, to her, honey that sure is a pretty blouse you'se got on, but, you clean done forgot to put on de skirt dat goes with it."

My brother went to see de show, dat Angeline was in when he was in New York. He said, that gal didn't have on a thing, but a little skirt of feathers, and from the looks of dat skirt, de bird dat furnished dem feathers must have been a canary.

I don't want my Sally speaking to dat Angeline, deed I don't. Now, you aint goin' so soon, Miss. Smith? I aint had a chance to talk to you none, and you must come to see me again real soon. Good-bye.

"Sally did you see dat dress she had on, up to her knees, de idea, an at her age too." See who dat is at de door Sally.

Well, bless my soul! if it aint Miss Green, and her dear little Angeline. Come right in, I sure is glad to see you both. Why Angeline, I didn't even know you was in town! You'se been all de way to New York. Miss Green you sure should be proud of dis chile, she is so smart.

I sure wish my Sally could get into one of dem shows. Angeline couldn't you teach Sally some of dat show stuff? I guess it jes' aint in her to be smart lak' dat. Sally you must copy some style from Angeline, she looks jes' too sweet for words, wid dat short skirt, and her hair fixed up dat way.

"Now, don't think of goin' til' I fix you some lunch. Oh, you expecting company, now, I'se so sorry to see you hurry lak' dat." Brudder White comin' to call on you. Well, now I sure is 'sprise I heard that he wasn't goin' 'bout much since all dat talk 'bout him preparatin' de church money las' month.

Co'se I never did b'lieve dat he did it, but folks seemed to think dat it was strange, dat he bought a new suit right after it was gone. But, don't mention my name, if you say anythin 'bout the suit 'cause I don't never want to get mixed up in no talk.

You must call again Miss Green. And Angeline do come and see Sally real soon, good-bye. I'll be over real soon to see you.

Sally! thar now dey's gone, I'd think her and her flapper daughter would stay away from decent folks. If I ever catch you going 'round wid dat gal, I'll break your neck. HEAR ME.

Goodness sakes dere's somebody at de door. Sally! jes' look who has honored us wid a call, brudder White. It sure is a honor to have you drop in brudder White, jes' sit right down, Sally and me is goin' to fix you a little lunch, aint we Sally. Excuse us a minute.

Sally, do help me scrape up something, for dat old grafter to eat. Here I'se spent de whole mornin' listenin' to a lot of gossipin' hens.

"I sure am glad I aint no hand to talk."

CHIP OF THE OLD BLOCK

You Ephrem—come here to me boy. I declare it aint no use to talk to you. I'se talked and talked till my throat is sore, and I aint gonna talk no more, 'bout your low down trifflin' ways. You jes' aint no good, and to my name you is a disgrace. Goin' 'round here 'er shootin dem craps, and de worst of it is, you don't never win nothin' at dat. Here, I'se your daddy and deacon too. You sure aught to be 'er shame. Got the folks all 'er lookin' at me, and saying I'se to blame, for sending you to dat high flulutin school. "Den when you comes back here, all de thanks I git, is for you to make yourself a fool. You jes' hangs around dem poolrooms from mornin' til night, wastin' your time drinkin', dis here hootch." Now does you think dat's right?

You won some money last night! Now, dat I jes' can't b'lieve. You gonna give me twenty bucks, huh. I guess it's time. How much is you got? Come on now, I don't want no lyin', what's dat you got in your hand? Let me see dem bones man, is dat de way you roll 'em? Well, wid all de practise you'se had, I'm surprised, you don't know nothin', dem bones. Man I can see dat wid my eyes, hand 'em here. Now, dar, look at dat ten, how much you bet I can make it again?

Ten bucks! boy you'se on. I know I aint got rusty, tho' its been mighty long since I talked to dese bones. But, I b'lieve I can still make dem hear. "Don't fail me now, make it for pappy, jes' lak' you use to long ago." Ten more you say, boy I'se heard you. Come on now baby mine, huh, ten now, aint dat fine, dat ten spot is mine. It's jes' too easy, but you see it's done jes' dis way, huh. Oh, I never miss what's dat shoot ten more. Alright let 'em roll, I'se heard 'em before. What's dat you'se broke, well, who's to blame, ah, no it aint no luck. I jes' naturally knows how to play 'em.

"Lend you five bucks? land sakes alive you think I'm gonna lend you money to waste on craps. You'd better get yourself a job, and leave dem dice alone.

You got all dese hypocrites 'round here sayin' now, dat dey aint shocked, dat you'se turned out to be jes' a chip of de old block."

OUT-SIDE O' DAT WE HAD A WONDERFUL TIME

Goodmornin' Miss Jones, how is you dis mornin'? Now aint dat too bad. I had a sister dat had de self same thing, and one mornin' de found her dead, in her bed. Yes, indeed, they did. Dey said that her penderlum busted, she was always complainin' of a pain in her right side, right whar yourns is, but den, you might not go so sudden lak' dat.

Oh! I'se jes' feelin' torable, kinder tired lak' this mornin'. You wasn't out to Miss Brown's parlor social, last Saturday night, was you? Yes, deed I was dar, we sure had a good time, b'lieve me we did.

Well, I jes' stopped in on my way, I aint been home since de party you know. "Why, well to tell the truth, I was kinder detained,—detained, you don't know what I means? Well, kept in jail, 'twasn't much tho."

You should 'er seen Bessie Snow at de party. Yes, she was dar, jus' lookin' as fine, all dressed up in that green dress o' her'ne dat has de yellow trimin's.

I'se goin' by de hospital when I leaves here, to see how she is. Yes, she's in de hospital. De doctor says dat her leg's broke in three places once at de knee, and once below de knee, and once at de ankle. But, it'll mend in 'bout six months, I guess.

"Trouble, why we didn't have no trouble, dat is to speak 'bout. De boys was jes' playin' a little game, dey calls blackjack, and somebody snatched somebody else's money. No dey wasn't gamblin', nothin' lak' dat, but dey was kinder friendly layin'."

Drinkin' goodnes, no Miss Jones. De idea, and dis is probation times, dey jes' had 'bout three gallons of home made hootch, and a little gin. 'Bout twelve quarts, dat's all. Well, Mr. Brown came in, and somebody wacked him on de head wid a chair, and he runned right into a razor. I don't know who had it. The cops found 'bout a dozen of 'em 'round.

Oh yes, de cops comed' in and dat's how Bessie got to

break her leg, she went right outer de window, and 'couse you know Miss Brown lives on de fourth floor.

Well, dey took everybody to jail, and fined us all twenty-five dollars apiece. Dat is all, but, my old man and de Jordon boys. Yes, de Jordon boys is out, but now dey's in again, and dey is holdin' dem and my old man, to see whether or not Mr. Brown dies. Doctor says his skull is busted in three places and dey had to take seventy-five stitches in him. "Well, I must hurry Miss Jones, I'se goin' to Miss Brown's furnell, dey says she died from shock."

"But out-side o' dat, we had a wonderful time." Good-bye Miss Jones.

AINT MEN DECEITFUL

Lord Martha Johnson, I sure am glad you stopped in for a minute dis mornin'. I'm jes' itchin' to tell somebody what's happened. Lord no chile. 'Taint nothin' serious, its worse den dat, but I'm so happy.

Well, you know dat dear man Deacon White was over here yesterday, came right up, so sudden like, Lord chile I jus' had luck 'nough to be lookin' out de window, when he came up on de porch. Chile! I had to run in my room, dat quick, and grab my teeth out 'er de glass of water, and get 'em in place, and pat my bangs on in no time. But, by the time he had knocked twice, I was right at dat door, to let him in.

So he comed' in. Chile, I sure could see from de look on his face, when he walked in dat door, dat dere was something on his mind. He was dat 'barrassed, so I jes' smiled, dat sweet, and said kinder friendly like. "Well, well, Deacon dis sure is a pleasant 'sprise, to see you, and took him by de arm. I made him sit down in my most comfortable chair. He jus' sit dar and looked like he couldn't bring his 'self, to say what he wanted to say." And pretty soon we was sittin' dat close together, jes' like two turtle doves, as folks dat write books says. 'Couse I seein' dat he was nervous I had moved my chair, kinder over near his 'en. Then in no time, we was holdin' hands. Dat is, I reached over and took his hand. Jes' to make him feel at home you no'.

"Well, he said to me." sister Black, I'se got something to axe you. I knowed what it was, so I said, jes' to make him feel comfortabel, dar aint no need to hurry, 'bout askin' deacon. Den he started gettin' all nervous, like, and I said. "deacon, wont you have some lunch." 'Cause I 'membered what folks says 'bout a man's heart bein' near his stomach. He kinder 'jected like, sayin' dat he wasn't hungry, but I insisted. 'Cause I know dat bein' a widower for eight months, he don't get no good home cooked grub. Pretty soon, I had him sittin' down to de table, and it bein' hot I 'sisted on takin' his coat.

'Couse he didn't want 'er pull it off, but I 'sisted him, and what you think, dar was a button off. So I grabbed a needle and in no time, had it sewed right on again.

That man was 'barrasses, dat he didn't eat a thing. Jes' kept sayin' he had something to axe me, and every time he said dat, I talked him out of it. Till finally he rushed out.

But, I knew he wanted to axe me to marry him, and I didn't want to 'pear to anxious. "What's dat you say Martha, dat he wanted to axe me, to come to his weddin' next month." Is you sure, 'er dat? Um, now who's goin' marry dat old skinflint? Sally Peck!

Well, it serves her right, I don't like her nohow, and as for him, I wouldn't have him, if he was the last man on earth. Hypocrite. But, Lord aint men deceitful.

THE AIR WAS MADE FOR BIRDS

I'se been gettin' so many letters here lately, from great folks all over de country, to talk on de subject of Flyin'! I'se made up my mind, dat maybe I could jes' say a little something, on dat all arsobent subject. Course I aint no 'navator myself. But everybody is so het up over dis thing dat dey's even got up in de air.

Course folks think dat dis flyin' is something new. But, it aint, and dey's given lots of folks, de credit for startin' it, but, de fust man dat started it, was Elizha, when he flewed away in dat chariot. Course I don't know what makes it anyhow.

But, I'se always thought dat after all de room dat us folks is got down here, on dis earth, it sure is a shame, to be so selfish, as to rob de poor birds of de air.

But, I'll admit it must be mighty fine, to soar through de air. Jes' 'er dippin' and curvin' 'round dem clouds, and scratchin' yo' head on dem stars. Dat must be mighty fine.

'Specially when you can look down here at dis world, and see de folks, jes' 'er rushin' 'round. And you'se sailin' along wid nothin' to worry 'bout, but, whether you'se comin' down, where folks can say, here yo' is. 'Er where dey'll have to be sayin' where am you.

And then it must be 'er mighty sight, to fly 'round and look on de big blue ocean, wid de waves jes' a rollin' and tossin', nothin' but water, everywhere.

'Cause water is one thing dat everybody should 'naturally like, why, de doctors say dat you jes' can't drink too much of it. De doctors say you should love it, and Mr. Volstead thought so too. It's good for you.

But when de doctors said dat, dey sure didn't say dat salt water was good for you. I don't b'lieve dat dey was figurin' on folks tryin to drink up none of dese oceans. Dey wasn't figurin' on navator folks nohow, and if you should land plump in de middle of one of dem oceans, and dar didn't happen to be nobody dar to pick yo' up—Umm, umm, jes' use yo' own judgment.

I had friend dat flyed one time, and de aint found all of de pieces of him yet. So I'm gonna stay right here on de ground.

Anyhow, too much air, might not agree wid me, I aint 'tall worried 'bout 'zamining none of dem stars, and I sure aint in love wid nobody's Venus, nor Mars. And 'til dey builds some kinder track up dar, where I can ride on a buss, or 'er trolley, my 'pinion is allus gonna be. "Dat de air was made for birds, —not me."

ENVIRONMENT

A DRAMA

IN

THREE ACTS AND FOUR SCENES

CHARACTERS

Mary Lou Williams ....*The mother*
Edna May Williams ....*The daughter*
Carl Winters ....*Edna's sweetheart*
Henry Williams ....*A son*
James Williams ....*The father*
Eliza Louder ....*A neighbor*
A Detective
A Police Officer
Teddy Smith ....*Henry's friend*
Rosa Lee ....*Henry's girl*
Millie Brown ....*Rosa's friend*
Charles Jackson ....*A disbarred lawyer and realtor*
Margaret Jackson ....*His daughter*
A Stenographer
Samuel Blackwell ⎱
Richard Mooney ⎰ ....*Jackson's handimen*

SCENES

ACT 1

(Scene)   The dining room in the Williams basement apartment.

(Time)   At present.   Around 9 P. M.

ACT 2

(Scene 1)   The same as Act 1.   Four months later.

(Time)   Early evening.

(Scene 2)   Jackson's office, in a down town section.   The next day.

(Time)   Afternoon.

ACT 3

Mary Lou's home in Durham, N. C.

(Time)   Two years later, early afternoon.

Environment

ACT 1

SCENE 1

(*A poorly furnished combination dining room and kitchen, in a basement apartment. A delapidated table in the center of the floor. A few chairs, a small stove in one corner, and a cupboard with dishes in another corner. Mary Lou is discovered wrapping up a bundle which she is trying to conceal, as Edna and Carl enter room. She has on hat and seems anxious to make her exit*)

EDNA

Oh! here is mother.

CARL

How are you Mrs. Williams? (*Crosses to shake her hand*)

MARY LOU

Just fine Carl. I'm going out for a minute.

EDNA

"Let me go for you mother." I know you must be tired.

MARY LOU

No dear, I'm not tired and I think a little air will do me good. I'll be right back.

(*Exits quickly with bundle under coat*)

EDNA

(*Looking thoughtful*)

Gee, mother acted queer. I wonder what was in that package, that, she seemed so anxious to hide.

CARL

"Goodness only knows." Edna I do wish you would listen to reason. I'm leaving tonight, and I have talked to you for three whole days, and haven't been able to make you see, that, it's all wrong, your staying here and—

EDNA

Now, Carl, please don't start all over again. I've told you it's impossible for me to leave them like this, when they need me so much.

CARL

But don't you see dear, that, there is no earthly reason for you, to sacrifice yourself like this.

EDNA

"What would become of mother?" Father has spent every cent we had, he can't get work.

CARL

You mean; won't stay sober long enough, to try.

EDNA

I won't deny that, but, mother wouldn't admit it, and she wouldn't leave him. And then she has her pride.

CARL

Pride? in these environments. How long will pride last? It will effect you too Edna, just as it has your father and brother. Even your mother has changed, she left home a beautiful woman, full of hope, and now; she is broken in health and mind.

EDNA

Oh! I know Carl, haven't I seen it all. We came here with money, we received from the sale of our farm, and for awhile lived in a better neighborhood. Then, when father could not get work, and the money was all spent, father started drinking and then, this. (*Indicating surroundings with her hand*). I don't know how it will end.

CARL

"Let me take you out of it Edna." You promised to marry me. Say, that you will tomorrow, and then go home with me.

EDNA

No Carl, I can't, oh! can't you see that I can't leave mother now, like this.

CARL

"Very well, I will go now, my train leaves within an hour. If you need me, you can just wire. I've got our home all finished, and a nice business, and no matter what happens, I will be waiting." I love you sweetheart. Oh! so much.

(Embraces her, and turns to go, as door opens and Mary Lou enters with arms full of packages)

MARY LOU

Leaving so soon Carl?   I was going to fix you some lunch.
(Places packages on table)

CARL

(Taking out watch)
Yes, Mrs. Williams, I must catch my train, which leaves within an hour.   I will write as soon as I get home.

EDNA

I'll go to the station with you Carl.   Wait until I get my hat.
(She exits into bedroom left)

CARL

"Mrs. Williams, I've just been trying to persuade Edna to marry me tomorrow, and go home to Durham, but she won't consent.

MARY LOU

Oh! I wish she would Carl.   Sometimes, I feel so afraid for her here.   I don't know why; but, this dreadful place has done us so much harm. Just think, only one year ago we came to this city, and since we have been here, just look how our lives have changed.   "My poor James," he is no longer the man he was, and Henry, why, I hardly know the boy.   He keeps all kind of late hours, and his companions are just street ruffins, and I am so tired.   Oh!
(She reels as if about to fall, Carl catches her in his arms)

CARL

Are you better now?   Let me get you a chair.

MARY LOU

I'm alright, just a weak spell.
(Edna enters)

EDNA

"I'll be back soon mother.   You lie down and rest."
(Kisses mother and takes Carl's arm and exits)
(Mary Lou seated at table, drops her head on table and sobs.   Door opens and Henry a boy of eighteen enters, walks over to table, and places hand on mother's shoulder)

HENRY

Mother, are you ill?

MARY LOU

No dear, I'm only tired.

HENRY

"Has father been home, mother."
(Henry busies himself over stove, looking for food, turns and looks at mother)

MARY LOU

Yes Henry, your father was here, an hour ago.

HENRY

And was he—

MARY LOU

Don't say it Henry, I know, yes, he was drunk.

HENRY

And?

MARY LOU

Oh! he didn't do any harm. I had to give him money, that's all.

HENRY

Give him money, or take a beating. I know, I can't believe that he is my father nowadays. He is so different. But, mother, I have decided to quit school and go to work.

MARY LOU

What! no Henry you cannot, you must not! I want you to finish, you will need your education, and you have only one more year. "I will not hear of it."

HENRY

But, mother, I can't stand to see you working, like this night and day. I must help you.

MARY LOU

No Henry, I won't let you do that, and suppose you did not get work. "It was not being able to get work, that first started him, doing as he does that, and these environments. Nothing to do, job after job, turned him down, he became discouraged, and then this."

HENRY

But, what about you? You have grown twenty years older, and you're working yourself to death.

MARY LOU

Oh! I'm alright, I don't mind it a bit, as long as I know that, I have you to fall back on, some day. *(Embraces boy)*. Now, you run along to bed, and Henry promise me, that you will always, be a good boy.

HENRY

"I certainly will, mother."
(Starts toward bedroom door)

MARY LOU

Henry, there's something that, I want to ask you. Why, do you keep company with that boy Teddy? He's not the kind of a boy that I like to see my son with.

HENRY

"Why, mother, what has he done? He's my best pal, and he's promised, to help me find a way to make some money after school. Big money, not the dimes I make now."

MARY LOU

I've never seen him do anything Henry, but, he's no good. I know it. I've always been a good christian Henry, and some how God! always shows his children, where there is danger. I feel it Henry, he will get into trouble.

HENRY

Mother you are excited and suspicious. Teddy is alright, and besides, I must have some friends, and he lives in the same house. So how can I shun him. But, I must go to bed, goodnight, mother.
(Kisses mother and exits into bedroom, Mary Lou starts sewing, seated at table)
(Knock is heard at door)

MARY LOU

Come in!
(Woman enters)

ELIZA

Oh, here you are, I just dropped in for a little chat.

MARY LOU

Glad to have you come in Eliza.
(Continues to sew)

ELIZA

"Well, you don't seem to like it. You're still sewing. Say, Mary Lou, why don't you snap out of it. Come on upstairs, we're having a party, and I want you to join us."

MARY LOU

Thanks Eliza, but, I have some work to finish.

ELIZA

That's all you know, work. Cut it out and have some fun, for a change. There's a bunch of good boys, up in my flat, and plenty of good liquor, and the night is young, who, knows what might happen.

MARY LOU

"I don't care for liquor, and I don't want to meet any boys."

ELIZA

Alright, Salvation Army Ann, I guess your old man wouldn't turn none down though.

MARY LOU

"I think," I can sew better alone.

ELIZA

Now, don't be upish, it don't become your basement surroundings. You're just a fool to sit here and sew, while that man of yours makes whoopee, on the money you make.

MARY LOU

Please leave my affairs alone.

ELIZA

"Affairs," you ain't got no affairs. That's what I'm trying to start for you. An affair that will get you more than that sewing will. Why, one of the boys, is dying to meet you, on the strength of what I told him, "How you looked."

MARY LOU

Please go—

ELIZA

Oh! well if you are dumb, it ain't my fault. But, you've turned down a good time and money.

MARY LOU

(Goes over to door, and opens it)
Now, get out. I mean it.

ELIZA

Alright. But say, Mary Lou, won't you lend me a cup of sugar, to make some punch? I'll give it back tomorrow.

MARY LOU
(Goes over to cupboard, fills cup)
"Here it is, good night."

ELIZA
Well, Mrs. Prim, here's how.
(Lifts hand as if taking a drink, laughing, exits)

MARY LOU
Oh! Lord! how much longer, will I have to endure this?
(Goes over to stove and starts to pour cup of tea, as knock is heard on door, opens door, Jackson enters)

JACKSON
Good evening, Mrs. Williams. I was in the neighborhood, so I thought I would drop in. How are you?

MARY LOU
(Looking frightened)
I'm alright, but, is there anything wrong with the work?

JACKSON
"No, everything is O. K. I just dropped in, as I was on this street."

MARY LOU
That's nice of you, Mr. Jackson.

JACKSON
Mrs. Williams, I wish you would take one of the upstairs apartments. I don't think it's healthy for you here. I could arrange it.

MARY LOU
But, my husband is the janitor, and this is the apartment, we are supposed to occupy. Isn't it?

JACKSON
You mean, you are the janitress. I know that you do all the work. "You are a fine woman, and I want to help you."

MARY LOU
Thanks, but, I don't think we can afford it. "It would cost some rent, wouldn't it?"

JACKSON
I could fix that for you.
(Walks over and puts hand on her shoulder intimately)

MARY LOU
I'd rather not, Mr. Jackson.
(Looks frightened)

JACKSON

Very well, but you think it over. I'd like to help you, and you may see it different some day. These are my houses, and I could do a lot for you.

MARY LOU

"Please, don't say any more about it, Mr. Jackson."

JACKSON

Well, if you should change your mind, or need my assistance, here is my card. "Let me know personally."

MARY LOU

The agent trys to get me everything to work with, and is very nice.

JACKSON

Oh! the agent's alright. But, this is between you and I. "Good night, my dear." (*Exits*).

MARY LOU

Insults, insults, everywhere. Oh! God, how can I bear this. (*Walks up and down floor in despair, door opens stealthly, and James Williams enters, looks very much frightened, stands with back to door, and places finger on lips. Mary Lou startled, speaks*). James! for God's sake, tell me quickly, what has happened?

JAMES

Hush, don't talk so loud—"hide me,—they are after me,—do you hear,—they are after me."

MARY LOU

Who? what do you mean?

JAMES

The police, I haven't much time, I must hide, a man was killed, in the place where I was. Before God, I didn't do it. "Don't look at me like that. I was asleep, and when I awoke, the cops were there, and I had the gun, in my hand." Before God, I do not know how it got there. I got away in the excitement, and I must hide. They will be here any minute now, do something, don't stand there and look.

MARY LOU

"No, James you must go away." It would never do for them to find you, it would mean imprisonment, or maybe death." Think of daughter and son, disgraced for life. Here, take this money and go."

(Goes over to stove, takes from coffee pot, a small roll of money. Gives it to James, who, takes it hurriedly and puts it in pocket, they embrace. Starts apart frightened, as a loud knock is heard on door. James exits on opposite side of stage. Mary Lou opens door, two cops enter, pushing her aside, and she starts toward other door, she to delay them, knocks cup off of table. They turn and address Mary Lou)

POLICE

"Well, where is that husband of yours?"

MARY LOU

"I do not know."

DETECTIVE

"Now, listen here, you had better come clean. We saw him come in this house, and if you are hiding a murderer; it will go hard with you,—see.

MARY LOU

I tell you. I do not know where he is—

POLICE

Well, we will get him, and when we do, you had better look out,—let's search the place.

(Starts toward bedroom, Mary Lou strikes cup from table, causes crash, also police and detective to turn)

DETECTIVE

What, was that?

POLICE

I thought it was a shot. See, it was a ruse of this woman's. *(Walks over to Mary Lou, catches her wrist and twists her arm, until she drops to her knees).* You devil, you know where he is, now, come through with it.

MARY LOU

(Crys out from pain)

"I swear, I don't know. Oh! you are hurting my wrist, please stop."

POLICE

Not until you tell us where he is. You search the place. *(To detective).* Now, will you talk or not. We'll take you to headquarters.

MARY LOU

"I don't know where he is."
(Crying)
(Henry comes out of bedroom, rushes toward mother)

HENRY

Mother!

POLICE

(To Henry)
"Get back there, you."

DETECTIVE

(Enters room)
It's no use. He's made his escape. What are we going to do with her?

POLICE

I won't take her down, I've got a better plan. We'll station a man here.

DETECTIVE

"Well, you helped him to get away, and you will pay for it."
(Police and detective exit)

HENRY

(Rushes to mother's side, catches her in his arms)
Oh, mother this is terrible

CURTAIN

ACT 2

SCENE 1

(Time: Afternoon four months later. Place: Same as first scene, in Act 1. Henry enters the kitchen with bag, crosses over to bedroom door, leaves bag in bedroom. Comes out with books, takes a seat at the table. Opens book and tries to study. Gives gestures of impatience and brushes books to floor)

HENRY

Oh! How can I put my mind on lessons, when my conscience is worrying me to death. Why, did I do it? How could I ever have brought myself to listen to Teddy. It would break my poor mother's heart. If she knew, oh!—

(Lays head on arms at table, door opens and Teddy a boy of a few years Henry's senior enters, with cap in hand whistling)

TEDDY

Oh! there you are, mamma's little school boy. How is tricks?

(Henry starts as Teddy speaks, but, looks away)

"Is mamma's boy getting ready for night school, ha, ha, night school, and some school eh, Henry?"

HENRY

Don't bother me, haven't you done enough harm? Oh! I'm sick of it all.

TEDDY

Now, there you go blame me if you want to. I didn't make you do anything. I only tried to do you a favor, when I got you in with the gang. And now, what you squawking about. Don't you get your share?

HENRY

Oh! I didn't mean anything, forget it.

TEDDY

Now, you are talking turkey. "I met a girl, that is just nuts to meet you. You old shiek, she's coming here this afternoon.

Works downtown in a small night club, and makes money to burn."

(Teddy makes a few steps in imitation of girl, turns and extends hand to Henry, laughs, then Henry bows and laughs)

HENRY

But, Teddy I don't want to meet any girl, that is, that kind of a girl. "Some day I mean to get out of all this stuff. I met a girl last week, that, has made me feel ashamed of what I am doing, and these surroundings and everything."

TEDDY

"Say, cut the sermon." How you do talk. You said that the law had run your father off, and that you was going to get your revenge. Now, you are squawking your head off, because everything is coming your way."

HENRY

Yes, but sooner or later, the law triumphs, it always does.

TEDDY

Oh! you make me sick.

(Goes over to bedroom, returns with bag, just as knock is heard on door. Rushes back to bedroom with bag and comes back on stage, just as Henry admits two girls. Girls loudly dressed and too much makeup on their faces, smoking. Shakes hands with Teddy who in turn introduces them to Henry, nods head toward one and winks)

Well, Henry, here are the little dolls. Now, what can we do to make them happy?

ROSA LEE

"I am more than pleased to meet you Henry." "For my part I suggest a little party, with everything that goes with a party, eh, Millie."

MILLIE

Suits me, right down to the ground.

(Takes out vanity case, begins to put on more paint, hands Teddy a small mirror to hold)

ROSA LEE

Of course, I want it understood, I stand the expenses. So here.
(Pulls out roll from purse, and starts to hand it to Henry, who waves it aside. Teddy steps between her and Henry and takes money, gives Henry a kick on the foot)

TEDDY

"Why certainly Rosa Lee, it shall be just as you desire."
(Starts toward door)

HENRY

Teddy, you know I cannot pull any party here. Why, mother
and Edna will be here soon.

ROSA LEE

Well, boys I'll tell you what we'll do. Come on over to my
little shack, and we can have all the fun that we want, and
the skies for the limit, eh, Millie.

MILLIE

"You said it Rosa, and besides it's so exclusive. So let's go."
*(They all exit. Henry takes books from floor and hides
them in oven)*
(Mary Lou and Edna enter)

EDNA

"Mother, you sit down. I'll fix you a bite to eat. I know you
are tired."

MARY LOU

No more tired, than you are dear. "Why, you look like a
ghost. My poor baby." Pounding on an old typewriter all
day, is harder than sewing.

EDNA

Oh! I don't know about that. But, you see, I've got to go
back and do some extra work. I only ran up here to let you
know where I would be, so that you would not worry.

MARY LOU

"Why, Edna! it's after ten o'clock." I won't let you do that.

EDNA

Now, mother this will mean five dollars more, and goodness
knows we need it.

MARY LOU

"But child, your health." Why, you are not well.

EDNA

"Oh! I feel fine. I did have a headache. But, one of the girls,
who goes around with the boss, gave me a pill, of some kind,
and bingo, my headache went, just like that."
(Waves hands and both laugh)

MARY LOU

Well, be careful Edna. I don't know what I'd do if I didn't have you, to cheer me up. "Henry's so wrapped up in his books."

EDNA

"Yes, his books and Teddy. Mother, I don't like that boy, and Henry's been acting very queer lately. Ever since that night he said, he met that girl, that he rescued in the night club. By the way, what became of her?"

MARY LOU

"Henry, said," that she went south. She and her mother. He says that she was a very nice girl. But, I can't see how she can be nice, and in a place like that.

EDNA

(Placing food on table)

My dear old fashioned mother. The best people go to night clubs here.

MARY LOU

But, you mustn't Edna. I just couldn't stand to have you go. You won't, will you?

(Sits at table)

EDNA

(Kissing her)

Of course not. But, I must hurry back, to the office, see you later, bye.

MARY LOU

"Bye, bye, dear, hurry home as soon as you can." I'll be lonely with you out, and Henry at night school.

(Starts eating)

Well, Henry's gone to night school. I didn't know it was so late. *(Looking at clock, nearby).* I have so much ironing to do. *(Gets up, puts up ironing board, and starts ironing).* *(Knock is heard at the door).* Come in. *(Eliza enters, takes seat at table, helps herself to a cup of tea and other food, eating with great gusto).*

ELIZA

"This is good tea, Mrs. Williams." *(Sips tea).* I was just going to borrow some from you, but you've got some already made. It will save me the trouble of making it.

MARY LOU

Just help yourself, don't mind me.

ELIZA

Do you happen to have any more biscuits around?
(Takes last one from plate)

MARY LOU

I have only one, for my son's supper.

ELIZA

Now, that's too bad. "Say, you'd better watch that son of yours. He's running in some mighty bad crowds." I saw a gal down here this afternoon, that was in court the same time I was there for fighting, for peddling dope. She's a bad egg.

MARY LOU

I know Henry would not touch dope. But, I'll speak to him about that.

ELIZA

"Well, I'm just wising you up. Of course, I ain't no angel, but I'd hate to see anybody on that stuff. I tried it once myself, but, I didn't go far that way. By the way, I saw Jackson down here last week, and what's he up to. Sweet on you or Edna."

MARY LOU

These houses belong to Mr. Jackson. I guess he can come around whenever he wishes. As to anybody being sweet on me, you should know better than that by now. I'm still married.

ELIZA

Oh! that ain't nothing, and besides old Jackson's got money and the Lord knows that's what you need.

MARY LOU

"Let's talk about something else."

ELIZA

Alright, how about lending me a little tea.

MARY LOU

(Goes over to cupboard and puts some tea in a small paper)
Here you are Mrs. Louder.
(Hands her tea)

ELIZA

"Thanks," pay you back soon.   Good-bye.
   (Exits)

MARY LOU

Oh! but I'm tired.   I worked hard today, but I must work hard, to just barely live.   I could write home to father for aid, but, I do not want the folks at home, to know about James.

(Knock is heard at door, Mary Lou opens door and Heury staggers into room, and sinks to floor.   There is blood on his sleeve, Mary Lou rushes to him and starts to bathe his forehead.   He is shaking with pain and fright)

MARY LOU

Oh! my poor boy.   How did this happen?   Are you badly hurt?   Tell mother all about it.

HENRY

   (Brokenly)
They told me to watch, while they went inside.   The cops came, I didn't see them, and when I did, I ran.   They shot. I am not hurt much, only my arm.

(Loud knock is heard at door, two cops enter)

POLICE

"Well, here he is."   So it's you again.   I told you we'd get you.   Now, it's your son, a gangster.   But, what can you expect, with such a father.

(They address these remarks to Mary Lou, who gathers Henry in her arms)

MARY LOU

"You can't have him," he is mine! mine!   I tell you.   He hasn't done aynthing, he's hurt.

DETECTIVE

That's what they all say.   *(Calls to police)*.   Come on help me here, let's get him to a hospital.   He's our prisoner.

(Police and detective starts picking boy up, Mary Lou still on her knees, holds on to him, they try to push her away and she fights back, crawling to keep up with them)

MARY LOU

"Oh! please don't take him," leave him here until he is well. Let me nurse him.   I'll turn him over, when he is better, I swear it. "For God's sake," don't take him away like this, he's my baby! Oh! my boy! my boy!

(Mary Lou's voice rises higher and higher, until it is all a scream. The two officers push her away and take boy out of door. Her voice dies away into a sob, as she falls prone on the floor)

CURTAIN

ACT 2

SCENE 2

Place:Lawyer Jackson's office, furnished with upholstered easy chairs and a mahogany desk. Time: The next morning.

JACKSON
(Seated at desk dictating a letter to stenographer)
Mrs. Smith, this is to inform you that the mortgage, that I hold on your home, is past due. And I am giving you until tomorrow to either pay the same, or vacate the premises. Respectfully yours.

ALICE
Mr. Jackson, please don't send that letter. I know that Mrs. Smith is in trouble, and her husband is in the hospital, not expected to live another day.

JACKSON
"Well, what has that got to do with me?" I must have my money, that's my business. I'm not here for my health, hand me the letter, I'll mail it. From now on, you do as I tell you, or someone else will. See, who's in the outer office?

ALICE
Yes sir.
(Alice leaves the room, Jackson turns to desk, Alice enters room)
There's a woman out there, seems sort of crazy. Says, that she must see you at once. A matter of life and death.
(Jackson, looking up from paper he is reading)

JACKSON
Is that so? Does she look as if she has money?

ALICE
No, sir.

JACKSON
Tell her, that I can't see her. I'm in a conference. By the way, Miss Ross, my wife's gone away for a short time, and I

want you to send her a check every Saturday. "Don't bother me with it, I'll make out a few." If you should hear anyone saying anything about her leaving, just say that she is in a Sanitarium in North Carolina, for her health. That's all. Oh! yes, Miss Ross, you can go to the bank now. Finish these briefs, that you are doing, and then go.

(Alice crosses room to typewriter and starts writing. Samuel Blackwell and Richard Mooney enter, walk over to Jackson's desk, all shake hands)

JACKSON

"Glad to see you." You are on time, what's up boys?

SAM

Oh! there's plenty stirring.

RICHARD

You bet your boots there is.

JACKSON

Just a moment. *(Turns to stenographer).* You may go to the bank now, Miss Ross. *(Puts up hands to men to be quiet until she leaves)*

Have a cigar boys. *(Offers them box of cigars, the men each take one and lgiht them. Stenographer leaves room).* Well, boys, shoot the works. You're first Dick.

RICHARD

"Well, to start with, that woman you had taking care of the flat, took on too much of the stuff, and ran wild." "This morning the bulls got her, and of course, they tried to make her tell, where she got the stuff, but, she wouldn't. Then they searched the flat, but they didn't find a thing. She's in the jug."

SAM

There's about five thousand dollars worth of the stuff, in that flat. The bulls are watching the place.

JACKSON

We've got to figure out a way, to get it out of there. Let me think.

(Meditatively)

RICHARD

I don't believe we are going to get Scotty in again. The people have found out that our gang is back of his election.

[73]

Yes, and boss, you are none too popular with folks around here.

JACKSON

You two get busy and round up the others. "Get around to my tenants, promise them things, anything, until after election. I've got to run this district, and with Scotty on the bench, everything is turkey."

RICHARD

What's going to be done about the girl in jail?

JACKSON

I've got a plan. Get Jones on the phone.

(Sam goes over to telephone, calls Monument 6253, gets number and hands receiver to Jackson, Jackson speaking over phone)

Hello, Jones. I want you to go down to the jail and see about Rosa Lee: what's that! oh, yes, she got charged up, and they canned her. Get her bonds for her, and send the girl, I just put there with you, over here. I can use her. That's none of your business, just do as I say, and be quick.

SAM

(Aside to Richard)

The boss is tight today.

RICHARD

Yes, and Jones ought to know better than cross him. What he's got on that fellow, could get him the chair.

JACKSON

You boys, clear out.

(Millie rushes into office)

MILLIE

Gee, I had a time getting in here. "How you guys feeling?"

(Sits on desk)

JACKSON

How did you get up here?

MILLIE

Used the stairs. You don't catch little Millie taking any chances. I guess you know Rosa Lee's canned.

JACKSON

Yes, you lay low for awhile. Take a few days out in my place. Long Island.

MILLIE

Alright, but, say Jack.—

JACKSON

Mr. Jackson.

MILLIE

"Mr. Jackson, some stew." I want to know why do you want me to slip the stuff to that girl over at Jones office? What's your game?

JACKSON

I don't want none of that sob stuff, from you. I can use the girl and her mother, and I mean to do it. Now, all of you, "get out."

MILLIE

Yes, you can use everybody, and God! how you do use them. But, some day, you'll get yours.

RICHARD

Cut it out Millie. It's our living and the boss is good to every one of us, and you know it.

SAM

Oh! she's just setimental, over that kid Rosa Lee's been tagging around, some Henry. "He's in the hold-up racket."

MILLIE

He's not in any racket, and you know it. It's these environments that's got him. Just like it got me. Then there is Teddy to push him on. "God, I'm tired of the whole business." When I think of that innocent girl whose very soul I've damned with dope. *(Pacing floor)*. Some day, I'm going to turn on all of you! *(Shakes finger in Jackson's face)*. And when I do, God, help you.

JACKSON

(Catches her by shoulders and shakes her, both men spring to their feet)

"Shut up, you little fool, don't you know if you try any of that stuff, I've only got to say the word, and you go out like a light."

MILLIE

Oh, don't worry, I know that. Give me the keys to the Long Island place.

(Jackson hands her keys, she turns and leaves the office)

RICHARD

She's alright now. I guess she took one pill too many.

SAM

I don't know about that. She's dangerous.

JACKSON

Just keep your eyes on her boys. Now, you both had better
go.

RICHARD

Alright, we'll take the back stairs out.

(They exit, just as Miss Ross enters other door)

ALICE

Mr. Jackson. That woman is still out there.

JACKSON

Send her in.

*(Mary Lou enters shabbily dressed and in great distress.
Jackson gets up, and meets her, places her in chair)*

JACKSON

My dear Mrs. Williams. What has happened?

MARY LOU

Oh! Mr. Jackson, I'm in so much trouble.

(Bursts into tears)

JACKSON

(Patting her on the shoulder)

Now, calm yourself, tell me what is the trouble?

MARY LOU

"My boy's a prisoner, and in the hospital."

JACKSON

What happened?

MARY LOU

Oh, Mr. Jackson, he's been running with a bad boy named
Teddy. I warned him, but he would not listen. Last night,
he was with a gang, who was robbing a store. He was outside
watching for them.

JACKSON

And the cop got him.

MARY LOU

He tried to run, when he saw them coming. They shot him.

JACKSON

Bad, bad.

(Shaking head)

MARY LOU

Yes, and it will go harder with him, because, they suspected
his father of murder, and he got away.

JACKSON

Yes, the law never forgets.

MARY LOU

You'll take the case, won't you Mr. Jackson?

JACKSON

Well, it depends.

MARY LOU

What do you mean?

JACKSON

I can clear your boy, and put him on the street. What of
my pay?

MARY LOU

Oh, I'll work night and day and Edna's working. We'll pay
anything you ask.

JACKSON

I don't want money.

MARY LOU

Oh! (Looking frightened). How can I pay you then?

JACKSON

Listen Mary Lou. "You may have guessed that I love you.
Now, don't interrupt me. I'm not trying to make love to you.
I have a business proposition, for you to consider."

MARY LOU

Oh, I'm so glad it's that. Of course I'll accept.

JACKSON

But, you don't know what it is yet. I might as well tell you
now. It's outside the law.

MARY LOU

I can't do anything, that would be breaking the law Mr. Jack-
son.

JACKSON

Well, you don't want your boy out.

MARY LOU

Oh, yes I do. Please Mr. Jackson, let me pay you. I do not
want to do anything wrong.

JACKSON

It's all up to you. I have an apartment in one of the best parts of the city, and must have a nice quiet woman to keep it. I keep stuff there. I don't want the police to suspect the place.

MARY LOU

"If they do find it there, then what." Oh, I can't, can't do that, I can't.

JACKSON

Well, there are other lawyers.

MARY LOU

Yes, but, I haven't got a penny right now. They want their money in advance. Oh, I thought you were a friend.

JACKSON

And so I am, you are acting foolish, you get a good home and everything. What am I getting out of the bargain? Maybe some day you'll let me be real nice to you, eh?

(Gets up and puts arms around her shoulder)

MARY LOU

Please don't. What is it you keep in this apartment?

JACKSON

Thousands of dollars worth of dope and liquor, and my name must never be connected with the place, no matter what happens.

MARY LOU

My God! I don't want to be a criminal. I must get my boy out, I must.

JACKSON

I'll have Jones take you to the place. I'll pay all bills, and he will visit you there. "You are to pose as a widow and Rosa Lee's mother. Rosa Lee is in jail, Jones will take care of her case."

MARY LOU

Oh, Mr. Jackson, I do not want to get mixed up in this. I'm in bad enough now, then there is my Edna. What about her?

JACKSON

I am giving her a job here, as my stenographer. She will bring the stuff here to me. Then I will pass it out to the boys, who will sell it.

MARY LOU

No, I can't, I won't.

JACKSON

There's no risk in it for people like you. I can just say the word to Scotty, the district attorney. Then your boy goes free, otherwise he can go up for several years.

MARY LOU

Oh, my God! that would kill me.

JACKSON

Well, will you accept my proposition, or not?

MARY LOU

Yes, for his sake.

(Spoken in tense whisper)

CURTAIN

ACT 3

SCENE 1

Time: Two years later. Place: Durham, North Carolina.
Setting: Living room in home of Mary Lou Williams.
Furniture: Large settee, comfortable chairs and living
room table, piano, and a general air of comfort, and pros-
perity.
(Henry is discovered, hanging up hat, takes off coat and
calls)

HENRY

Mother, mother dear, where are you?

MARY LOU

Coming, dear.

(Mary Lou enters room, neatly dressed, they embrace,
and Mary Lou holds Henry at arm length, looking at
him lovingly)

How is my big baby? Just look what a fine man you are.
Then to think just as mamma has really gotten acquainted
with you, she is about to lose you. "Oh, well, that is the way,
we mothers just raise you for some other woman to take."

HENRY

"There, there, mother of mine." To hear you, one would
think you were jealous of Margaret, you need have no fear.
You will always hold first place in my heart, every day you
grow dearer and dearer to me. When I think of all the trouble
that I have caused you, and how you have suffered. "It makes
my heart ache."

MARY LOU

Don't Henry, it is just opening an old wound for both of us.

HENRY

You know mother, I've been here just six months, and have
had two raises in salary. All of this, this home, sometimes,
mother I feel as though I should tell Margaret about the time
I spent in that terrible place. I hate making a new start, and
still living a lie.

MARY LOU

"Don't do it Henry." Some things are better untold. Just imagine that you are beginning life, and let it rest there.

HENRY

I guess you are right mother. Oh, I wish Edna would come home. Sometimes I feel mother, that I am the cause of all the suffering, she is going through.

MARY LOU

Henry, don't say that, it's my fault. Had I not consented to keep that awful apartment for Jackson, my darling child wouldn't be what she is today. Oh! it's too dreadful to believe, my lovely baby, a—dope fiend. It's my fault!

HENRY

Mother, do not say that, you know—

MILLIE

(Standing in doorway, very pale and shaking.)
"Mrs. Williams and Henry." I have a confession to make. I hope you will forgive me.
(Comes into room)

HENRY

Here, sit down Millie. "You're still very weak and sick."

MILLIE

Well, I don't deserve the kindness you two have shown me. I am the one,—who gave Edna, her very first—dope.

MARY LOU

You! why! Millie.

MILLIE

"That devil made me do it. He's got so much on me until I dared not disobey him. Oh, I wish you had left me where you found me to die. I ought to be dead. Before God, I had to obey him."

HENRY

God! I'd like to kill that man.

MARY LOU

Henry, don't say that.

HENRY

But, I mean it. Look how he's treated me, Edna, this girl and how he lied about getting me out of jail. I even found out, he used his influence, over that district attorney, to get me a year.

MILLIE

I'm so sorry, will you ever forgive me Mrs. Williams?

MARY LOU

"Of course I will. Didn't I risk my life to save you, when I heard them plotting to take you out,—and kill you. I put you wise and scared them away. They'd killed you, but I slipped in blanks.

MILLIE

Jackson would kill us both, if he knew, where we were.

MARY LOU

Well, we don't have to worry. We are safe here.

(Henry helps Millie from room. Mary Lou sits at table very thoughtful. Henry returns immediately)

HENRY

Mother, I am going over to call on Margaret. How are the rehearsals coming on? I saw our preacher downtown, and believe me, he is expecting your concert to be a big success. "You know the church needs a lot of money, to finish the Community House."

MARY LOU

They shall have it. I am having just a few here tonight. Just the ones that need to rehearse most, as some know their parts so well. Tomorow night is the big night. Henry is Margaret going to sing for us?

HENRY

Why yes mother. I am going over to get her now. She is expecting her father on the midnight train.

(Mary looking into space wistfully)

MARY LOU

Her father, oh, Henry, are you going to ask him tonight?

HENRY

I don't know mother, I've got to see how he looks first. He might be a bear *(laughs)* and eat your little boy's head off, just like this—*(both laugh, as he imitates how bear would bite, as he growls and springs at mother).* *(Henry moves over to door).* So long mother, I'll be right back.

(Mary Lou busies herself round room, as Henry throws her kiss, and exits meeting Carl at door)

CARL

How are you Mrs. Williams?

MARY LOU

Very well Carl.   You don't look so well yourself.

CARL

I'm not sick, just almost crazy with grief.

MARY LOU

You poor boy.   I know, you mean about Edna.

CARL

Yes, I've made up my mind, to go to New York and find her, and bring her home.   No matter what she is doing, or what she has done, I love her.

MARY LOU

I wish you success Carl, with all my heart.

CARL

"Pray that God, will help me to find her Mrs. Williams.   If I am not successful, I will never come back again."

MARY LOU

God bless you, my boy.
(Crying, starts towards door, meets Henry with telegram, who comes in joyously)

HENRY

I met the boy at the corner with this telegram.   "Listen," mother and Carl, it's from Edna.

MARY LOU

Read it, quick!
(They both collapse into chairs)

HENRY

Haven't written because I've been West, found father he is cleared, guilty man caught, will be home tomorrow safe, well and cured.   Edna.

CARL

Thank God.

MARY LOU

God is indeed good.   Oh!   I am so happy.

HENRY

So am I.
(Catches mother and Carl by the hands and dances around, Margaret enters looks on happily)
Oh, Margaret, my sister and father will be here tomorrow. We are so happy.

MARGARET

And I'm happy, because that you are, I just ran over for a few moments. I've got to hurry back, to be at home, when father comes. Do you want me to sing Mrs. Williams?

MARY LOU

No Margaret, I will not have any rehearsal tonight. Everybody knows their parts, and then, I am just too happy to bother.

CARL

Well, I'll go home and try to realize this happiness. Goodbye folks.

(They all bid him goodbye. Carl exits)

MARY LOU

Excuse me children.

(Mary Lou exits into bedroom)

MARGARET

It's all so strange Henry. Father coming here, I haven't seen him in over two years. Mother and I have tried to forget all about him. That's why, I never mentioned him. As we have only been in Durham a few months, we don't know many people. No one here knows him, so mother was taken for a widow. We let it go at that.

HENRY

Will he and your mother become reconciled?

MARGARET

I guess they will.

HENRY

What if he objects to our marriage?

MARGARET

But, I know he won't. He'll think you are just grand.

HENRY

I do hope so.

MARGARET

Then when I tell him, how you saved my life in New York, when that terrible man got after my cousin and I. "Well, he will say *(pokes out chest and puts thumbs in waist, as though it was a vest)* take her boy, she's yours.

HENRY

Margaret, you never lived in New York, did you?

MARGARET

Why no, I always lived over on Long Island. Mother and I went to New York seldom. Why, is it such a terrible place?

HENRY

Oh, no. Some parts are a bit rough, I was just wondering, why I didn't meet you before I did.

(Starts to embrace her, knock is heard at door)

Come in—

(Jackson enters. He and Henry stare at each other angrily. Margaret runs to her father and embraces him)

MARGARET

Oh, father! I'm so glad to see you. *(Looks from one man to the other)*. Why, what's the matter? Do you know Henry father?

(Father pushes her away)

JACKSON

Go home, Margaret.

MARGARET

But, father.—

JACKSON

Don't argue with me. Go—

(Points sternly to door, Margaret exits). (Jackson turns to Henry, just as Mary Lou enters from bedroom, and as he raises his cane to strike Henry, Mary Lou steps in between them)

MARY LOU

"So it's you Jackson."

JACKSON

Yes, my wife told me I'd find Margaret at this house. To my surprise, I find her with this thief and ex-convict, son of yours.

MARY LOU

Be careful, Jackson.

HENRY

Yes, you had better be careful. You have caused my mother and sister enough trouble.

JACKSON

Not near as much as I will cause you, if the whole bunch of you don't clear out of this town. When I get through telling these people who you are, it won't be big enough to hold you.

MARY LOU
(Pushing Henry away and facing him)
Now, you've had your way and say. I'll have mine. Mr.
Jackson, you say one word to anyone about me or mine, and
I'll start telling the world and your wife, what I know about
you. You! hypocrite, you unspeakable beast, how you ruined
my daughter's life and tried to ruin mine. Tried to make me
do things, that I would be ashamed to mention. You dope
peddler, I should kill you, where you stand.
(Her voice rises hysterically)

HENRY
Let me do it, mother.

MARY LOU
No, let me handle this Henry.

JACKSON
And who do you think you are, that people would believe your
word against mine.

MARY LOU
Oh! I've got proof enough. Edna worked in your office, she
has duplicates of your code messages and Rosa Lee's signed
confession before she died or how she smuggled the dope in
for you, and how you tricked her and other girls into selling it.

JACKSON
Yes, Edna's dead, so what good can she do.

MARY LOU
"She is not dead." She will be here tomorrow, and I'm telling
you Jackson, if you want peace, it shall be peace. If you say
one word, if you try to disgrace my boy and I, and send him
back to the life, he has just got away from, I'll kill you.

MILLIE
(Entering quietly from the other room)
If you don't kill him, I will. *(Points gun at Jackson, Henry
takes it from her.)*

JACKSON
Millie, I thought.—

MILLIE
That I was dead. I know you did, but I'm not. You know
I've got a plenty on you. I am beyond caring what becomes
of me now. I will see that you get yours.

MARY LOU

Now, Jackson, what shall it be? Peace or war.

JACKSON

(Walks away, stands thinking, turns to Mary Lou.)
"Peace, you win Mary Lou." Henry do you still love Margaret, now that you know she is my daughter.

HENRY

Yes, that is not Margaret's fault. She's an angel.

(Millie sits down feebly)

JACKSON

Go and find her boy. May God bless you. *(Henry extends hand, Jackson takes it and they shake. Henry exits.)* Mary Lou can you and Millie ever forgive me.

(Goes over and takes Mary Lou's hand, places other hand on Millie's head)

MARY LOU

Yes, Jackson. Maybe God will forgive you, and the rest of us. We can all start life anew.

JACKSON

"Yes, in better environment."

CURTAIN

AUNT SARA'S WOODEN GOD

Sincerely
Mercedes Gilbert

Bruno
of
Hollywood
n.y.c.

AUNT SARA'S WOODEN GOD

BY

MERCEDES GILBERT

The Christopher Publishing House
Boston, U. S. A.

[92]

TO
MY FATHER

FOREWORD

Miss Mercedes Gilbert, who comes from Florida to Broadway as one of America's leading Negro actresses, returns again to the deep south for the scene of her first novel, "Aunt Sara's Wooden God." This is an authentic every-day story of thousands of little families below the Mason-Dixon line, bound to the soil by poverty and blackness, but living their enclosed lives always in the hope that some-day some one of them may escape the family group and go on to higher things. Their tragedy is that there is so small a foundation on which to base such a hope. The wooden god of Miss Gilbert's novel is a mulatto country boy, worshipped by his mother, but himself unable to fulfill the faith and belief she has in him, balked as he is by poverty, the color-line, and his own inner weaknesses born of conceit and fear. That he lives and dies a hero to Aunt Sara, although he tortures and hurts so many others, constitutes the ironic tragedy of this book filled with little pictures of the rural and small-town life of the South.

Those readers who enjoyed "Jonah's Gourde Vine" or "Ollie Miss" will find in "Aunt Sara's Wooden God" a kindred volume.

Langston Hughes

vii

AUNT SARA'S WOODEN GOD

CHAPTER I

"Ah'm gonna lay down my burden
Down by de river side
Down by de river side
Down by de river side
"Ah'm gonna lay down my burden
Down by de river side
Ain't gonna study war no more."

Sara Lou's song trailed off to a whisper as William's voice, raised angrily, broke the silence of the early morning.

"You're a liar! and a meddlesome black fool! and I've got a good mind to smash your ugly face in," William shouted.

"Mister Gordon jes' tole me yuh done borried money from him an' said Ma sent you to get it, an' ah know he wouldn't lie on nobody," Jim retorted.

"Yes, you know it's the truth 'cause Mister Gordon said so, and he's a white man and can't lie," William sneered.

"No! It ain't dat, ah jes' knows yuh, an' what a liar yuh is!" Jim's remark raised William's fury to a murderous pitch. Picking up a long stick that lay near by, he raised it threateningly.

"Shut up, you black fool, before I knock your head off."

"You ain't gonna let your wooden God an'

9

corn-stalk Jesus fool you into hittin' me," Jim taunted; his voice, though quieter than William's, carried a convincing quality of determination that William knew meant more than mere words.

Sara Lou ran as swiftly as her two hundred pounds would permit towards the barn from where the angry voices of her sons seemed to be coming. The early July morning had dawned hot and oppressive, and Byron, a small farming village in Central Georgia, stirred itself sleepily. Dew lay like carpet upon the green grass that covered the surrounding woods. Overhead numerous brightly colored birds flitted from tree to tree chirping loudly, unheard by Sara Lou as she called:

"Yuh Will-y-um! Yuh J-i-m! Will-y-um! Stop dat fussin' dis moment!"

William dropped the stick he held quickly, and turned to greet his mother, his face still flushed with a dull angry red that showed to the roots of his dark brown wavy hair.

"Yuh boys aught'er be shame uh yo'selfs, blood brothers an al'lers fussin' an' fightin', jes' cause yo' pa done died an ain't nobody but me to try an' keep yuh straight," Sara Lou scolded, as she stood between the two boys, looking directly at Jim.

Jim started to speak, but changed his mind and walked slowly away. What was the use, he thought. He could gain nothing by trying to tell his mother of William's latest deception. No matter what he said, his mother would take William's side. He was slow of speech, while William had answers ready before questions were asked, and their mother hung on every word he uttered. He was her God. Next to her religion, she worshipped him. To her his words were always soft and honey-coated, while to Jim, William used a patronizing tone which made the younger boy's blood boil. But their mother could not detect the underlying sneer in his smooth words and she usually blamed Jim for the frequent quarrels between the boys.

Sara Lou watched Jim as he walked away in the direction of the Gordon plantation. A little pucker in her usually smooth fair brow showed plainly the anxiety of her thoughts. In the depths of her large black eyes lurked the troubled expression which for the four years of her widowhood had dimmed the bright cheerfulness of former years, when her husband, John, had been the staid prop on which she leaned and watched her boys grow to young manhood.

A sigh escaped her lips, as Jim's figure receded in the distance. How like his father he was, she thought—the same slow steady tread, his father's height and color, the same quick flare of temper, and equally quick forgiveness.

Her mind drifted back over the years to the day, twenty years before, when she first met John Carter. He had come to Byron, to pick cotton, and had lingered on after the cotton picking season had passed. Owen Gordon, the richest white farmer in Byron, had hired him as a steady farm hand, but that had not been the main reason for his sojourn in Byron. He had seen Sara Lou, then a tall, fair young woman of twenty; her large black eyes had looked beyond him the evening he first saw her standing in her little cabin door on the outskirts of the Gordon place, but something sweet and soulful in their depths had made him want to talk to her and know her better.

He had asked about Sara Lou, that night, as he sat out in front of the little log cabin where he boarded with Lucy Salisbury, the village midwife and root doctor. (Aunt Salisbury, as she was lovingly called by the villagers,) gave her snuff brush, a tiny oak twig, a swish as she pushed it with her tongue from one side of her bony cheek to the other, and spat out a long string of brown snuff before she answered. Then, turning her feeble, squinty eyes heavenward, her jet black face seemed to take on a purplish hue as she exclaimed:

"Lawd uh mercy man, yuh ain't gone an' took no notice uh dat strumpet is yuh?" and without giving John time to answer she continued. "Dat gal jes' naturally ain't no good, cain't ever be no good, none uh her folks fore her was no good, dey was jes' a bad lot an' dat's all dere is to it."

"Whut yuh mean, a bad lot?" John questioned, mildly enjoying the distressed look on Aunt Salisbury's bony black face, almost invisible in the dim moonlight except for the white string with which her hair, short and thin, had been wrapped so tight, that her homely face looked strained and witchlike.

"Jes' dat, son, yuh see ah done knowed dem all, from her great grandma down to her, an' all uh dem 'cept Sara Lou's ma, done had half white bastard chillun."

"How did Sara Lou's Ma escape?" John asked laughing heartily.

"Well, to start wid, her great grandma, Hester, b'longed to de Saunders family back 'fore surrender. She was a pretty yeller gal jes' like Sara Lou

is, an' de fust thing you knows she had a baby for
old mister Frank Saunders, old missy Saunders gits
suspicious 'bout it bein' his chile an' makes him sell
Hester. Owen Gordon's father, Charles Gordon,
bought her and put her to keepin' house for um.
Well, Charles Gordon had a half brother who was
jes' de limit when it comed to women, white or
black. Wid him it didn't make no difference. It
was jes' any woman who he could lay down wid,
so he took right out after Hester's daughter, Ida,
soon as she was knee high to a duck, an' when she
was fourteen she had a baby for that man and they
named her Charlotte. About a year after dat Ida's
Ma Hester died, an' old man Charles Gordon went
to live in Macon an' Ida stayed at de Gordon house
to work for his son Owen Gordon, who had jes'
got married. Well, Owen and his half uncle had a
big fuss, an' the Uncle skinned out an' went some
where up North, dat was de last heard uh him.
Ida took charge uh de Gordon house and raised
Charlotte right dare on de lot."

Aunt Salisbury interrupted her recital with a loud
chuckle as reminiscences of Ida passed through her
mind.

"Lawd, son, dat Ida was a caution. Twan't long
'fore she was sure runnin' dat Gordon home, an'
when Owen Gordon's sons was born, first Lawrence
an' den some years later Franklyn, Ida jes' took
dem in charge and raised dem so dey wouldn't mind
nobody on earth but her. She was a strong-willed
woman as ever I seed, Ida was. Well, her gal
Charlotte grew up right pretty an' 'bout de time
she was seventeen, Owen Gordon had given us a
little piece uh land an' de logs and some uh de men

had built a church, our Calvary that we still wor-
ships in, an' de next year durin' cotton pickin' time
a young preacher named Sam Smith come here to
pick cotton an' decided he'd jes' stay on an' preach
in de church an' farm. Well, den de fun started,"
Aunt Salisbury laughed, as she produced a box of
railroad snuff from the pocket of her apron, and
putting the stick she had been chewing into the box
she moved it back and forth as she nodded her head
on her bony neck with a gluttonous sound of sup-
pressed mirth.

"Lawd, son, when Ida found out dat de new
preacher, Sam Smith, had his eyes on Charlotte,
she didn't let no grass grow under her feet. She
started plotting right den how she was gonna marry
Charlotte to dat black man so as to try an' live
down dem half white bastards hur ma and hur done
had, an' den she figured dat would be a good way
to git back at us Byron colored folks dat had all'ers
called dem de Gordon Niggers. Heh, heh, heh,"
she chuckled.

"Ida had dat preacher sneakin' up to de Gordon
place every night to dere cabin back uh de Gordon
kitchen, where she'd feed him chicken an' all de
good things she could sneak out to him, an' den she
ranged it for him and Charlotte to run off to Macon
an' git hitched."

"What happened after they got married?" John
asked as Aunt Salisbury paused in her story to rub
her snuff brush over her few charred teeth and spit
out her long brown string of snuff.

"Well, when the folks found out what had hap-
pened, dey got powerful mad and planned dat dey
would stay away from de church, de next Sunday,

but heh, heh, heh," the low chuckle shook Aunt Salisbury's shoulders, and when she got her breath she continued.

"Well, son, dat fust Sunday dey stayed away, but de next Sunday Ida had got a note from Owen Gordon sayin' dat effen dey didn't 'tend dey church meetin' he would take de church away from dem, and dat settled things, an' de darkies was glad enough to meet de new Misses Smith. Well, den Charlotte an' de preacher got long jes' fine. Folks was running over each other to meet dem an' make dem welcome. A year later Charlotte had a baby boy; a little ill-formed thing dat hopped 'round like a frog, an' 'twasn't long 'fore de pore little critter died, an' a year later, when Sara Lou was born, pore Charlotte died in child birth, an' de Reverend Smith raised her all by himself. Course, when Sara Lou was old 'nough she started working for Owen Gordon, and when she got to be twenty an' hadn't had no mishap ev'rybody believed she would marry respectable and like her Ma, but no, what did she up an' do but have a baby by Owen Gordon's son, Franklyn."

"Dat's 'bout all dere is to it, son"! Aunt Salisbury concluded, stretching her bony arms above her head and yawning sleepily.

" 'Cept dat Sara Lou's trouble done killed her pore old Pa, he died foh her baby was two months old, it was bad enuff her havin' a bastard chile, but when as de pastor uh de church he had to turn her out de church, well, it was jes' more den de old man could stand so one night he jes' sleeped away." Aunt Salisbury ended her story with a sigh, as she rubbed her knees vigorously and hobbled towards the cabin door.

"Well, de gal is jes' human, an' ah sur' ain't blamin' her so much," John said as he knocked the ashes from his pipe and walked slowly towards the gate and called back "Ah'm sure gonna try an' git dat gal tuh marry me, eff'en she'll have me."

And John Carter kept his word. It was several weeks later when he got his first opportunity to talk with Sara Lou, he had walked around her cabin and found her sitting in the back door, her baby William held tightly in her arms, tears falling freely upon the face of the sleeping child.

It was a cool Autumn afternoon and when Sara Lou looked up to find him smiling at her, the serious expression in his eyes had brought a quick smile to her lips as she asked.

"Whut yuh want, Mister?"

"Nothing special, sister, ah was jes' passin' an' ah thought I'd jes' stop an' git acquainted," John answered, his smile broading to a grin.

"Well den, you better be on yo' way, cause dey ain't nothin' yuh nor nobody else kin do fuh me," Sara Lou answered, wearily passing her hand over her straight black hair that hung to her waist.

"Ah ain't so sure 'bout dat, dere's lots ah kin do. In de fust place, dis garden is all runned down, ah kin fix dat," John assured her, glancing over the little ragged garden that grew near the cabin.

Sara Lou had argued and tried to send him away, but he could not be gotten rid of, and thus their friendship had started, but to all of John's entreaties that she marry him, she turned a deaf ear.

"No, John, ah'se got my baby William, an yuh

ain't gonna take him an' me an' ask no questions,
an' ah ain't gonna answer none," she would always
answer to his pleading.

"Listen heah, Sara Lou, ah swear ah won't never
ask yuh nothing 'bout William an ah'll treat him
lak my very own long as ah lives if yuh'll marry
me," John promised from time to time. But it was
a year later before Sara Lou consented to become
his wife, after the news had reached Byron of
Franklyn Gordon's death in an automobile accident
in New York. Owen Gordon had spoken quietly
that morning when she came to bring his laundry.

"I'm leaving this morning for New York, Sara
Lou. Mister Franklyn has been killed in an acci-
dent," he said simply. And Sara Lou, not daring
to answer, had nodded her head and abruptly left
the house.

She had heard from time to time about Franklyn's
escapades in New York. Owen Gordon had never
mentioned him to her but news somehow travelled
in the small village, and Franklyn's wild drinking
and gambling had drifted back to Byron.

A week later, Sara Lou became the wife of John
Carter; and until the day of his death he had kept
his word, never to ask questions about William.
He had treated the child as his own son, even
spoiling him to some extent, for which Sara Lou
rebuked him with:

"Now, John, yuh'se spoilin' dat boy, an' dat
ain't right, 'cause he got hard 'nuff disposition now
to fight down."

"Don't yuh worry 'bout William, Sara, he's uh

smart chile, an' nuthin' ain't gonna spoil de young 'un", John would excuse.

A year after they were married, Jim was born, as black as his father, but a good-looking little chap. But even the birth of a son of his own did not change John towards William. Until the day of his death he had never shown any difference in his treatment of the boys, and William had loved and honored him with all his heart. If he had ever had any doubt that John Carter was his father, because of the neighbor's children's hints and jibes, he never showed it and for sixteen years life ran a smooth course for the Carters. John was a beloved Deacon in the little Calvary Baptist church, and Sara Lou's kindness to the villagers soon won their love and respect. Her ever-willingness to aid them in their trouble, answer the call of sickness and distress among them, had made her a favorite, and they lovingly called her "Aunt Sara."

She turned a deaf ear to the taunts the neighboring children threw at William, and when he came to her sobbing that they had called him a half white nigguh, consoled him with:

"Sticks an' stones kin break yo' bones but names ain't never goin' to hurt yuh, son."

Even as a small child he showed tendencies of a willful tempestuous nature, but she enthroned him in a place in her heart that no other human being could ever reach, excusing her partiality with the thought that he would need all the love and tender care she could give him to help him overcome his faults.

And thus life had run along, smoothly and happily for Sara until her husband's death. But, for the last few years the frequent quarrels between William and his brother had distressed her more than she cared to admit.

Jim loved William with all his heart, but he could not overlook the streak of deception that he saw, more plainly than anyone else, under William's smooth exterior. His fear for his mother's happiness was greater than anything else in his life. He knew that she worshipped William and did not want her to be disappointed in him.

On William's part, there was a deep dislike for Jim that had always been latent in him from early childhood. The realization irked him that Jim was legitimate and had a real father. He would be tortured with jealousy whenever John Carter cast a kindly glance at little Jim. And he would take any little remark directed at himself as bitter criticism. These flaring feelings had persisted with the years, but after John's death, he had stopped trying to conceal them, but allowed them to burst out in frequent quarrels and disagreements with his half brother.

Sara Lou had watched the growing dissension with fear and foreboding. Her eyes filled with tears, as she laid her hand tenderly upon William's shoulder, and asked:

"What's the matter, son? What makes you and Jim can't get along? Don't yuh love one another?"

"Oh, it ain't me, Ma. Jim is always fussin' 'bout me stayin' in Macon—going to High School," William answered, placing his arm affectionately around her waist.

"Thar yuh go—makin' love to yer ole mammy, as usual", she chuckled, her face showing the pleas-

ure she always felt when near her handsome elder
son.

William, a head taller than his mother, was
straight and slender; his features, like hers, were
finely molded; his hair dark brown and curly, match-
ing well his smooth fair skin.

With a pleased little sigh she clung to him, loving
the way he petted and fussed over her.

"Ah been wantin' yuh an' Jim to come an' git
yo' breakfuss. It's nigh on to five uh clock an' yuh
gotta git to Macon to yo' business," she said, push-
ing him before her towards the house.

"Ain't much doin' in my pressing shop right now,
Ma. Folks wearin' overalls lots an' they don't need
no pressin' shop for 'em," William remarked.

"What was that Jim was sayin' 'bout Mr. Gor-
don?" Sara Lou asked. A note of concern crept
into her voice.

"Oh, nothin', Ma," William answered hastily.
"Only he and Mr. Gordon both think I should be
here workin' on the farm instead of tryin' to get
a better education."

"That's all right, son. Some day me an' Jim goin'
to be mighty proud of you when you'se carryin' the
Gospel."

William was silent for a moment. Then, looking
toward the Gordon plantation he observed: "Mr.
Gordon's sure left lots of work for Jim while he's
in Europe!"

"An' Jim'll git it all done. Dat sho' is a smart
boy!"

"But he'll be gone a long time, Ma. There ain't
no need 'er Jim tryin' ter do it all in a day when

there's so much right here on our place that needs bein' done," William complained.

"Now Willyum, yuh jes' leave Jim do things his own way. Dass how come Mr. Gordon laks dat boy lak he does. White folks laks things don' right 'er way an' not put off ontell de las' minute."

"Well, can't we have our breakfast right 'er way, Ma?" William asked with a laugh.

"We sho' kin!" Sara Lou smiled and a few moments later they were seated at the table, before them a steaming breakfast of fat side, hot corn bread, molasses and coffee.

Sara Lou bowed her head as William prayed—a routine never neglected in their home.

"I'm goin' to ride to Macon this morning with Reverend Johnson. He's going in to see the doctor," William was saying.

"Ah'm glad he is caise he ain't been feelin' so well lately," his mother replied, full of concern about her ailing pastor.

"He's a good un for yuh to pattern atter, Willyum, when yuh starts preachin'," she added, looking at him proudly. Her desire to make a preacher of William was the greatest thing in her life, and although William wasn't so keen about becoming a preacher, he made her think he was, and after all it would afford him a chance to lead a life of ease and he hated work.

"He's all right, 'nough, ma, but he ain't educated and when I starts preaching, I'm goin' to be well prepared," he answered.

"But he's chuck full 'er religion, and dat's whut counts wid de Lawd, William."

"And the Lawd ain't 'gainst us preparing our-self to carry His word either, Ma."

"Ah knows dat, William. Dat's why ah let yuh go to Macon to high school, but jes' de same, don't yuh git all puffed up wid pride caise pride goes 'fore a fall, de Lawd says."

William's face flushed over his mother's rebuke, as he lowered it over his plate, but when he raised his head again, he was smiling.

They had finished breakfast when Jim entered the kitchen. Placing a basket of fresh vegetables on the table, he seated himself to eat his belated breakfast. Sara Lou smiled fondly as, passing, she patted his shoulder, and hurried away to her many morning tasks.

Jim, a reticent boy of medium height, stocky and as his mother put it, 'the spittin' image of his father', claimed only one resemblance to his mother and brother—his eyes which were large and black. Un-like William who was a brilliant scholar, he had learned little in school; his brain just did not seem to grasp even the simplest rudiments.

The farm had been his teacher. He loved it, un-derstood cattle, could doctor them when sick and bred them better than the oldest farmers around Byron. Since his father's death he had become the head of the house as far as earning the living was concerned.

Sara Lou's home like the other Negro cabins, had at first consisted of two rooms in which they lived, cooked their meals and slept. Her husband, John Carter, had however, enlarged it with two rooms built under the eaves known as a jump, adding a front and back porch downstairs and a little shed-like kitchen. It was by far the best of the Negro homes for miles around.

"See the garden's doing nicely, Jim," William ventured, as Jim settled himself at the table.

"Could do bettuh, if Ah had some help."

"You spend too much time working over at Mr. Gordon's. Maybe that's why you can't get more done here."

"Not half as much time as yuh spend sittin' 'round in dat school or foolin' 'round in Macon loafin' and pretendin' yuh wanna learn something so as yuh kin preach," Jim retorted hotly.

"You don't know what you're talkin' 'bout. Jes' 'cause you're ignorant ain't no reason for me to be. I'm tryin' to be better myself."

"Yuh ain't never goin' to better yo'self! It jes' ain't in yuh. Ah done heard 'bout yo' carryin' on in Macon," Jim threw over his shoulder, as he rose and walked away.

"Don't you talk to me like that, you black ape. I've got a good mind to smash your face in, anyhow," William cried, catching up with him and shaking his fist under his nose.

Sara Lou, coming in to clear away the breakfast things, saw the situation.

"Now whut y'all fussin' 'bout?" she asked pushing them apart.

Jim turned and walked away.

Sara Lou watched him, a sigh escaping her lips as she said to William:

"Dat boy sho's got uh temper!"

"Yes, he's always fussin' wid me 'bout attending school. You should speak to him about it, Ma, once and for all."

"Ah sure will, son. He ought to be sham'er his-self an' yuh studyin' to git ready to carry de gospel but dat comes uh him not havin' religion an' dere by de needed grace to carry on."

"I wish Reverend Johnson would come on by. I wanna get going," William said, anxiously looking in the direction of the minister's home.

"It is funny he ain't sho'ed up yet. Yuh bettuh run over dere an' see whut's hol'in' 'im, Willyum," his mother advised.

William hurried away, anxious to visit the parsonage anyway, as it afforded him a chance to see the minister's sixteen year old daughter, Ruth, whom he and Jim had both loved since they were small tots.

His mother watched him walk jauntily away, hatless, the sun now high in the skies beaming brightly down on his curly brown hair. A sigh trembled upon her lips, as she wondered what the future held in store for her two boys so different in body and mind.

CHAPTER II

The Reverend Peter Johnson's little log cabin built near the Calvary Baptist Church was little more than a mile from the Carter home. Reverend Johnson and his daughter, Ruth, whose mother had died in child birth, eked out their meager living working in the cotton fields and in their own little garden and with the few dollars the members of his church grudgingly gave him from time to time.

Ruth was a pretty dark brown skin girl. Her short black curly hair framed a small oval face, the chief attractiveness of which lay in her large black eyes set wide apart, sparkling roguishly beneath long silky lashes. This morning an anxious look was in their depths, as she faced William, who greeted her with:

"Hello, Ruth, you look brighter 'en the sun."

"Go 'lon' wid you, William. You'se all'ers making pretty speeches," she smiled, alluring dimples playing hide and seek in her cheeks.

William's heart beat rapidly, as he looked into her eyes. An almost overwhelming desire to take her in his arms sent his blood coursing wildly through his body.

"Ah was jes' about to come to yo' house to tell you dat pa is too sick for drivin' to Macon dis morning, an' our ole horse Bess to top it off, done tooken sick las' night," she was saying.

"I'm sorry to hear that, Ruth, but I'm glad I gotta see you agin 'fore leavin'."

"You jes' seed me las' night in church, William," Ruth laughed.

"Yes, but I ain't had no chance to talk to you wid Jim moonin' 'round lookin' at you like a dying calf."

"An' how does uh dyin' calf look, William?" Ruth asked sweetly.

"Just like Jim does when he looks at you."

They both laughed heartily and Ruth, anxious to change the subject, remarked.

"When yo' school goin' to open, William?"

"In October, an' I'm gonna try and make two terms in one this year, if I can", William replied, a trace of pride in his voice.

"You sho' is smart and allers was. Ah ain't never seed a body dat kin learn fast as you kin nohow."

William's voice was low and tender when he replied: "I want my success to be yours, Ruth. Promise me you'll marry me when I finish school." He pleaded, trying to look into her eyes which she had lowered to her feet, restlessly digging little holes in the soft earth. Visions rose before her of a barefoot boy and girl driving home a cow. The boy, William's brother, Jim;—in his slow passionless voice had said, as he lifted her to the broad back of the cow.

"Ah loves you, Ruth. Les' you an' me git married."

"Ah loves you too, Jim, but us ain't old'er 'nough," she had answered, hanging her head.

"But we could git engaged," Jim had urged and

explained the process of becoming engaged accord-
ing to something he had heard Aunt Salisbury say
that if two strands of hair from the heads of two
people in love were tied together and buried at the
roots of a tree, as the tree grew, they would grow
closer. They had buried the strands of hair at the
roots of a tall hickory nut tree. That was four
years ago and even if Aunt Salisbury's charm was
not always productive of love and harmony in other
lives, in theirs it had become a sacred ritual which
even William with his good looks and education
could not shake.

Ruth raised her eyes and smiled brightly into
William's face, as she replied evasively.

"You jes' go on an' git to be uh preacher. All
us folks gointer be wid you. Pa wus jes' sayin'
tu'ther day that he wish you'd preach yo' fust ser-
mon in our own church, an' Ah kin jes' see you now
walkin' up an' down, wavin' yo' arms an' preachin'
'bout Zekiel an' de dry bones an' uh wheel in uh
wheel, an' ole sister Spencer jes' uh singin' her
little song, 'preachee, brudder Willyum, preachee,
preachee.' "

"I declare Ruth, you're a sight for a minister's
daughter, but I think I'll start preaching in Genesis
and work up to Revelations," William laughed.

"Anyhow, good luck to you an' may Sister Spen-
cer sing longer an' louder," Ruth smiled, turning
to go into the house.

William spent a few moments with the sick min-
ister and left promising to send Jim over to see
about his horse. He was soon on his way to the
Railroad station. Sara Lou watched him until the
bend of the road hid him from view, his goodbye

kiss making a warm glow in her heart, a prayer for his safety on her lips, as the shrill whistle of the train slowing down at the station faintly reached her ears. Far out in the cotton field she could hear Jim singing loudly as he wielded his hoe.

"Umph! Dat boy's all'ers happy," she commented giving her churning extra speed. Up and down the dasher plunged, as she hummed her little song.

The village now fully awake, was alive with the noises of cackling hens, quacking geese and turkeys. Children ran to and fro in play, their happy cries rising above the barking of the neighborhood's many mangy dogs.

Sara Lou, a clean bandanna tied over her neatly coiled hair, prepared to go forth on a mission of praying with a neighbor's sinful husband.

Jim sat down heavily on the back steps, the bucket in which he kept medicine for ailing horses by his side. He had just returned from Reverend Johnson's.

"How's de Rev's horse?" his mother asked, noticing his dejected expression.

"Ah, b'lieve she gonna die, Ma."

"Umph! Dat's too bad. Fo' de lan's sake whut ails de ole cuss?"

"Ah don' know but ah done give her uh dose uh every medicine Ah got an' it ain't done uh mite uh good."

"Well, you don de best you could do an' dat's all dat's 'quired uh anybody. But Ah gotta go over to Sally Brown's. She done sent fo' me tuh come an' pray wid dat triflin' Luke. Ah be back tuhrechly."

"Ah hope he gits 'ligion dat'll last 'im longer den de last he got, Ma," Jim laughed.

"Go 'lon' boy, youse all'ers pokin' fun atter somebody's 'ligion. You bettuh git some yo'seff," Sara Lou chided.

"Don't worry 'bout me kaise when Ah gits it, ah'm gonne keep it sho'nough."

"Dat's zackly whut Luke done said, but last Sad'day night dat low corn liquor he drinked done tole 'im to beat Sally nigh 'bout to death an' he promised if she wouldn't jail 'im he git some mo' an' Ah goin'ter help de pore debil keep his hocks outter de jail house."

Sara Lou moved toward the gate, as Jim rolled on the porch with laughter.

"Umph, dat boy sho is uh causon," she grumbled, walking down the road, the crunching grass beneath her feet making even rhythm in her ears. On each side of the road tall leafy trees threw fitful shadows across her path.

Occasionally, a wagon passed her, the driver calling a greeting or offering her a lift for Sara Lou was the most loved person in the little settlement. Hurrying on, her voice floated back in snatches of her favorite song.

"Ah'm gonna lay down mah burdun,
Down by de ribber side
Down by de ribber side
Ah' gonna lay down mah burdun
Down by de ribber side
Ah ain't gonna study war no mo'."

A thin column of smoke curled up from the one room cabin that was Sally Brown's home.

"Huh!" Sara Lou grunted, as she looked over the sordid wreck the place had become, "Lawd, ain't it jes' terrible how triflin' some folks kin be."

Sally, a tall, black woman of twenty-five, standing in the door, greeted her happily.

"An' Sara, Ah sho' was scared yuh wuzn't comin'."

"Well, Ah's heah. Whar's dat no 'count Luke? Ah thou't last 'vival when he confess 'ligion we wasn't gonna have no mo' trouble wid dat scamp."

"He's sleepin'. Come on in!" Sally whispered, leading the way into the cabin, where Luke lay fully clothed upon a wooden bunk built to the wall.

"Now look'uh heah, Luke Brown, you wake up an' do it rite now," Sara Lou demanded.

"Awrite An' Sara," Luke muttered sitting on the side of the bed rubbing his eyes with his tightly balled fists.

"Come on an' git yo' vittels, Luke!" Sally called from the hearth where a pot of peas was cooking over a small bed of glowing coals.

"He don't need no vittels, Sally," Sara Lou said impatiently, catching him by the shoulder. "Whut he need is de grace uh God, an' he don't need no full stomach to git it on. Git down on yo' knees, Luke, an' pray!"

Luke knelt sheepishly, and Sara Lou started her prayer.

"O Lawd, come intuh dis house an' call Luke
    Brown by his natrul name.
Make 'im know dat you is God,
An' 'side you dere is no odder,
Dat he gottuh die,

An' dat he got an ebber dyin' soul to save,
Paralyze his throat agin' dat poison liquor dat's
   killin' his soul an' drivin' 'im from yo' presence.
Lawd, Ah knows dat you kin unlock doors dat's
   locked,
An' Ah want'uh ask you dis mornin' *heah me
   Lawd,*
To unlock de door uh Luke Brown's heart
An' walk in an' take yo' riteful place.
Wake 'im up dis mornin' Lawd to de sense uh his
   duty.
Ah know you is a prayer answerin' God,
An' Ah want you to bend down yo' ear,
An' hear my prayer for dis heah sinful man."

Sara Lou prayed on and on while Luke fidgeted
from knee to knee, at times sitting back on his heels.

Five minutes passed.   Sara Lou's voice rose
higher and higher, as she called down every kind
of calamity on Luke's head, if he refused to change.
Sally from her corner amen'd and moaned.

Luke peeped slyly from one to the other and
groaned aloud.   Sara Lou's voice rose louder, be-
lieving the groan came from a contrite heart.   Rais-
ing one knee slowly, Luke gave a loud shout and
springing to his feet, darted out of the door, Sally
turned just in time to see him disappear.

"Look uh Luke, An' Sara," she shouted.   Spring-
ing to her feet she started in hot pursuit of the flee-
ing man.

Across the field Luke raced with Sally close be-
hind him and Sara Lou waddling after them as fast
as her feet would carry her two hundred pounds.
But he had a good start and soon vanished from

view. Sally, realizing her defeat, waited for Sara
Lou, who soon reached her side.

"You think he got 'ligion, Sally?" Sara Lou asked
breathlessly.

"Ah don' know An' Sara, but Ah sho' does thank
yuh for comin' an' trying to save de po' debbil."

"Well, anyhow, we got ole Satan on de run.
Praise de Lawd for dat!" Sara Lou rejoiced.

"How's all yo' folks, An' Sara?" Sally asked, as
Sara Lou turned to go.

"Jes' fine, Sally. Willyum done gone back to
Macon dis mornin'. He's doin' fust strate in his
pressin' business dar, an' learnin' lak uh house afire
in school."

"Ah sho' glad to heah dat, we'se all crazy 'bout
dat boy."

"Yeah, he de top uh de pot an' some day he
gonna make his ole Ma mighty proud uh 'im, Sara
Lou smiled.

"Ah heah dat de Rev. ain't so spry, An' Sara."

"No, he ain't so good. Ah'm goin' tuh stop by
dar on my way home. De sisters uh de Chu'ch aid
gonna meet at my house dis atternoon so Ah gottuh
hurry. So long, Sally!"

'So long An' Sara!" Sally called, as Sara Lou
walked hurriedly away and was soon out of sight,
hurrying back home to the many duties that awaited
her.

CHAPTER III

The day began to show signs of intense heat. Swarms of flies made buzzing sounds overhead. The midday sun beamed mercilessly down upon the hard, dusty, red clay road.

The door of Reverend Johnson's cabin was propped open with a pine wood knot. In the clay fireplace a low .fire glowed, over which Aunt Salisbury bent, stirring a pot of boiling roots which sent out a sickly bitter aroma.

Reverend Johnson, a little dried up brown skin man, propped up in a large armchair near by, watched her wearily, pain distorting his wrinkled face.

For over forty years Aunt Salisbury had doctored the village ills and as she expressed it, "catched dere babies for dem." Her anger rose in hot heat against anyone who dared call Doctor Clark, the white physician, who lived down in the village.

"Yuh all jes' don't b'lieve in me kaise Ah'se yo' own color," she would complain when anyone suggested his aid was needed on a case.

Sara Lou's entrance brought a bright smile to the minister's face. She'd always been his best friend even in the days when the church had been arrayed against him, and had prevented his little family from going hungry many times.

Aunt Salisbury grunted a greeting from the hearth and turned again to stir her pot.

"Mah Rev. you sho' do look pert for a sic' man,"
Sara Lou beamed encouragingly.

"Yeah, but he was 'neih dead an' Ah'se had a
hard time pullin' 'im through. Ef dat dere Doc
Clark had'uh come 'roun' heah wid his no 'count
pills, he'd uh been gone for sho'," Aunt Salisbury
complained.

"Aw he ain't so bad off, An' Salisbury," Sara
Lou smiled. "But whar's Ruth?" she added, look-
ing around the neat, sparsely furnished room that
served as bedroom and kitchen for the minister.

"Ah sent her to de village for lin'ament. Mine
done bein' run out," Reverend Johnson explained.

"Lawd! Ah could uh sent Jim for it, Rev. Dere
ain't no use uh de chile walkin' all dem miles wid a
strong boy lak Jim nearby," Sara Lou said, bustling
around, looking into the cupboard to see what was
on hand for dinner. Seeing that they were well
provided with food, she expressed her willingness
to be called upon any time she was needed, and de-
parted for home, grumbling to herself that the sick
minister needed a doctor.

She would send Jim to summons Doctor Clark,
she decided, as she walked around the back of her
house, where Jim was busily engaged drawing
water from their deep well, to fill the large wooden
tubs which were used to do the family wash every
Tuesday morning.

"Lawd boy! You sho' don't forgit nothin', does
you?" she chuckled.

"Nothin' dat concern you, Ma."

"As soon as you'se through, run down for Doctuh
Clark to come see 'bout de Rev. He rite sick dis

mornin' an' Ah ain't gonna let 'im sit dere an' die 'thout me doin' what Ah kin for 'im."

"Awrite ma, ah'se on de las' tub now," Jim replied speeding up his work.

Jim's information when he returned some time later, that the doctor had gone to Macon and his wife did not know when he would return greatly disturbed his mother when they seated themselves for dinner at noon.

"Lawd! Ah'se sho' sorry to heah dat!" she commented, as she dished up a large plate of collard greens and fat side for Jim. "Willyum sho' would 'joyed dese greens an' corn bread if he wuz heah", she finished regretfully.

"An' he would uh found fault wid dem bein' too greasy for 'im to digest," Jim replied before he thought.

"How come you allus findin' fault uh yo' brudder?" Sara Lou asked regarding him with a frown.

"Aw, Ah ain't findin' fault uh 'im, Ma, ah'se jes' tellin' de truth", Jim smoothed, bowing his head as a signal for his mother to bless the food.

Sara Lou prayed a lengthy prayer instead, in which she asked God to give her boys understanding hearts toward each other. Jim knew it was a rebuke for what he had said, and ate his meal hurriedly.

Pushing his plate back, he rose, stretched his arms above his head, and gave his body a vigorous shake.

"Ah jes' can't eat no mo', Ma. Ah ain't got much appetite nohow," he explained.

"Lawdy boy! You done ate two plates full. Yo'

appetite bound to go when you gits yo' belly full."
Sara Lou laughed looking up at him affectionately.

Jim reached over and patted her shoulder and
turning abruptly, left the room. Sara Lou's eyes
filled with tears. She had never showered affection
upon him. His touch had somehow had the feeling
of a starved animal begging to be noticed.

"Dat boy is as steady as an ole mule," she
mused, brushing away a tear.

"Jes' lak his pa, po John, I know he ain't happy
in heaven wid nothin' to do but flyin' 'roun'."

An hour later the living room that was usually
kept closed, was almost filled with the members of
the Church Aid, wives of hard working farmers.
The meeting every Monday afternoon was a great
event in their monotonous lives.

Ella Jones, a tall, skinny brown-skin spinster,
who, when she walked, made you think of many
bones loosely put together, was secretary of the club.

Sally Ann Peck, a portly woman with a rather
pleasant round face, a shade darker than Ella,
seated herself in the far corner of the room. She
was a newcomer in Byron, having lived most of
her forty years in Macon. Coming to Byron dur-
ing cotton picking season to work, she had decided
to stay. She and Martha Green, a thin, little black
woman lived together in a little one room cabin
over by the branch. They both were grass widows,
their husbands having left them several years
previous.

From the first day of their acquaintance the two
women had never agreed on any subject. There
had been constant fights between them for five

years, but to the amazement of the settlement they continued to live together.

Sadie Smith, Mary Ella Lawson, and a few others made up the membership of the club over which Sara Lou presided as president and treasurer. The women had been working hard for five years, trying to raise enough money to fix the parsonage but money was scarce and hard to get, and after five years of hard struggle, there was little more than fifty dollars in the treasury. Today they would decide on some way in which twenty dollars more could be added.

After a lengthy prayer by Martha Green, Ella Jones adjusted her glasses, and holding her book at arms' length before her, started reading the minutes of the last meeting.

"De meetin' ob de Church Aid met las' Monday atternoon at An' Sara Lou Carter's house, she bein' de pres'dent and trea-sure. Two dollahs an' ten cents was turned ober to de trea-sure An' Sara, leabin' ten cent mo' to be turned ober by sis'ter Martha Green."

Ella lowered her book and looked at Martha Green over the top of her horn rimmed glasses meaningly and continued:

"Fifty dollahs was den paid to brodder Slack Henderson for work he gwine to do on de parsonage, leabin' two dollahs an' thirty-five cents in de trea-sure. Dat's all sis'ters," Ella Jones said, dropping back into her chair.

"Dat's good, Sis Ella. All in favor notifie by sayin' Ah!" Sara Lou said taking over the meeting.

"Now while ah'se on my feets," she continued,

"Ah want to ast whut you'all 'cided to do to git dat twenty dollahs balance fuh Slack."

"Ah move we gib uh barn party", Sally Ann suggested.

"We ain't gonna do nothin' uh de kind! De las' un we gib de young folks danced an' dat's agin de church rules," Martha Green objected vigorously.

"Shucks, dem whut danced ain't 'long to the church nohow. Dat's de trouble wid you folks. You jes' too narrow. When Ah lived in Macon de church was allus givin' parties an' de young folks allus dance an' Ah ain't seed no harm it done 'em," Sally Ann came back sharply.

"How 'bout givin' uh donkey party?" Sadie Smith asked timidly.

"Aw we kaint, kaise somebody done stole de donkey an' Ben Johnson whut allus draws de donkey, done gone off an' don't nobody know when he's comin' back," Martha Green informed.

Jim's entrance at this moment interrupted the meeting. He had just come from the parsonage, where he had found Reverend Johnson prone on the floor of his cabin; having fallen there while trying to get into bed.

Before he finished speaking, the women were on their way to see about their stricken pastor, their hearts filled with fear that they might be too late.

Eager, loving hands undressed and laid him between cool, clean sheets. They then rushed around getting in each other's way in their anxiety to help. But Reverend Johnson lay still with open, unseeing eyes, his mouth twisted to one side, unable to utter a word. A deep guttural sound came from his throat, as a tiny froth moistened the corners of his mouth.

Ruth, coming in a few moments later, hovered close to his bedside, as Sara Lou bathed his head with cold water and tried to force a few drops between his lips. Some of the women rubbed his hands with hot salt and did all of the many things they had heard would help in a case that plainly showed paralysis.

All afternoon neighbors came in steady streams. Women busied themselves brewing coffee and laying out the food they had brought over for the watchers at his bedside. The Church Aid members sat huddled in a corner of the room softly singing spirituals and offering prayer for their sick pastor.

Slowly the afternoon faded into twilight. The long hot summer night with many sounds from the dense woodland that surrounded the little settlement closed in around them. Owls hooted in the trees near by. Crickets filled the air with their screechy song. Near the cabin a dog howled dismally, sending a shiver over the waiting household. Night passed and the first faint streak of early dawn sent many of the farmers and their wives home to do their chores.

There was no change in the sick man's condition except that he seemed weaker. A cold sweat had accumulated upon his forehead, which the neighbors observed with a sad shake of their heads.

Sara Lou sent a message to William by a farmer driving into Macon asking him to come home at once.

Another hot miserable day came to add to their misery. To Sara Lou's distress nothing had been heard from Doctor Clark, who had not returned from his visit to Macon.

The sun again hid itself behind the Western horizon. Stark dark midnight encompassed them. Sara Lou patted up the sick man's pillow and straightened the bed covers in an effort to make him more comfortable and passed quietly into the next room for a cup of coffee. Finishing her drink, she again seated herself at the head of the bed, noticing that the covers she had straightened before leaving the room, were again thrown aside. She leaned down to pull them into place, and drew back with a scream.

"Lawd sakes, folks! De Rev. is gone! He done slipped away from us jes' as quiet," she cried, tears streaming down her face.

Ruth fell sobbing across his body. Women added their cries to the din and soon the cabin was a swaying mass of screaming people, lamenting the passing of their pastor and friend.

CHAPTER IV

Wednesday morning a light rain fell mercifully, cooling the dry, hot day. The farmers breathed a prayer of thankfulness. The summer had been intensely hot and dry. Long before noon many of them had finished their work in order that they might be on hand early for the wake to be held that night.

At the parsonage Martha Green and Sally Ann Peck, their dresses tied high around their waists, were diligently scrubbing and cleaning the two rooms. Food had been stacked high in the cupboard to be cooked and served during the night at intervals between the singing and praying. Sally Ann tucked a clean sheet over the one mirror the Johnsons owned, as she remarked to Martha.

"Lawd sake, Martha, dis gonna be de biggest wake we'se had since Ah been libin' in Byron."

"Huh! T'ain't nigh as 'portant as de Rev. Smith's wuz," Martha grunted, walking over to the open door and spitting out a long stream of snuff.

"Yeah, but Ah wuzn't heah den an' dis 'un goin' to be mighty good anyhow wid all de local preachers 'tending eben down to dat personable Reverend Bruce Hanson from Iron City."

"Ah guess dat's all you thinkin' 'bout, dat Rev. Hanson. Ah done see'd you makin' eyes at 'im de las' time he wuz heah durin' de big meetin'. You'se de forwardest 'oman whar mens is concerned, Ah eber did see, Sally Ann Peck."

"You ain't 'exactly blind yo'self, Martha. Anyhow you jes' jealous kaise he don't pay you no mind."

"No Ah ain't. Ah jes' ain't forgot dat he's got uh wife. Ef'fen she is done gone off an' lef' 'im."

"Yeah, you jes' 'members dat kaise he don't notice you."

"Ah ain't nothin' uh de kind. You'se jes' uh fresh 'oman, Sally Ann Peck. H'it ain't no wonder yo' husband done gone an' lef' you."

"Lis'en to dat!" Sally laughed loudly. "Whar's yo'un gone to and why, when he lef' you six years ago? Folks sho does say some curious things 'bout why he packed hisself off."

"Aw shet up, loud mouf!" Martha grumbled, unable to find words strong enough to silence the laughing Sally Ann.

Much to Martha's relief, Sara Lou put an end to their argument when she entered the cabin to see how they were getting on. Both women went about their tasks and were soon chattering together again pleasantly.

Out in the little Calvary Churchyard men were busy digging a new grave in which the Reverend Peter Johnson would be laid to rest Thursday afternoon. Night found everybody from miles around gathered to keep the wake. Ruth, worn out with crying, lay quiet upon a cot in the corner of the room.

William, who had arrived from Macon during the afternoon, helped his mother get the people seated. At his word the singing was started and through the long summer night their songs, low and mournful, wafted out upon the air.

The day of the funeral dawned bright and clear. Long strings of wagons wended their way to the Church. Ministers from the adjacent counties took their places on the rostrum. William had been chosen to read the scripture and sit with the ministers on the rostrum, looking down upon the crowded church with solemn eyes in which gleamed the pride he felt in his position. Jim, looking up at him seated there, could not help feeling proud of his intelligence and importance.

The sun had begun hiding itself in the west behind mountains of soft pink clouds when Reverend Johnson was finally laid to rest in the Calvary Churchyard, and Ruth became a member of the Carter household.

William, placing his hand tenderly upon her shoulder, as she stood later that evening ready to accompany Sara Lou and Jim to the parsonage to get her things, said consolingly:

"Now, don't worry yourself sick, Ruth. You can't do your father any good by worryin'. He was prepared to go. You'll just have to give him up, and try and meet him in Heaven some day."

"Ah know, Willyum. Ah want to be brave an' should oughter be to show An' Sara Ah 'preciate her givin' me uh home. But rite now Ah jes' can't help missin' Pa," Ruth replied, her eyes misty with tears.

"You must feel it's just as much yo' home as it is ours, Ruth, an' we're glad to have you heah," Sara Lou told her kindly.

William watched them walk down the wide road, Ruth between his mother and Jim, her slight form swaying in perfect rhythm as she walked. A mixture of jealousy and fear filled his heart—jealousy of Ruth's and Jim's proximity and fear that Jim, whom he knew had heard about his gambling and other misdemeanors in Macon, would some day tell his mother, gripped his heart.

There were times when religious fervor held and swayed him under its spell. But his was a changeable nature, cold, hard and calculating, ready to move heaven and earth to have his way. He loved money; pitting his wit against the other fellow's to gain something for nothing thrilled him, and made him a slave to gambling. Of late his luck had been bad. He had lost in continually trying to win back his losses, and had lost money his mother and Jim gave him from time to time to buy things for the farm. These thoughts haunted him as he sat alone on the steps of the front porch where he had seated himself when the trio left him.

Sally Ann Peck and Martha Green spoke to him from the front gate.

"We ain't aimin' to 'tain you brudder Willyum, if you goin' out, only we'uns 'thout dat y'all would kinder enjoy dese hot rolls and preserves for supper. An' brudder Willyum, we wants to tell you how grand you wuz at de Reverend's funeral," Sally Ann continued, beaming with one of her brightest smiles on William.

When he answered he was once more the suave young deacon they all loved.

"Come on in, sisters, the folks will be back soon," he called, leading the way into the house.

Sally Ann and Martha followed eagerly.

"Ah 'clare things sho is happenin' roun' heah. One time dar wuzn't uh thing goin' on. But now de

Rev. done tooken sick an' died almost de same day. Minds me uh de sayin' you'se heah today an' gone tomorrow," Sally Ann said with a resigned air.

"Ain't it de truth?" Martha echoed.

"Yeah, Martha, jes' de odder day you wuz sayin' you wished somethin' would happen an' you sho' done got yo' wish. An' Salisbury done tole you 'bout wishin' up things," Sally said, turning to Martha scornfully.

" 'Nother thing. You wished up dat storm las' month sayin' dat it wus so dry. You wished it would rain so de ground wuz soaked through an' it rained steady one whole week."

William laughed heartily as the two women glared at each other, and Martha, not wanting to be rebuked before William, retorted angrily.

"Aw, shucks, An' Salisbury's allus beatin' up hur gums an' cookin' roots. Kain't nobody wish up nothin' nohow, kin dey brodder William?" Martha asked turning to William.

" 'Course they cain't," William smiled.

"When you goin' back to Macon?" Martha asked, anxious to change the subject.

"I haven't decided yet. I might go tomorrow but Ruth is so upset, I feel like staying and trying to cheer her up in some way," William answered.

"Dat's you, brudder Willyum, allus tryin' to help odder folks," Sally Ann commented.

"Ah wish lot uh other folks wuz lak dat," Martha said, casting a meaning glance in Sally's direction.

"Dar you go, Martha Green," Sally spoke up hotly. "Castin' yo sly remarks. You kain't speck us to be lak brodder Willyum, he lives close to de

Lawd kaise he gonna carry de Gospel. You ain't bent down from carryin' too much 'ligion nohow."

Martha started to give Sally a sharp reply, but William cut in.

"Now sister, you mustn't quarrel an' you shouldn't judge for fear you be judged by the same judgment the Bible teaches us."

Sara Lou and Ruth's voices, as they came up on the porch, cut short the discussion. William stepped forward quickly, to help them with their bundles.

"Lawd Ah'se tired!" his mother gasped, sinking into the nearest chair.

"We came ober to bring you some vittels," Sally informed.

"Ah sho thanks you sis-ters. Me an' Ruth is purtty much hungry Ah 'speck."

"Ah ain't hungry," Ruth said listlessly.

"But you must eat an' keep up yo' strength, chile. Dar ain't no need uh you gittin' all sick and skinny," Sara Lou said kindly.

"Yeah, jes' brace up an' be cheerful, Ruth. De Rev. is done gone an' you kain't live by de dead. You'se young an' got uh long time 'fore you, so enjoy yo' life while you'se able," Sally Ann added cheerfully.

"Dar you go, Sally Ann Peck," Martha snorted. "Dat ain't no way to talk to Ruth kaise she got to moan 'bout her Pa's death. You jes' cry much as you want to, Ruth. Don't you try to be careless lak dis 'oman heah whut ain't got no heart a-tall."

"Let's talk 'bout somethin' else, sisters," Aunt Sara begged. "Ruth's awrite an' ain't got no cause to moan 'round. She's in good hands an' 'course she gonna git cheerful."

Sally Ann and Martha soon bid the family good-bye and hurried home to the many duties that awaited them. Sara Lou refused Ruth's offer to help get supper.

"No, chile, you jes' sit down an' rest," she said kindly.

"I tell you what we'll do, Ruth. Come on out and let's take a walk," William offered, taking her hand in his. They walked through the sweetly scented woods that surrounded the farm. At their heels, Jim's old dog Towser ran barking loudly.

William tried to cheer her with vivid descriptions of his last school term, and his plans for the future, but Ruth was silent and unresponsive, the deepening shadows of dusk gathered around them, and Ruth complained of a headache, so they returned to the Carter home in silence, each busy with their own thoughts.

When they entered the yard, Jim was seated on the front porch and greeted them with a happy smile.

William's heart filled with jealousy as he saw the happy light in Ruth's eyes and the animation he could not arouse became evident when she seated herself beside Jim.

Excusing himself early, he went to his room determined to leave the next morning for Macon, where he hoped work in his pressing shop, and lively nights in the Broad Street haunts he frequented, would obliterate the unhappiness he suffered seeing Ruth smiling and happy with his brother Jim.

CHAPTER V

The early morning sun cast fitful shadows through the half-opened window upon the floor of the little back room behind William Carter's pressing shop on Broad Street in Macon.

The room was close and filled with a musty odor, mingled with a smell of stale beer, bad liquor and decaying food. The floor of rough dirty boards was strewn with bottles and bits of a torn deck of cards. In the center of the room stood a rickety table covered with a mixture of bottles and bits of bread and drying sparerib bones. Swarms of flies made their invasion known, as they buzzed from place to place and rested for brief spells on the face of Slippery, William's helper, who stirred occasionally to brush them away, and settle himself in a more comfortable position on the cot pushed close to the wall on which was thrown a dirty quilt. His face, a brick colored yellow, covered with dirt and freckles, was thin and wrinkled, not so much from age as from sickness and exposure, for Slippery was still in his early thirties—a thin, stooped, medium-sized man, whose past life was little known to the crowd around Broad Street, where he had recently drifted, from where, no one, not even William, knew.

Turning with a groan, his feet slowly struck the floor, as he sat up on the side of the cot and stretched his arms above his head. For a moment he sat looking around the room, his hands pressed tightly to his aching head, then slowly he dragged himself over to the back door of the shop which opened into an alley running the length of the block behind the dingy front negro business places. Hanging on a nail just outside the door was a rusty basin which served as bath tub and dish-pan for the place.

Slippery took it down gingerly, filled it with water and started washing his face with his hands, scooping up the water and letting it run down over his face and neck. Someone passed down the alley and helloed. He answered gruffly without turning to see who the speaker was.

Loud knocks came from the front of the place. Someone was banging to get in. Slippery slouched into the room wiping his face on the first thing that his hands came in contact with, which happened to be an old shirt, and with an oath, started hurriedly towards the front door.

"Hey, Slippery, whut you tryin' to do, sleep all day?" The query came through the door.

"Who de hell's business is it, if Ah do?" Slippery answered, as he opened the door and faced Cotton Eye, who stood grinning with a pair of pants hanging on his arm.

"Well, lil' ole business man, is dat any way to greet uh customer whut comes all de way pass dozens uh cleanin' shops to bring yuh work?" said Cotton Eye grinning broadly.

"Whut you want done to dese pants?" Slippery asked, taking the pants and throwing them on a chair piled high with crumpled suits.

"Want 'em scrubbed, man, an' pressed. Dat's whut Ah wants."

"You would want dat today when my head is achin' an' Ah feels nigh ready to die."

"But you'se in business, ain't you? An' how you gonna pay de rent ef we'all don't fetch you work?"

"Oh awrite, Cotton Eye. Sho I'se glad to have yo' work but dat don't make me not feel sick, does it?"

"Sick or well, Ah wants dem pants tonight. Daddy Jenks is openin' up his place back uh de pool parlor wid dancin' an' he's got some purtty gals whut'll be 'round an' one uh dem gals is uh humdinger. Ah done seed hur. She's from Chicago. Whew, some gal, Ah says."

"From Chicago?" Slippery asked, turning quickly to face Cotton Eye.

"Dat's whut Ah said. But whut's dat to you? You ain't neb'ber said you come from dere."

"An' Ah ain't said yit. Ah jes' wanted to make sho whut place you mentioned."

"Ha, ha, ha! You sho is a slick 'un, Slippery but Ah almost got yuh den, didn't Ah?"

"Whut you mean almost got me kaise Ah didn't quite git whut yuh said?"

"Well, we'll let it go at dat. Say when is William de Parson comin' back?"

"You bettuh not let him heah you call him dat. Dat's one sho thing."

"Huh! ·Ah ain't scared uh 'im even if you is. Ah'se done knowed him since we wuz babies dere in Byron an' Ah'll call him anything Ah wants to. Who is he, anyhow? Everybody in Byron knows dat he ain't born rite."

"Whut you mean, ain't born rite, Cotton Eye?"

"Why, Ole man John Carter wuzn't his Pappy. He's uh white man's chile—jes' uh plain bastard."

"Whut diff'rence does dat make? How does you
know dat you ain't one nor me nor eve'ybody. For
whut we knows. We all know who our fathers wuz
'spose to be but can we prove dat dey wuz? You
ain't sho uh nobody but yo' Ma an' even if uh pusson
is born, what didn't habe uh lawful pappy, does it
hurt 'em any? An' if dey wuz lawful, did hit help
'em any? My Pappy wuz 'spose to be lawful an'
uh preacher, an' whut am I? Nothin'. It's up to
us all whut we make uh ourselves not who our Ma
or Pa was."

"Awrite, Friday, youse rite to take up fo yo' Rob-
inson Crusoe. He sho is been uh friend to you but
Ah ain't neber been crazy 'bout no half white nigger.
Dey's tuh biggity, an' thinks dey is better den us
blacks, an' Ah jes' don't lak 'em."

"Dat de trouble now. We ain't satisfied fo de
white folks to fin' fault wid us, we'se jes' got to fight
one 'nothur jes' kaise we all ain't de same color.
Whose fault is it, anyhow? Kain't nobody make
demselves, don' you know that? An' to white folks,
whether you is black or yellow or brown, you is jes'
uh darky, so shut yo' trap up 'bout color."

"Awrite, us ain't gwine fight. How'd yuh make
out in de game las' nite?"

"Rotten. Loss every penny Ah had to dat ole
pusley Sugar Kid."

"Whew! Dat boy sho is lucky."

"Oh! Ah don't b'lieve it's jes' plain luck. Ah
b'lieve he's crooked but none uh us can ketch him,
dat's all."

"It sho is funny he don't never start winnin' 'til
atter he's had de deck in his hands. Den if he picks

uh queen, it's right on de bottom.   Do yuh think he
nails de cards dat quick?"

"Well, yuh knows dat's why Ah went on home.
He cleaned me right quick."

"Yeh but if Ah eber finds him nappin', he's a
gonner fo sho."

"Dat's it.   How you gwine ketch him nappin'?"
Cotton Eye asked dubiously.

"Ah'll ketch him, don't yuh worry an' when Ah
does, dere'll be plenty uh trouble stirrin'," Slippery
answered menacingly glancing towards the desk in
the corner of the shop, where despite William's ad-
vice to the contrary, he kept his revolver loaded
and pushed carelessly under some papers in the
drawer.

"Well, Ah got to hurry on, Slippery.   Ah'se
workin' today," Cotton Eye remembered, moving
slowly towards the door.   Ah jes' had to have some
money kaise dat new gal's ober at Daddy Jenks an'
she's some queen, b'lieve me," he sighed.   "Hur
name's Ethel Myers but see heah Slippery, I ain't
figurin' on no opposition in dem quarters."

"Don't worry.   Ah ain't interested," Slippery
assured him.

"Well, Ah'll be pushin' on.   So long.   Have dem
pants all slicked up by five o'clock," Cotton Eye
called over his shoulder, as he sauntered slowly
down the street, both hands in his pockets and
whistling a popular blues.

Half-way down the block he met William walking
rapidly with his small bag swinging at his side.   They
had known each other from infancy but there had
never been any friendship between them.   In fact, Ed-
ward Knowles, which was Cotton Eye's real name,

had been the worst boy in Byron and had spent so
much time in jail that Marshall Bailey had asked
him to just leave Byron and not come back, as he
was an expense to the county. He had been given
the nickname Cotton Eye because of his large eyes,
which seemed to sit on his forehead and were a
glaring white except for their small black pupils.
He was extremely tall and slender, almost skinny,
his color a shiny black but his broad smile, which
showed all of his even white teeth, usually won the
hearts of the fair sex and made him many male
friends as well.

William merely tolerated him as there was noth-
ing else to do, but it was a superior tolerance which
Cotton Eye felt and resented. His lips parted in
a quick smile at sight of William.

"Gee, boy, glad to see yuh back. How's Byron?"
he asked quickly.

"Oh, Byron's fine, Cotton Eye," William an-
swered, as he tried to pass on down the street.

"How's my Aunt Sofia an' yo' ma?" Cotton Eye
continued almost blocking William's path.

"Yo' Aunt Sofia's right poorly, Cotton, but Ma's
fine."

"Now dat's too bad 'bout Aunt Sofia. Sho wish
Ah could see hur," Cotton Eye replied earnestly.

"Well, I guess in a case like this you could run
down to Byron. I don't believe old Marshall Bailey
would object to you seein' the only mother you ever
knew when she's sick."

"Yeah, Willyum, Ah mought try it but say, whut's
to become uh Ruth now dat hur pappy is dead?
Who's she gonna stay wid?"

"With Ma, of course. Who else would she be likely to stay with?" William answered.

"Well dat is de truth. Aunt Sara is a kinder mother to all de folks down dere. Pore li'l' Ruth. Is she as purtty as eber, Willyum?"

"Yeah, Cotton Eye, she's even prettier than ever and a wonderful girl."

"Which one uh you boys is gonna marry hur— you or Jim? Ah 'member dat yuh both is allers been sweet on hur," Cotton Eye smiled.

"I don't think we had better discuss that, Cotton?" William answered with acerbity, and walked quickly away.

Cotton Eye's laughter echoed in his ears, as he walked on down the block.

"Black fool!" William muttered, and disliked Cotton Eye more than ever.

Slippery looked up from his task of cleaning the front of the shop as William walked in the door and threw his bag down on the nearest chair. William's face showed he was not in a very pleasant mood, and Slippery merely helloed as he continued hurriedly to the back room for the broom to sweep the floor and sidewalk.

William followed him into the back room and stood for a moment viewing the upheaval condition of the place.

"Say, Slippery, you must have had a mighty rough bunch here last night to get things in such a mess. Whew! Open the window, the place smells bad. How on earth could you sleep in such a mess?" he asked disgustedly.

"Ah don't guess Ah could uh slept if Ah hadn't

been dead drunk when Ah went to bed," Slippery answered shortly.

"You'd better lay off that bad liquor. It don't do nobody no good," William warned.

"Don't Ah know it, but whut else yuh gonna do when you'se disgusted an' broke, Bill?"

"Had bad luck last night again, eh?"

"Yep and how! In fact, been havin' it ever since you went to Byron. A new guy blowed in town Wednesday nite dat's cleaned eve'ybody but Daddy Jenks an' he jes' won't play him."

"Who's he?"

"Oh, some fellow dat calls himself Sugar Kid. Brought plenty dough wid him an' done 'tached ebe'ybody else's to his'en since he's been heah."

"What does he play, Slippery?"

"Georgy skin an' whut luck!"

Slippery had been sweeping all through his talk with William and started out the front door to sweep the sidewalk that ran in front of the shop when he remembered that he had a letter for William. He leaned the broom against the wall and hurried back into the place, and after searching through the table drawer for a moment, handed William the letter.

"Jes' came yistiddy, Bill. Ef yuh hadn't come back today, Ah wuz gonna send it on down to Byron to you."

"No, Slippery," William spoke up quickly, after he had scanned the postmark. "Don't ever send my mail down there. Jes' keep it 'til I come back."

William sank into one of the two rickety chairs and frowning, read the letter which was from one of his creditors. A sigh escaped his lips. Slippery coming in from his sweeping, looked at him with deep concern.

"Whut's wrong? Anything Ah kin help straighten out?" he asked.

"No," William answered trying to pull himself together. "There isn't anything that anyone can do."

"Must be very serious, Bill."

"No, Slippery, jes' a man I owe, wants his dough. Have you got any money?"

"Not uh lousy cent. Ah got cleaned out for sho las' nite.

"That's bad news but I guess I can find some way out."

"We'se got lots uh work hangin' 'round an' if de folks calls for it, dere'll be a little money on hand," Slippery informed.

It was Friday. Most of the people who patronized the shop, got paid on Saturday and the work would have to be ready so they spent the remainder of the day working steadily.

Evening brought a good many customers in for their clothes. To most of them it was the only suit they had, and they all would attend Daddy Jenk's blow-out, dressed in their Sunday best. Cotton Eye appeared promptly at five and retrieved his pants which were all scrubbed and pressed and looked nothing like the dirty rag he had brought in earlier in the day.

"Lawd, Slippery, ole boy, you sho' did do uh good job on dese pants, but shux dey don't look nothin' lak de coat now. 'Speck Ah better fetch it over an' let yuh knock hit off wid yore hot iron. You wouldn't mine doin' dat, would you?" he asked.

"No. For fifteen cents Ah wouldn't mine doin' it at all," Slippery answered.

"You sho is tight, Slippery. Heah Ah brings yuh all my work an' yuh 'fuses to do me uh li'l' favor."

"Cotton Eye, you knows we charge forty cents for a suit. Why do you want to try an' get it done for the twenty-five cents you paid for your pants?" William asked.

"Awrite, awrite, we won't argue 'bout it," Cotton Eye answered disappointedly.

"An' anyhow, whut yuh want to weah a coat for?" Eddie Nolan, known to the bunch as Red Shirt, asked from the chair where he had sprawled in his underwear waiting for Slippery to finish pressing his pants.

"Yeah," Slippery echoed, "you ain't been wearin' no coat. Why de big desire to dress up?"

"Shirt sleeves is awrite far as dese Macon Janes is concerned." Cotton Eye explained. "But ain't Ah done tole yuh dat uh queen from Chicago gonna be ober dere an' maybe she ain't use to seein' de boys in shirt sleeves an' Ah want to make uh hit wid hur."

The boys all laughed heartily and Cotton Eye grabbing his pants, left in a huff.

"Wear uh red silk shirt. Dat'll make uh hit wid hur," Red Shirt called after him.

"Ah'll leab dat for you to do, Red Shirt. Dat's how you got yore name," Cotton Eye called back.

William's pressing business was located across the street from Daddy Jenks' more imposing pleasure emporium, a large building with a pool parlor in the front and a large room in the back used for dancing. Overhead were furnished rooms and a large room

in the rear for gambling.   Here every night the
boys played dice or Georgia Skin.

Daddy Jenks seldom gambled.   When he did it
was for high stakes and he was generally lucky.   He
had bought the building in which he ran his business,
with his winnings many years before.   Money was
plentiful then, and he had gone from place to place
all through Georgia and Florida, to saw mills and
other public works on pay day, returning with his
pockets bulging with money.   His poolroom brought
him in a good profit and also his furnished rooms,
but he depended mostly on his club room from which
he gleaned a neat profit.

Anything from soda pop to corn liquor could
be bought in the place, and upstairs in the gambling
room, anything from a nickel to a thousand dollars
could be played over the tables.

Daddy Jenks' imposing figure could be seen early
and late as he walked around, keeping an eye on his
boys, as he called them.   He was a large light-brown
skin man with heavy jowls and small twinkling eyes,
always dressed in a suit of expensive clothes, pre-
ferably grey with a huge horseshoe pin set with small
chips in his tie, which he claimed was his lucky
charm, and wore faithfully.   Across his bosom his
watch chain stretched.   At one end his watch with
its large solid gold case was tucked in a pocket and
a gold penknife in the opposite pocket.

A half smoked cigar always hung between his
lips and his black Stetson hat was usually pushed
far back on his head.   He was known to everyone
in and around Macon.   His real name, George
Jenkins, was seldom heard.   He was Daddy Jenks
to everyone, white and colored.

His prosperity was an unquestioned fact in the community. He even boasted a brand new Ford sedan and a chauffeur. Kongo, the misshapen mute who drove for him, was more or less his own property. Daddy had rescued him from the gutter when a lad of ten, whose half-witted brain seemed only to emerge from its stupor where cars or machinery of any kind were concerned, but the mere fact that Kongo drove the car for him and did his every bidding made Daddy Jenks quite a personage among his associates. He had visited New York the previous summer and had come back with new ideas for his place, had brought a second-hand piano and hired a trap-drummer.

Three girls from a show that had been stranded while playing the colored vaudeville house had appealed to him for aid, and he had taken them in to help entertain his guests. Ethel Myers, one of the girls, had been rather glad to remain in Macon for a while. It was a new field and Ethel, for certain reasons, did not want to go back to New York nor home to Chicago, where she was always getting into trouble. She was a clever dancer and a good-looking girl, light-complexioned and medium height, with a mass of short curly hair, framing a face of small fine features. Ethel knew her good points and made the most of them. She could sing as well as dance, and had a dashing personality. The word conscience meant nothing to her. She was out to get what was coming to her. Of the three, Ethel was the star with undisputed rights.

Daddy Jenks, a good business man, had struck a good bargain with the girls, who were to receive rooms, board and a percentage from the drinks sold for entertaining and keeping the place lively by dancing for and with the customers. He realized in trying to run his dance hall at a profit to keep the men spending, there had to be girls around—girls that could be depended upon to stay until closing time.

The place had been newly painted, and colored lights hung from the wall. In one corner stood the second-hand piano and drums. Little tables lined the sides of the wall with a space left in the center of the room for dancing. A crude counter had been built across one side of the wall. The small ice-box behind it held soft drinks. White mule could be obtained by giving a certain sign. The room, a fairly large one, running the full length of the building, could be entered through a door from an alley that ran behind the place.

At nine o'clock the music started, and the place was soon filled with sweating, swaying bodies.

CHAPTER VI

Across the street William and Slippery, tired from their day's work, finished their supper of fried mullet fish and hominy, and sat out in front of the little pressing shop, watching the crowd pour into Daddy Jenks' place.

Because of Daddy's opening, many pairs of pants had been scrubbed and pressed, but for all their hard work, the day's receipts had amounted to a very small sum. To William it was nothing. He needed money, and lots of it. His gambling had gotten him into a tight place. He would have to pay or be exposed to his mother. To lose her confidence would mean the end of the lazy, care-free existence he now enjoyed. It rankled him to see money pour into Daddy Jenks' hands for which he didn't have to make a struggle, and he voiced his thoughts to Slippery sitting quietly smoking a cigarette beside him.

"Sure's a shame how some folks get money so easy and others have to work so hard for it, ain't it, Slippery?"

"Yep. Dat's whut Ah allers thought, Willyum," Slippery replied and after a moment's silence, continued. "Dat would make uh fine racket for you. De dance hall business is easy money."

"No, Slippery, not for me. I jes' wasn't cut out for anything like that," William answered quickly.

"But why, Willyum? You know Ah allers wondered why you wants to preach anyhow. You'se uh good talker an' is educatid awrite, but outsider dat, you ain't nothin' like uh preachin' man aught'er be!" Slippery said, eyeing William closely, his brow slightly wrinkled in an effort to read William's mind.

"It's 'cause Ma wants me to be a preacher, I guess, and because in my heart or somewhere, there is a part of me that loves honor and right livin' and helpin' others."

"Ah knowed dat by de way you helped me. Ah was nigh 'bout dead and everybody but you was scared uh me, sayin' dat Ah had de con. Ah sho was down when you picked me up."

"Well, to be truthful, there was some selfishness in that. I figured if you ever got well, you could help me with the shop."

"Yeah, but de chances was sho slim uh me gettin' well but you tooked me in an' got uh doctor for me and everything. Paid out yo' good money and didn't even know me. Youse awrite, Willyum, ah'll say dat for you an' Ah ain't never gonna fergit you."

"I try to be, Slippery, but I certainly do make a mess of mistakes for all of that."

"Us all makes mistakes. Ain't nobody perfect."

"Yeah, but I suffer for mine because they worry me. I feel ashamed of some part of me, the part that holds me back when I want to do right and makes me do wrong."

"Lawd, boy, to heah you talk a body would think you'd killed somebody."

"Maybe I have."

"Whut!" Slippery almost jumped from his seat.

William laughed long and loudly at Slippery's agitation.

"Sit tight, Slippery," he said between the laughter that shook his shoulders. "I was only joking. 'Course I ain't killed nobody and sure hopes I never will."

"Boy, you sho had me scared!"

"No, Slippery, it's money that's worryin' me. I needs lots of money right through here. I've got to have it or all my plans are busted. That's all!"

"Well, you might git lucky an' win it. Dere's Sugar Kid 'roun' heah dat's got gobs uh dough. Maybe you'll be de one to break 'im."

"Yeah, maybe, with the luck I've been playin' in lately, there's a fat chance of me breakin' anybody."

"Well, at least it's worth tryin'."

"No, I guess I'd better let well 'nough alone. I sometimes wonder why some people have all the luck and others never seem to git anywhere," William mused, continuing. "There's my brother Jim. Everything he touches seems to prosper. He's lucky with our crops even when other folks' cotton fails or the bugs eat it up. He gets good money for every bale he turns out. Then 'sides Mr. Gordon pays him to take care of his place. Now that he's in Europe, Jim's in full charge. He's gonna sell the peaches and keep the money 'til Mr. Gordon gets back. He never asks any questions—jus' takes Jim's word for everything. I couldn't get a break like that."

"Gee! Dat sho is some break. It's uh wonder dis Mistuh Gordon wouldn't have uh white man lookin' at'ter his place."

"Not as long as Jim is around. He's known Ma

all her life, and my folks as far back as my great grandmother was born right on his place. He thinks uh lot of Ma and likes Jim because he took to farming. He don't like me much—thinks I want too much education and as Jim don't crave none, he's right down his street."

"Does Jim make much money for him? Maybe dat's why he's so crazy 'bout 'im," Slippery asked, setting his chair which had been tilted against the wall, firmly on the sidewalk, while he rolled a cigarette.

"Well, he don't make any too much, 'sides Mister Gordon's rich and don't have to depend on his place any, but he likes to make it pay something. Jim will make over a hundred dollars when he sells his peaches. 'Course he'll have to pay some of it out to get them picked, but not much."

"Lawd! I'd be scared to keep dat much money 'round me, but maybe Jim banks it."

"Well, he should, but he don't. He keeps it over at Mister Gordon's house in his safe."

"Dat sho' is a mighty risky thing to do, seems to me."

"That's jes' what I'm thinkin', Slippery. Jim thinks it's the safest place. Maybe it is. But Mister Gordon's place is right on the main road and lots of no 'count people travel that road."

"Even if dey was to break in an' take de money, nobody would blame Jim, would dey?"

"Gordon wouldn't, but old Bailey, the Marshall, and the other white folks might. They ain't got none too much good blood for Jim 'cause Gordon left him instead of a white man in charge of the place," William replied.

Slippery, his chair tipped back against the wall again, watched the stream of women and men pouring into Daddy Jenks' place. Now and then a cough shook his slight form from which he quickly recovered rather breathlessly.

"You'd better put on your coat," William advised.

Rising slowly he entered the shop to return shortly with his coat and hat on. William looked up, as he stepped out of the door.

"Goin' over to Daddy Jenks' to see whut's up an' to get another look at dat Sugar Kid's dough. Kin yuh let me have uh dollar?" he asked.

William handed him the dollar and taking his chair, started for the door.

"I b'lieve I'll mosey over there too and see the sights. Wait a minute," he called over his shoulder.

A few moments later they walked into the crowded dance hall where the fun was at its height. The center of the room had been cleared of dancers and Ethel Myers had the floor. She was in the middle of a song, a low, moaning blues which she sang, as her body swayed back and forth to the rhythm of the music. Couples sprawled at the tables, others stood in knots around the room. White mule and soda pop flowed freely.

Everybody was watching the girl, who, when her song was finished, broke into a wild dance. The crowd applauded loudly when her dance ended. Turning to bow to her appreciative audience, she saw Slippery standing just inside the door. Her eyes dilated as if she had seen a ghost.

The piano and drum started up a loud jazz number and Slippery walked quickly to her side.

"Want 'er have dis dance?" he said loudly. Then under his breath he spoke closely to her ear. "Don't lose yo' head, Ethel, Ah wanna talk to you."

She quickly recovered herself, as Slippery guided her around the room in a slow drag.

"Ain't dere some place whar we kin talk?" he whispered.

Ethel nodded and they danced over towards the door that led into the pool parlor. There they slipped into a dark hall.

"What you want to say, Jessie?" Ethel asked, as she slipped free from his arms.

"Nothin' much—only dat you don't know me. Git me? An' if you say you do an' start shootin' off yo' head an' beatin' up yo guns Ahm gonna make Macon too small to hold yuh, dat's all."

"Well, I ain't got no call to go 'round here braggin' 'bout knowin' you. You ain't no prize package to know, nohow."

"Ah jes' wants to warn yuh, kaise 'round heah Ah'm jes' Slippery an' nobody don't know anything but dat—not even whar Ah comed from, and it ain't gonna be none too healthy for you if you put 'em wise," Slippery warned.

"Don't worry. I'm out to 'tend to my own business, Jessie, and that's about all I kin do."

"Not Jessie, jes' Slippery. Yuh git me?"

"Awrite, say, who's the slick-lookin' guy dat you was standin' next to over dere by the door? I mean de high yellow boy wid de good clothes on," Ethel asked, nodding her head towards the dance hall.

"Dat's de man I work for—Willyum Carter."

"You wouldn't mind knockin' me down to him, would you, Slippery?"

"He don't wanna meet no tramps lak you."

"Now be a good boy, Slippery. I'm crazy to meet 'im. Why, he's got all dese guys 'round heah skinned uh mile in looks, and besides, how do you know he don't want to meet me? I sho could go for him all right!"

"Well, ah'll introduce you to him, Ethel, but remember he ain't yo' kind, so go slow," Slippery agreed reluctantly.

"I might be lots uh help to him for all you knows kaise ah'm de little gal dat's gonna put Macon in my pocket." Ethel laughed as she and Slippery crossed the room to where William was standing, leaning against the wall.

Ethel and Slippery were a strange pair—both outcasts and without conscience. They were from Chicago, and for many reasons neither was desirous of going back there. With Slippery it was the law that he feared and the many cases that they held against him. For many years he had been a terror on the South Side, always up for stealing. The last affray he had been mixed up in, a killing had been pulled off that could have been easily traced to his door, had he waited for the tracing. That had been several years ago, and he had finally drifted to Macon, sick and broke, and had met William, who befriended him. A friendship grew between them that had become almost worship on Slippery's part. There was nothing in the world he wouldn't have done for William.

William liked him because he could use him for his pressing business. He knew the fellows around Byron and Macon, if he had gotten any of them to help him in his shop, they would have had to be paid.

With Slippery he only had to say he needed the
money for something and Slippery would make out
on just enough money to buy his food or a few dimes
with which to gamble. At times he was lucky, and
shared his winnings with William. For thief though
he was, he appreciated the kindness William had
shown him when he was a stranger and down and
out.

Ethel had no actual crime lurking in her past—
just general worthlessness. True, she had been
picked up several times in Chicago, for street soli-
citing but had drawn only minor sentences. Her
brother, a prominent Chicago attorney, had become
disgusted with her way of living, and paid her to
leave town because of the disgrace she had brought
her family. She had gone to New York and pro-
cured work in an uptown cabaret as an entertainer.
Soon tiring of that line of work, she had drifted
from the chorus of one small show to another,
until she finally left town with a small troupe that
had gone on the rocks in Macon.

Daddy Jenks' proposition had come as a God-
send. At least it offered a place to eat and sleep,
and whatever could be picked up on the side, and a
certain amount of protection from the law.

Knowing her past, Slippery did not like the idea
of introducing her to William. To a certain ex-
tent William was his hero. He did not drink, and
was ambitious to study and better himself. That
he loved to gamble, he did not hold against him.
Why shouldn't he try his luck? He was a man and
if he didn't have a fault, it would not have been
natural. Besides, the temptation was too strong for
any real man to resist, especially when he needed

money so badly for such a good purpose as schooling. He felt that William was miles and miles above the other negroes with whom he was thrown in contact. With a certain reluctancy he guided Ethel over to where William was standing.

"Ethel wants to meet you, Willyum," he said as the three stood together jolted on all sides by dancers. "Dis is Willyum Carter—Ethel Myers."

William graciously acknowledged the introduction and Ethel smiled her sweetest, as she said:

"I certainly am pleased to meet you, Mr. Carter. Your friend here, Slippery and I were dancing together, and I had to beg him to introduce me to you. Do you like to dance?"

"I'm sorry, Miss Myers, I never dance," William answered politely with a smile.

"Well, now, can you beat that! I thought everybody in the world danced."

"I've never tried and never cared for dancing, and I'm in the world."

Ethel looked at William for a second without speaking. William returned her gaze unconcernedly. Ethel was plainly getting on his nerves and he did not try to hide the fact, which made her all the more interested.

"Well, big boy," she said, "You've got me there. I thought when I first saw you that you were a live one—different from the other tripe, but now . . ."

"Well, what do you think now?" William asked, stifling a yawn. A surge of anger swept through Ethel as she was made to feel his indifference to her.

"I've got just one more question to ask, then I'll be ready to give the verdict. Do you drink?"

"No, never tasted a drop in my life, and never cared to," William answered, moving away.

"Whew! How did your mother ever let you get out? Say boys," she cried making herself heard above the din of jazz music. "Look what we have here! It never drank a drop in its life, and don't dance. Where did you folks find it?"

Most of the dancers had turned to hear what she had to say, and when she pointed to William, a loud laugh went around the room. Cotton Eye, who had been watching her ever since she had walked over to William, guffawed louder than the rest. William turned a brick red and fire showed in his eyes, as he turned and faced the girl, who went on addressing the crowd.

"Say, where did y'all git dis 'un?" indicating William. "It hasn't got a fault in the world. Why, I believe it would think dice was number blocks made for children to play wid. Ha, ha, ha! Any more in Georgia like him?"

William, almost beside himself with anger, strode over to the laughing girl and caught her by the wrist.

"Say, you little rat!" he cried. "What you tryin' to do—make a sissy out 'er me? I've got a damn good mind to knock yore block off!"

"Don't mind her, William," Slippery said, stepping over to the girl and laying his hand on William's shoulder, "She's crazy!"

"I ain't crazy," Ethel exclaimed angrily. "He did tell me he didn't drink or dance, and walked away with that dizzy look on his face."

"Well, whut of it if he don't?" Slippery broke in. "He don't have to, if he don't wanna but Ah bet

he kin take uh pair of dice or uh deck uh cards an'
send you home barefooted."

"Who dat whut can do so much wid dice an'
cards?" A voice asked from the door. A mur-
mur went around the room. The speaker was the
stranger known as Sugar Kid, who, although he had
been in Macon only a few days, had gathered in all
of the boys' loose change and had them scared to
mention cards or dice in his presence.

Nobody knew exactly where he had come from
nor what his right name was. Some said that in
Jacksonville he called himself Sugar Kid and that
was all anyone knew of his identity. He was a
large pompous person with smoothed brown skin
and large features. His eyes were small and in
them lurked a crafty look. His large full lips hung
loosely on his mouth. His large flat nose with its
wide nostrils seemed to be always scenting some-
thing. There was an air of bravado about him and
from the day he came to Macon, the crowd around
Daddy Jenks' place had taken a dislike to him,
which grew as he cleaned the boys one by one of
their scanty bank roll. Daddy Jenks was the only
man who did not fear him, but to others he was
poison.

William had not met Sugar Kid, but intuition told
him that the speaker was the much-talked-of-
gambler. He realized that Slippery's bragging might
get him into a mess as he did not want to play with
the few dollars he planned to use otherwise. But
William loved to gamble and could not bear to be
thought beaten in anything. He had promised him-
self to lay off games for awhile, but with Sugar
Kid standing there glaring at him, his blood became

fired with a desire to put him in his proper place at
any cost. Then, too, Ethel's remarks had to be
lived down. The boys had laughed at him, a thing
he could not endure.

Her remarks caused them to look at him in a way
he did not like. In view of them, she had poked
fun at him. He would have to do something to
make them forget her insinuations or things would
be said that would cause him to have to flatten out
a few of them. He would show them that he could
meet the man they all feared.

Sugar Kid walked slowly over to where William
stood in the center of the room. There was an in-
dolent smile on his face, as he slowly looked him
over and winked to the others standing looking on.

"So, youse de guy whut craves to git rid uh some
dough?" he asked sneeringly.

"Well, I can't say that I exactly craves to git rid
of any dough, but I do crave annexing some of yours,
an' kin do it if I try," William answered nonchal-
antly, looking the gambler over.

"Atta boy, William!" Slippery shouted.

"Well, whut yuh say to playin' a li'l' skin?" Sugar
Kid asked.

"O.K. by me," William replied.

"Well, less go. Ah'll play any uh de odders whut
wants to take me on," Sugar Kid said loudly, look-
ing around the well-filled room.

"There's only one thing I want and it's such a
li'l' thing I know you won't object," William said
looking straight into the other's eyes.

"What's it?"

"I want someone else beside you to deal the cards,"
he answered slowly.

"How come yuh wants dat? Is dere any objection to us dealin' to one 'nothur?" Sugar Kid asked, a trace of annoyance in his voice.

"Yes, there is, and if Daddy Jenks will give us a new pack an' a dealer, we'll start!" William announced calmly.

"But I don't see any sense in havin' no stationary dealer," Sugar Kid objected.

"Well, I do, and if I don't get one, I don't play," William replied with finality.

A general murmur of approval went around the room, but none of the boys dared express an opinion that would in any way show their disapproval of the swaggering Sugar Kid. Sugar Kid, sensing their feeling and not daring to object, for fear of putting himself in a bad light with the boys, consented to William's demand.

Daddy Jenks placed a table to one side for the game, and called one of his boys to deal. The music struck up for the dancers to continue but everyone was absorbed in the game that was about to be started.

Ethel Myers sided over to William's side and placed her head on his arm. William turned and looked up into her face coldly.

"Don't play him, Carter," she said softly. "I hear he's plain poison around here."

"Don't worry 'bout me," William retorted. "I've got his number." And then announced loudly. "I'm goin' to bet on the queen, Queen Ethel, and when I wins my first five dollars, it goes to buy a present for the Queen."

Everyone laughed and Sugar Kid frowned his displeasure.

"That's right, William, yuh got de best go," they all shouted.

Slippery stood a few paces away with a worried look. In a way he felt responsible for William's plight. If he lost, it would be his fault for mentioning the game.

William looked at him and smiled, and Slippery thought that whatever faults William might have, he was not lacking in courage and admired him for that.

The game was on. A few of the other boys took a hand betting quarters and half dollars. William won and won again. The few who had joined in the game were soon frozen out and only Sugar Kid and William remained. Sugar Kid won a few hands and William won again and again. Sugar Kid had laid aside his coat and then his vest for he, unlike the rest, had come well-dressed, in fact, overdressed, for he had also hoped to impress Ethel.

Sugar Kid lost a big bet, and swore loudly. William coolly played on. Everybody, including Daddy Jenks crowded around the table where the game was being played. Sugar Kid, never a good loser, continued to swear.

"Say, listen heah, Carter, I won't stan' for nobody dealin' all de time. Ah wants de deal to walk."

William, the winner by fifty or more dollars, slowly gathered up his money saying: "When the deal walks, Sugar Kid, I walks. I done told you how I'd play an' I means it!"

The game ended at daylight. William crammed the money he had won in his pocket and prepared to leave the place. Everybody had gone except

Ethel, who walked over to his side and placing her hand on his arm, said:

"Please forgive me, William, for whut Ah said. Ah was jes' mad cause you didn't fall for me lak de rest uh dese tramps round heah, but I sho done took uh tumble for you, honey!"

"Heah's five dollars. Maybe that'll pick you up," William answered disdainfully, shoving the bill into her hand.

"Ah don't want yo' money," pushing the bill away.

"All right, I'll buy you a present with it, I said I'd give you the first five I won, and I always keep my word."

"Ah knows you'se dead tired, William, playin' heah all night. Why don't you come up to my room. Ah got uh little stove in dere an' Ah'll fix you some breakfast," Ethel pleaded, her body pressed close to William.

William looked at her for a moment in silence. What difference did it make with whom he ate breakfast. Ethel had a nasty tongue and a rotten character but she certainly was good to look at.

He sat in a small rocker as she made coffee and cooked eggs on a small oil stove in her poorly furnished room upstairs. They laughed and talked about the happenings of the night before, of Sugar Kid's disaster, and when she turned her back, William tucked the five dollar bill under the dresser scarf. She would find it there, and have to keep it.

"Tired, William?" she asked, taking his hand and pressing it gently to her face.

"Yes and sleepy too," William answered, trying to shake off the sleep that was creeping on him.

"Why don't you lay down heah den?" Ethel said, sitting on his knee and running her fingers through his thick curly hair.

"No. I think I better go to my own room," trying to get up.

"Whar's yo' room?"

"Er, 'bout ten blocks from here—with my cousin."

"Why walk ten blocks when you kin stay heah?" kissing him. "Come on, William, don't be so mean. Ah ain't so bad, an' Ah sho is strong for you hot papa!" Ethel coaxed, turning back the bed and patting the pillows into place.

William stood up and stretched, and made a step towards the door. Ethel playfully caught him and pushed him until he sat on the side of the bed. Sitting beside him, her arms stole up and rested around his neck. Pulling his head to her shoulder, she kissed him passionately again and again.

William accepted her caresses with no pretence of returning them, his blood tingling with passion, hot and overpowering. Ethel talked softly as she removed his shoes, and unfastened his shirt and removed it. Throwing her arms around him she pushed him back across the bed. Her body soft and warm lay close beside him for a moment. His arms reached out eagerly and drew her to him in a long, warm embrace.

CHAPTER VII

William's eyes opened lazily, and slowly traveled around the unfamiliar room. The cheap muslin curtains fanned in and out of the small open windows. Slanting shadows of late afternoon shed an ephemeral light across the dingy uncovered floor. His eyes found and rested on the form of a woman aranging a tray on a small table near the center of the room. Yes, it was Ethel. It all came back to him with startling clearness. He sat up quickly on the side of the bed. Ethel, looking up from her preparations of the tray, saw him.

"Come on, William, an' eat yo' dinner while it's hot," she called pleasantly, siding up to him.

"I don't want no dinner," he answered shortly.

"Whut's de mattuh, William?" Ethel asked anxiously, noting his frowning countenance.

"Oh, nothin'. I jes' don't like being here when there's so much work over at the shop to do."

"You just as well eat now, it's all fixed. Dere ain't much you kin do nohow. It's pretty nigh six uh clock."

William ate sullenly and hurried away with a gruff good-bye. He was thankful for once that the usual crowd that blocked the sidewalk in front of Daddy Jenks' place gossiping and telling jokes, had taken a recess.

Slippery looked up from his pressing, as he entered the shop. Neither spoke; but Slippery easily guessing where he had spent the day, felt vaguely

uneasy.   He realized William was in for a world of
trouble getting mixed up with Ethel.

One by one the gang dropped in for their things
that had been left for cleaning, and to loll around
and talk about William's triumph over the brag-
ging Sugar Kid.

"Boy, oh boy, dat's one snake whut ain't so pop-
ular roun' dese diggin'," Cotton Eye laughed.   "Ah
sho is glad yuh took 'im for his dough, Willyum!"

"Me too," Red Shirt added.   "Ah thought sho
some uh us was goin' uh hafta step on his head an'
flatten 'im out 'fo 'lon', but Ah guess dis'll kind uh
cool him off."

"Yeah, but he'll be rarin' up agin, don't you
worry!" Slippery reminded them.

The laughter and talk went on about the game
of the night before, the boys counting up their small
store of change with which they hoped to give Sugar
Kid his next battle later that night.

Ten o'clock Daddy Jenks' Juke was crowded.
Music and dancing was in full sway.   Sweaty bodies
pressed close together, moved squirmingly to hot
jazz tunes, perspiration running down their faces.
Women twisting their bodies, working their hips up
and down seductively, dragged themselves around
the room, every movement an invitation.   If ac-
ceptance occasioned an absence of a few moments,
each couple boldly returned unashamed.

A close sour odor hung in the room, sickeningly
oppressive.   There was a heavy smell of bad corn
liquor, stale beer, unwashed bodies and dim lights
blotted out by the shadows of the dancers, swaying
back and forth through the fetid air.   Loud tin-
panish music was heard from a broken instrument

pushed against the wall on which an overalled in-
dividual beat unmercifully, his feet stamping out
what his hands failed to bang.

Ethel slowly dragged herself around the room in
Sugar Kid's arms, her eyes turned expectantly to-
wards the door every time it opened to admit a
newcomer. Sugar Kid, noticing her agitation, asked
sneeringly.

"Whar's yo' high yaller boy friend?"

"Who you mean, Sugar?" Ethel asked, innocently
looking up into his face.

"Go on gal! You know who Ah means—de high
yaller wid de white folks hair dat took my dough.
Ah seed 'im comin' out uh yo' room late dis after-
noon."

"Now look uh heah, nigguh, don't you go med-
dlin' wid my business," Ethel exploded angrily.

"Aw Ah ain't tryin' to queer yuh, kid. Ah laks
yuh an' could do heap more fuh yuh den he kin."

"Fat chance you'll git to do anything for dis sweet
mamma," Ethel laughed in his face.

"Don't be too sho, gal. Yuh may be glad to hang
on to sweet papa Sugar fo' long."

"Don't fool yo'seff. You jes' ain't my style an'
never will be," Ethel taunted.

"No, baby an' you ain't dat boy's style neither
an' nebber will be. He's high falutin' an' gals lak
you is jes' out, far as he's concerned. He thinks he's
a wooden God," Sugar Kid sneered.

"Ah'm good as he is. My brother's uh lawyer
an' uh big man in Chi," Ethel informed him with
spirit.

"An' his sister is whut? Ah'll let you say it."

Ethel jerked away from him angrily. "Yo big

black hunk uh nothin'," she hissed. "Lemme loose dis minute!"

"Not on yo' life, sister!" Sugar Kid avowed, taking a firmer grasp on her arm. "Yuh gonna dance an' lak it!"

Ethel danced on in silence until Sugar Kid pushed her away in disgust and slouched out of the room. A few moments later when William appeared in the dance hall, she nodded her head at him indifferently, and pulled Cotton Eye, who was standing near her, finished her dance determinedly.

"Well, Ah see you'se back to try yo' luck again tonight," Sugar Kid remarked, walking over to William, who stood looking at the dancers.

"Yeah, I'm sticking around," William answered nonchalantly.

"Well, yuh know dat luck is a mighty change-able thing. Take Papa Sugar's advice an' don't try to ride 'em too hard."

"Don't worry about me—just look out for yourself. I can take care of William."

"Awrite big boy. Whut yuh say we play up-stairs in de clubroom tonight?" Sugar Kid asked, a smile that could have meant anything, wreathing his smug countenance.

"O.K. by me," William answered, moving to-wards the stairs.

"Come on, fellows. Let's git de game started. My hands is itchin' an' dat's de sign uh money." Sugar Kid called to the fellows scattered around the room.

"Not so fast," Daddy Jenks remarked from be-hind the counter. "Eve'body's gotta drink to my health tonight. I'se jes' become a grandpa. My daughter done borned uh fine boy an' we gonna celebrate! Come on up, eve'ybody an' have uh drink on de house."

Murmurs of approval came from the crowd, as they rushed eagerly to get their free drink.

"Heah Willyum! Dere's uh glass uh gingerale for you," Daddy Jenks said, handing William the drink.

"Put a nipple on it, daddy"! Sugar Kid shouted.

"Shut up, you big loafer!" Ethel exploded. "Eve'ybody ain't a gin lapper lak you is."

"Atta gal, Ethel. Willyum sho' is got yo' number. You done fell lak de Walls uh Jericho". Cotton Eye laughed.

"Shut up all uh yuh black bastards!" Ethel shouted, her temper getting the better of her. "You ain't no good yourselves an' yuh hate to see anybody that got guts, try to be something."

William, standing at the end of the counter, said nothing. He felt miles above these ignorant riff raffs and their brawls.

"Ah leave de kid alone! He's awrite. Ah don't care much 'bout de stuff myself," Daddy Jenks ended the argument. "Anyhow Ah wants eve'ybody to be happy tonight. I'se got a good cause to be. Ah had uh hard time raisin' dat gal uh mine wid no woman to help me an' me bein' in dis kind uh business. Ah sent hur to Atlanta to school an' she comed out and teached. Den she married Sam an' he's a good, hard wukkin' man. Now dere little home is all paid for, an' my gal's in de best 'society 'roun' heah an' ain't nebber gived me a minute's trouble. Ain't dat somethin'?"

"Ah'll say it is!" the crowd shouted.   "Three cheers for dad's daughter and grandson."

* * *

Sugar Kid finally succeeded in getting his crowd together, and the game was on.

Ethel had had no chance to talk to William. She felt hurt. Daddy Jenks' recital had gotten under her skin in a way that she would not have admitted, as in her mind she turned over the incidents in her childhood. The environment and the advantages that had been given her, which she had thrown away to become a nobody. Walking over to the counter she called for a good stiff liquor which she drank hastily, then another and another. Her conscience numbed by the potent moonshine, she was soon dancing and laughing again. Finally, pushing the other dancers from the floor, she danced in a wild, primitive, sensuous manner. Her hips twisting, her body quivering, her mood changed to savagery. The crowd lining up, around the room, looked on, clapping their hands in delight. She pulled her dress higher and higher above her knees, her head thrown back in defiance. Pausing in the midst of her exhibition, she climbed from a chair to the top of the battered old piano; where she opened her lips to sing one of her course blues.

But the alcohol and dizzy twirling had gotten the better of her and she dropped heavily into the arms of some of the by-standers. Slippery, who had just come into the room, helped to take her upstairs to bed, where she lay in a drunken stupor.

In the clubroom the game went on steadily. The

atmosphere was tense. William was dealing, his small stack of money lay on the table before him. Slippery placed his small pile of change on the table, and took a card. The deal went around. Sugar Kid won. Again the cards were spread out. Each player picked his card. Swish—swish—the cards were turned from the pack. First Slippery then William lost and so on around the table. Sugar Kid swept their money in. Slippery, losing the last of his few pennies, stepped aside.

"You'se out 'fo you'se in," Sugar Kid taunted.

"Whut's it to you? Ah play my own money, don't Ah?" Slippery asked angrily.

"Awrite, Bo. Ah wasn't meanin' no harm. Ah was gonna let yuh have uh blind," Sugar Kid retorted.

"When Ah wants anyt'ing from you, Ah'll whistle!"

"Yeah. Yuh mought git yo' mouth puckered up an' my fist mought keep it dat uh way."

"Ah ain't gonna have no arguin' 'round heah. Dis is gonna be uh peaceful game so both uh yuh shut up!" Daddy Jenks reminded them.

Hour after hour the game went on, Sugar Kid taunting the boys spitefully, as one by one they dropped out, their money disappearing into his pockets. But he wanted to break William and although he was losing at almost every turn, he stuck with him longer than any of the others.

"They call dis game Georgy skin, but Ah'se a Florida boy whut kin teach you Georgy punks uh lot uh points," Sugar Kid grinned.

William was down to his last five dollars. Reaching over, he picked out a nine spot of spades and placed the five dollar bill on top of it.

"Ha! Ha!" Sugar Kid laughed. "De nin uh spades is whut digs de gamblers' grave. Ah'll take de ten uh hearts. An' say Carter, I wanna riffle dem cards."

"All right," William assented, handing him the pack.

The cards riffled and cut were handed to Daddy Jenks, who dealt them slowly. One, two, three, the cards were deftly turned. Sugar Kid glancing over Daddy Jenks' shoulder, said carelessly. "Wanna raise hit, Willyum?"

"No," William answered shortly.

A few more cards and then William's nine. Sugar Kid reached over and picked up the bill.

"Wanna play some mo'?" he asked.

"No. I think I'll go on home. I've got a headache."

"Bes' place in de world for uh headache," Sugar Kid laughed. "Well, Ah ain't got nobody to play me so, ah guess de game is all washed up."

"Aw no it ain't, Sugar Kid!" Daddy Jenks said slowly. "Put yo' money back on de table. Ah feels kinder lucky tonight."

The room was instantly tense. It had been years since any one remembered Daddy Jenks playing Georgia skin. Everybody crowded around as he spread and shuffled the cards. Daddy Jenks won the first bet then Sugar Kid won. Back and forth the money passed for almost an hour. Then Daddy Jenks' luck seemed to forsake him. He lost steadily, sent downstairs to the poolroom for more money, and lost that.

With the last money from the cash register be-
fore him, the gang begged him to quit, but Daddy
Jenks was fascinated. A power stronger than him-
self held him. He played on, sometimes winning
on a card only to lose again more than he had won.
His last dollar lay upon the queen of diamonds,
face up. He lost.

"Yuh wanna quit, dad?" Sugar Kid asked, cun-
ningly gorging him on.

"No, ah ain't nebber seen a meat man on earth
whut could clean ole Daddy Jenks," he answered
testily. "Ah'll write yuh uh check, Sugar Kid.
Let's play."

"Ah don't lak checks, daddy!" Sugar Kid an-
swered. "But Ah'll tell yuh whut, Ah'll play yuh
for dis clubroom, three chances each. If Ah win,
Ah runs it. If Ah lose, Ah pay yuh whutever it's
worth. Whut yuh say?"

"No. Ah won't do that!" Daddy Jenks answered
slowly. "Ah guess Ah'll quit!"

"An dey say dat you was de greatest gambler
'round heah—*was* is de rite word!" Sugar Kid
jeered.

"Whut yuh mean, was? Ah still is de best
gambler 'roun' heah!"

"But you sho is slippin', Daddy!" Sugar Kid
taunted.

"Ah ain't slippin' nothin' uh de kind."

"Well, yuh jes' damn scared den!"

"Ah ain't never been scared uh no man an' Ah
ain't yit. You put up uh hundred dollars an' if Ah
lose, Ah'll make yuh out uh lease for uh year on
de clubroom," Daddy Jenks replied coolly.

"Don't do it, Daddy!" William begged, laying his hand on Daddy Jenks' shoulder.

"Mine yo' business, son. When Ah want advice, ah sees uh lawyer!" Daddy Jenks flashed back.

"All right, Daddy, it's your funeral," William replied.

"Yeah, but Ah ain't buried yit. Whut yuh say, Sugar Kid, let's get started." Daddy turned to Sugar Kid impatiently.

"Sho thing. Let Willyum deal," Sugar suggested.

"No, not me!" William spoke up, quickly.

"Ah'll deal 'em," Slippery offered. "An' Ah'll deal 'em so Sugar Kid can't look through 'em lake he seem to been doin' all night!"

Daddy Jenks' card was the last to fall for the first deal. The crowd was jubilant. Again he and Sugar Kid picked their respective cards. Swish-swish-went the cards to the table. Sugar Kid won. The cards were again shuffled, and spread on the table face up. Each picked their card. Tense silence pervaded the room. It was the last deal. The on-lookers scarcely breathed. Slippery held the pack tightly gripped in his hand. Swish-Swish—the card fell to the table. One, another and another. Then Daddy Jenks' card flipped off, as a sigh went around the room. Sugar Kid had won.

Daddy Jenks sat as if in a dream. He had lost his clubroom, where he had reigned for many years, and with it went the best part of his profit. His body slumped in his chair, as his head rested on the table. Sugar Kid had slipped quietly from the room. Slippery examined the cards carefully. Yes, they were all right. The seals had been broken before their eyes.   Silently they filed out, leaving the old man alone.

William was the last to leave.   The first faint streak of dawn was coloring the sky, as he made his way through the semi-darkened streets.   After a ten minute walk he reached his Cousin Sissy's house and let himself into his room, where he lay for hours, thinking of his muddled life in the city.

CHAPTER VIII

Sunday was a great day among the simple farmers in Byron. They rose early and hurried to and fro, doing their usual chores before church time when everyone, saint and sinner, were wont to gather for worship. People came from far and near in wagons to which were hitched any kind of animal from horses to oxen. The settlers, who lived a distance from the little meeting-house, hitched their conveyance to the young saplings that grew in profusion around the church, and remained all day. Some brought their dinner in slat baskets and others, who were more fortunate, ate with neighbors, who lived nearby.

Between the services they gossiped and enjoyed the day like a group of children. The day showed promises of being a fair hot one. Jim and Ruth did their chores laughing and playing as they worked. Sara Lou standing on the steps of the back porch threw out hands full of corn and called the cackling chickens to their feed. In the distance birds sang airily. An air of peace pervaded the farm. The field of snow white cotton stood tall and erect, and as Jim put it, "nodding" to him to get ready for the picking.

Putting away the empty pan from which the chickens had been fed, Sara Lou bustled around the kitchen preparing breakfast and putting the finishing touches to the dinner, which had been cooked Saturday. She always entertained for dinner a good many of the farmers, who lived too far away to return home until after the last service.

A large cured pork ham lay on the table beside a fat hen that had been baked for the occasion. Sara Lou viewed with pride a large iced cake and two apple pies, as she tried to count her guests—her hand held before her checking off each one with a finger pulled down to her palm.

"Ah guess Ah'se got vittels 'nough!" she mused. "But dere's allus some dat jes' comes in whethur yuh ask dem uh not. Now lemme see—dere's Hilda an' hur husbun', Ben, an' dere four chillun, dat make six altuhgether an' dere's ole man Pettiebone an' 'Riher an' de Dausies. Now how many is dat? Lawd, Ah'se done lost track. Anyhow dere's de preacher. Umm, seems lak Ah done count uh hundred to say nothin' 'bout cousin Ella an' Jerimah an' dey six young 'uns. Ah guess Ah better let Ruth put 'em down on paper. Ah sho is sorry William ain't heah. He's allus such uh help when my ole brain ain't wukkin' rite."

She gave the big pan of batter bread an impatient push into the oven, and turned to lift the skillet from a hook behind the stove, smiling to herself, as she cut—a small chicken into four parts.

"Ah guess Jim'll purty nigh drop dead at de thought uh me killin' one uh my best pullets for Sunday breakfuss but Ah wanted to have somethin' real nice for Ruth. She's such uh comfort. Wonder whut could 'er keep Willyum in Macon anyhow? He done clean forgit dey gonna call uh new preacher today an' 'ull need his advice."

The chicken was soon frying and sputtering in the grease. The odor of bread and boiling coffee filled the kitchen, as Sara Lou moved to and fro stopping to mop the perspiration from her brow on the corner of her apron. Taking down three plates from the shelf, she wiped them carefully and put them on the table, pausing in her work, as a voice called from the front of the house.

"Yo hoo, is yuh in, cousin Sara?"

"Yeah, Ah'se heah", she answered loudly.

Turning, she gasped in amazement, as her cousin Ella appeared in the doorway. On each side of her clinging to her calico skirt were her two younger children, her husband Jerimah and the four older boys close behind her.

"Lawdy, cousin Sara," Ella exclaimed breathlessly, "Ah was dat scared we'un wouldn't git heah in time for breakfuss. Our ole hoss done took sick and we done had to leave home dat early we ain't had no time for vittels so we hurried on heah to eat wid yuh'all. Ah tole Jerimah it would be awrite wid you."

"Course it's awrite, Ella," Sara Lou answered not over enthusiastic at the prospect of having six more to feed, who would also be on hand for dinner, and it would be just like Ella to stop by for a late lunch after the evening services.

Jim and Ruth brought the two pails of fresh warm milk to the kitchen, and washed up for breakfast. Sara Lou grumbled inaudibly as she added six more plates to the table. Jim laughed softly at his mother's chagrin, and cast uneasy eyes toward the yard, where Ella's boys were playing.

"Yuh better keep yo' eyes on 'em, Ma," he warned. "De las' time dey was over heah, dey pulled up nigh all uh my new plants, an' if dey pull up dem geraniums dat Ruth brung over heah an' sit out, Ah'll skin 'em alive."

"No son, yuh mustn't do dat. Dis is de Sabbath an' you mustn't lose yo' temper on de Lawd's day."

"Sabbath or no Sabbath dey better b'have. Look uh dere!" he exclaimed, as the objects of their discussion were seen in the act of uprooting a plant.

"Hey, you young uns, come out uh dere dis minute!" Jim called.

Ella ran out and jerked the boys away from the little patch of plants, and set them down on the front steps.

"Now yuh'all stay dere," she warned. "You know yo' cousin Jim is fussy 'bout his ole yard so don't you young'uns touch uh thing!"

Jim boiled over, but a look from his Mother stopped the words that were about to pour from his lips.

At last they were all seated at the table. The children, hard to be kept quiet, rattled their knives and forks and fidgeted in their chairs. Sara Lou bowed her head to pray, but her prayer was brought abruptly to an end by a scream from one of Ella's boys.

"Ella, dem chillun is de worse Ah ever seen," Sara Lou complained, wiping a stream of milk from the table cloth, where little Jet had upset the glass that had been given him.

"Dey ain't no worse den nobody else's," Ella defended, turning on her angrily.

"We won't argue, but Jerimah should take 'em in hand rite away. You done rotten 'em ontell dey stincks," Sara Lou retorted, looking at Jerimah, who sat a little huddled creature afraid to even breathe when his two hundred and fifty pound wife was with him.

"Huh, Ah jes' wish Jerimah would tech my chillun," Ella remarked, giving him a look that seemed to wither him up like a flower beneath a scorching sun. He opened his mouth to speak, but closed it meekly. Jim looked at Ruth and they turned their heads to hide the laughter that showed in their faces.

"You allus talkin' 'bout my chillun, cousin Sara, but you ain't done sich uh good job uh bringin' up wid Willyum," Ella said, and the next moment realized she had tread on dangerous ground.

"Whut you mean, Ella, talkin' 'bout my Willyum lak dat?" Sara Lou asked sharply.

"Oh, nuthin', cousin Sara, but . . ."

Jim's hostile look cut her off. She changed quickly to:

"Folks says dat he sho is spendin' lot uh time in Macon dese days, not even comin' home most uh de time on Sundays."

"Well, Ah'se satisfied an' it ain't nobody else's business. Dey allus did pick on my Willyum jes' kaise he's got mo' sense dan de rest uh dese ignorant nigguhs 'roun' heah," Sara Lou replied with spirit.

"Dat's zact'ly whut Ah tells 'em," Ella said, looking at Jim sheepishly.

"Jim, we better hurry an' do de dishes for An' Sara," Ruth said, rising, looking down at the side of her dress which one of the boys seated near her had smeared with molasses.

"No, you ain't gonna wash no dishes, Ruth!" Sara Lou spoke up. "You an' Jim git ready for church. Ah can wash dese dishes in no time an

Ah'se ready 'cept for puttin' on my clean apron so
yuh'all run on upstairs an' don't be late."

Ruth looked reluctantly at the table filled with
dirty dishes and smeared with molasses and crumbs,
as Ella gathered her brood and herded them to the
back porch to wash them up for the meeting.

Jerimah, eager to get out of his wife's opulent
presence, slipped out into the yard to smoke his long
stemmed clay pipe.

Jim went quietly upstairs, his thoughts of Wil-
liam, wondering just what Ella had intended saying.
He had no doubt that she too had heard some of
the talk that drifted into Byron of William's life in
Macon. He wondered how long these stories could
be kept from their mother whose adoration and
faith in William was pitiful. At any rate, if he
could prevent it, nothing would ever reach her ears
that would tend to lessen that faith, he resolved,
hurriedly changing to his Sunday suit. He and
Ruth would be walking to church alone today.
William was usually along, making him look home-
lier than ever by comparison.

Ruth in Sara Lou's room across the hall, could
hear him moving around. Quietly she slipped
across the hall, and tapped lightly on the door of
his room.

"Come in," Jim called after a moment's silence.

"Whut you hidin'?" she asked, as he turned from
the dresser, where he had shoved something into the
half-open drawer.

" 'Tain't nothin'," Jim answered bashfully.

"Ah'm gonna look an' see," Ruth laughed, as she
pulled the drawer open. "Why, Jim, whut you

doin' wid dis mail order book?" she questioned, spreading it open on the side of the bed.

"Lookin' atter uh purtty marryin' dress," Jim answered, turning the pages.

Ruth looked in rapturous silence at the bridal array pictured there.

"Ah was jes' thinkin' how purtty yuh'd look in dis 'un," Jim said, pointing to the sheer white dress with sweeping train.

"Why Jim, you know we could never git uh dress lak dat. It'ud cost lotta money but it sho is swell," Ruth sighed.

"It's twenty-five dollars an' dat is uh heap uh money. Does yuh lak it, Ruth?" he asked, putting his hand caressingly on her shoulder.

" 'Course Ah do, Jim. Ah ain't never had uh silk dress nohow."

"Well, we'll jes' wait an' see. Maybe some day yuh'll wear it," Jim promised, taking her hand in his tenderly.

Sara Lou's voice called from downstairs, interrupted their dream. Ruth and Jim kissed, and ran downstairs to join her.

"Yuh'all sho does tak uh time to dress," she grumbled, as they walked briskly to the little log church nearby.

A low murmur went around the assembled worshippers as they entered the building. William had not entered with them and they were eager to find out why.

Reverend Thomas, a small, dried up man with a shiny bald spot, whom as Sara Lou remembered, had always conducted the services whenever the church was without a preacher, stood behind the rostrum, adjusting his horn rimmed glasses, which had a habit of sliding far down on his small flat nose.

"Well, sistuhs and brudders," he wheezed through his nose. "It's become my duty to take de place uh our dear departed pastor dis morning."

The congregation peeped at each other sheepishly. They all knew that Reverend Thomas would preach at least two hours, if some of the deacons seated on the rostrum did not stop him or he had to stop from sheer exhaustion.

"Ah'se gonna take my text in Revelations in de words uh John—

'An dese are dem, who done washed dere garments in de blood uh de lamb,' "
he announced, looking over his sliding spectacles.

The congregation settled themselves more comfortably. They knew when Reverend Thomas chose Revelations, they were in for an all-day session.

Sister Spencer, a little old dried-up, brown woman, who, ever since Sara Lou and some of the older settlers could remember, had held the place of honor as the best moaner in the amen corner, settled herself more comfortably, pushed her snuff brush to a secure corner of her mouth, and started her plaintive moaning, "Preachee, Brudder Thomas, preachee!" and kept it up except for the few moments she dozed.

Reverend Thomas preached on. Brave souls amened and every now and then shouted a loud "Hallelujah!" "Help 'im Lawd!"

Jim slept faithfully through the long sermon, refusing to awake even to Ruth's nudging. Even Sara

Lou snatched a few nods occasionally. Somebody started a hymn. The congregation joined in sleepily. Gradually they shook off their drowsiness and gained in volume in their singing until Reverend Thomas, no longer able to talk loud enough to be heard above their blatant voices, sank into his seat, wearily mopping his brow with his large red cotton handkerchief. The congregation now fully awake, sang lustily, swaying to the rhythm of the song. "In de morning when de Lawd says hurry . . ." until one of the deacons, Jaffus Simms, raised his hand, bringing their song to an end.

"Brudders an' Sisters," he began, and after clearing his throat several times continued. "Us done hearn uh powfull sermon dis mornin', an' 'fo Ah raise de collection, I wan' to ask yuh'all is anybody heah present got uh preacher in mind dat we kin call to pastor dis church now dat we'se widout uh leader uh dis flock? 'Course Brudder Thomas heah is uh ordain preacher, but we done asked him, as we'se allers done, in de pass when we was widout uh shepard an' he done refused."

"An' Ah rises to say, brudder Simms, dat de reason is dat Ah ain't so strong as Ah uster be, an' Ah couldn't stan' de strain." Thomas interrupted, rising from his seat, panting from his exertions.

"Thank yuh, Brother Thomas," Simms acknowledged, and continued: "I don't zackley see how we'se gonna git any whar wid brudder William Carter not heah, him bein' de junior deacon uh dis church as well as de clerk. Is dere anythin' wrong wid 'im, sister Carter?" turning to Sara Lou.

Sara Lou hastened to reply. "Lawd no, brudder Simms, I guess he done stayed in Macon 'count 'er 'portant business but he'll be heah bright an' early next Sunday."

"Well, Ah moves eff'en ah kin git uh second, dat we wait ontell next Sunday when we'ull have brudder Willyum wid us," Simms put to the congregation. After the members gave assent to their willingness to wait, the matter was put aside and the services closed with the benediction.

Ruth and Jim, taking advantage of Sara Lou's being besieged on every side with questions about William's absence, walked home alone.

"You know Ruth," Jim said thoughtfully, after they had walked a distance in silence, "Ah wish we could git married right uh way."

"Jim, you sho is for hurryin' up some things an' slow 'bout other things," Ruth laughed.

"Ah wants you, Ruth. Somethin' insider me is jes' cryin' for yuh honey."

"An' Ah done tole you it's bad luck to marry while you're wearin' black for yo' folks!"

"Ah don't b'lieve in dem signs. Ah wants to be sho uh you, an' 'sides Ah been havin' uh spell uh mighty bad dreams lately."

"Dat's b'lievin' in signs, Jim," Ruth reminded him. They both laughed at his contradictory moods and hurried home to start putting dinner on the table before Sara Lou's many hungry guests arrived.

Everyone Sara Lou expected for dinner came and almost as many more. They had to be fed in sections, the grown-ups first and a second table for the children. After dinner, the men strolled around the farm smoking their pipes, while Sara Lou and the women sat on the front porch stirring their neatly chewed brushes, deep in their boxes of rail-

road snuff, everybody enjoying themselves and re-
laxing for the big meeting to be held that night
when the much-talked-of "Swamp Angel" would
preach one of his stirring sermons at their own Cal-
vary. Excitedly they talked of the many things they
had heard about his fiery sermons, how he could be
heard for as far as a mile away, and the many souls
he gained for the Lord, how at the climax of his
preaching, he placed the Bible upon his shoulder and
walked the aisles of the Church, the building trem-
bling under his three hundred pound tread.

Thus the afternoon passed and the evening found
them again in the little church, where for more than
three hours the Swamp Angel preached his sermon
of fire and brimstone and lived up to all the things
that had been told about his mighty power to rock
the very depths of a sinner's soul.

Jim, his mother and Ruth walked home after the
meeting in silence, each busy with their own thoughts,
and Sara Lou hurried straight upstairs to bed. Dis-
appointment over William's not coming home or
sending a message to say why, filled her heart but
she would not for the world have let anyone, not
even Jim, know it.

"Come on, Ruth, less you an' me eat some vit-
tels," Jim, who was always hungry, suggested when
he and the girl were alone.

"Ah don't want nothin' to eat but Ah'll come an'
keep yo' company," Ruth consented.

Jim pushed her playfully into a chair at the table,
and placed a glass of milk and a slice of cake before
her, taking his place beside her a moment later
with a plate filled and overflowing with food.

"Ah had dis vittels hid in de stove. Ah was

scared dem starved out old stickin' plasters was gointer eat up everything today," he laughed.

"No wonder you dream all kinds uh dreams," Ruth smiled. "Jes' look whut you goin' to bed on."

"Dis ain't nothin' but uh bite. You ought'uh see whut Ah does eat som'times."

"Well, don't complain 'bout bad dreams den, Jim." "Gee, boy, you sho can hug!" Ruth complained a few moments later when Jim, having finished his meal, caught her in his arms.

"Ah loves you so much, Ruth, dat it makes me scared sometimes," Jim whispered, kissing her before he let her go.

"An' Ah loves you more den so much," Ruth returned, playfully pinching his round cheeks, and running lightly upstairs where she lay awake thinking for a long while beside his mother, who was sleeping soundly.

After a day of excitement and bustle, everything was still. Outside firebugs flitted to and fro, making the only light to be seen for miles.

Another Sunday had come and gone in the peaceful village. Everybody had put on their Sunday best and served God in their own simple way. Monday would find them again in their grimy rags —busy, hard working farmers intent on their daily tasks.

CHAPTER IX

To William in Macon, Sunday had not brought the peace his family had enjoyed in Byron. He had crawled into bed in the early hours of dawn broke, discouraged, ashamed of the life he was leading and disgusted with himself for not having the will-power to break away from the thing that was slowly but surely carrying him to disaster.

His cousin Sissy from whom he rented a small shabby room for one dollar a week, had called him in time for church, but receiving no answer, had decided he had worked in his shop late and needed rest. Of all her relatives, William was her favorite.

He had never shown by word or deed that he disapproved of her mode of living, and was always kind and encouraging. The others scorned her and called her a scarlet woman because when a girl of fifteen, she ran away with a man, whom she met during cotton picking time in Byron and had lived with him until he became tired of her and walked out. In the years that followed she had lived with any man who happened to suit her fancy, drinking and fighting her way down to the lowest ebb of morality.

William, on coming to Macon to attend high school, had looked her up, and made his home in her lop-sided hut in one of Macon's dingy alleys to which his mother while not approving, had explained to the rest of the family.

"William's stayin' wid Sissy might help to make de pore loose gal better."

But to Sissy's mind, it was proof that he did not think her so very bad, and she loved him for the thought.

William had dressed to go out Sunday afternoon when Sissy and her latest man, whom she had salvaged from a nearby poolroom, entered. She hastened to set the dinner of stewed chicken and rice on the table, and insisted on his eating dinner with them, but William ate so little she became alarmed and asked:

"Whut's de matter wid you, Willyum? You don't feel well?"

"No, Sissy, I don't. I've got a headache," William answered listlessly.

"Yuh see, Sissy, dat's whut Ah'se allers sayin'," Sissy's man remarked, boastfully slapping his chest. "Eff'en uh body'ud take on uh little liquor now an' den, dey 'ud never know dey had uh head. Look uh me. Ah feels fine, Ah does!"

"Aw shut up, you ole likker head. Willyum ain't yo' kind," Sissy snapped back scornfully.

"But you sho is, gal, an' Ah done brought long uh bottle for us to nibble on." Sissy's man grinned, setting the pint of corn at her elbow. Sissy reached for it eagerly and William, knowing the regular weekend fight would begin as soon as its contents were gulped down, put on his hat and walked out.

Hours later when he returned, the house was dark and silent, and reeking with bad corn liquor. Sissy and her man were asleep, but the over-turned table and broken chairs told a mute story of the battle that had previously raged.

Monday when William awoke, it was raining—
a steady down-pour. The dampness that seethed
through the partly paneless window had awakened
him. He searched around for a few old rags to
shut it out, and crept back into bed.

It was one o'clock when Sissy returned from
gathering up her numerous bundles of washings.
William had fallen into a heavy sleep. Hurriedly
she made a fire in the kitchen stove, and warmed
up the remainder of the Sunday dinner, adding a
batch of butter milk biscuits and setting the table
for two.

"Git up, boy, an' less eat. Lawd Ah ain't never
seed a body dat sleeped de whole day through
'thout' dey was sick," she chided.

William rose, stretching sleepily and soon joined
her in the kitchen.

"You bettuh drink some 'uh dis Sassfrass tea.
It'll bring yuh out," Sissy suggested.

William reached for the tin cup Sissy always
kept on the back of the stove and poured a cup of
the hot tea.

"Willyum, how come you didn't go home Sat-
tiday night?" she asked, setting the plate of hot
biscuits on the table.

"I didn't feel well and I know it would've wor-
ried Ma," William replied, busily helping his plate.

"Dat's you, Willyum, never wantin' to worry no-
body wid yo' troubles," Sissy agreed, looking at him
fondly and adding: "Ah sho wish som'times dat Ah
had uh thought uh somebody 'sides myself, 'fo Ah
ups an' runs off lak Ah did, but no, Ah jes' hated
tyin' myself down wid lots uh promises to one man
an' kaise Ah was sot on doin' my own choosin' an'

my own quittin', Ah ups an' does it, 'thout' carin' who it hurt."

"You ain't so bad, Sissy. We all makes mistakes. There ain't none of us perfect," William consoled.

"Anyhow, jes' you b'lievin' in me makes me happy; Willyum kaise Ah sho gotta lots uh faith in you an' some day you gointer make us all proud uh you."

"I sure hope so, Sissy," William replied, putting on his coat and hat.

As he walked down the narrow alley, Sissy's praise kept ringing in his ears. His mother, Sissy, everybody except Jim perhaps, expected great things of him, and he was getting deeper and deeper into trouble—gambling, mixing with a prostitute, even stealing, for in his heart, he could find no other word for losing money his mother had given him to purchase things with and having them charged when he had no idea where the money was coming from to pay for them later when the bills came due.

He walked rapidly down the street trying to still his accusing conscience but at the pressing shop trouble awaited him, like a menacing evil. One of his creditors, John Stevens, a white hardware merchant greeted him with a torrent of abuse, demanding his money immediately with threats of appealing to his mother if it was not paid before night.

"Give me a few more days, Mr. Stevens, and I'll pay you the money," he pleaded.

"You been owing me since way last Spring, William, and if I don't get my money by six o'clock, I'll go to your mother. I know Aunt Sara. She don't believe in owing nobody. I need my money. Every week you been telling me the same lie—you'd pay in a few days and I'm fed up with you," Stevens retorted angrily, shaking his finger under William's nose.

"Whew!" Slippery grunted, looking after the merchant when he walked away. "Dat white man sho is mad."

"Yeah, and I sure am in a tight place. Where'm I gonna get thirty-five dollars?" William groaned.

"Man, is you askin' me? Yo' goose sho is cooked kaise dat other white man whut you owes ten dollars done been heah an' said de self-same mournful words dis mornin'," Slippery informed.

"Instead of paying off those debts Saturday morning when I had the money, I had to hold it and lose it back Saturday night. I had just as well pack up and start traveling if Jim ever finds this out."

"Maybe you could borrow de money from Daddy Jenks," Slippery suggested.

"Not a chance, Slippery. I owes him now, and now that he's lost his club room to Sugar Kid, he'll be tighter than Nick's hat band."

"You think Sugar Kid 'ud loan it to you?" Slippery asked hopefully.

"No, he don't like me. Maybe I could borrow it from Ethel," William mused, his face lighting with hope.

"Don't make me laugh, William. Dat broad got pulled in dis morning for fightin'. 'Course Daddy Jenks got her out but whut li'l' money she did have, she done turned it over to him for payin' her fine."

"Well, that's that and to tell the truth I don't wanna get under no obligation to her nohow."

"Dat's one time you is so right. Ontell you is

perfect, dat gal's pizin. Whutever yuh do, stear clear uh dat drunken hussy. She'll git you in uh mess uh trouble," Slippery advised.

"Ah guess Ah'll take a chance and ask Sugar Kid. He can't say nothing worse than no," William ventured, ignoring his warning.

"Ah b'lieve he'll let yuh have it jes' for biggity. He's got gobs uh money an' loves notuhriety. He'll jes' love to brag 'bout havin' to help you out. Ah'll go over dere an' git 'im." Suiting his words to action, Slippery was gone, returning in a few moments followed by the swaggering Sugar Kid, who guessed that the cause of William's sudden desire to see him was to ask a favor. He was none too popular with the gang but William was, and it would be a good thing to have him under obligation to him so that he could use him to win the confidence of the boys to continue gambling in the club room he had won from Daddy Jenks. Yes, he would do whatever William wanted of him, provided it was not too large a sum, he decided, but he would be sure to get evidence of the favor in black and white. Then if William attempted to show off, he could put him in his place.

"Yuh craves to see me, Carter?" he asked, stepping into the shop, rolling the big black cigar he was smoking from side to side between his beefy lips.

"Yes, Sugar Kid," William answered, backed up by a wink from Slippery, who walked through to the back of the shop.

"Sit down," William offered, and continued pleasantly. "I want to ask you to lend me some money for a few days."

"How much money?"

" 'Bout thirty-five dollars."

"Whut's yuh got dat's worth dat much 'cause Ah gotta have some kin'er security for my money, yuh know," Sugar Kid said, shrewdly pulling out a roll of bills.

"I'll give you my word that I'll pay you in thirty days," William smiled.

"No suh'ree! Ah ain't dat dumb, Carter. Ah gotta have black an' white dat don't fool nobody, for my hard cash an' you gotta write it out dat effen you don't pay me in thirty days, ah kin take over dis shop," Sugar Kid replied, his eyes running estimatingly over the small stock of pressing equipment in the place.

"All right, Sugar Kid. I'll give you a note promising to pay in thirty days or turn the shop over to you," William consented.

Sugar Kid made himself comfortable, puffing his cigar in hard quick puffs, as William hunted in the drawer of the table for pen and paper, and in a few moments passed the note over for Sugar Kid to read. He studied it carefully, spelling out the words slowly and passed it back to William.

"Now sign it, William, good an' clear in big letters," he directed.

William signed the note, as he laughingly retorted, "You're a good business man, Sugar. I'll grant you that."

"Tries to be, Carter," Sugar Kid admitted, counting out the bills and placing the note carefully in his wallet.

"Ah don't want yuh to think dat Ah don't trust you neithur jes' kaise Ah ask for dis note. Ah jes'

laks to be on de safe side but Ah'm glad jes' de
same to do you uh favor."

"And I sure thanks you," William acknowledged,
almost having to grit his teeth to hold back the
words he would have liked to say to the big brag-
gard.

"Dat's de way to feel, Carter. Ah wants all uh
you boys to feel dat when you plays wid me, every-
thin' is on de up an' up. Now dat Ah'm de boss over
dere at de club room, Ah'se yo' friend an' Ah wants
you to help me make de boys know dat kaise Ah
b'lieve you for one done been thinkin' diffunt,"
Sugar Kid hinted.

"Forget it, Sugar Kid! That girl's remarks up-
set me Friday night. You're all right with me."

"Dat's how Ah loves to heah you talk kaise Ah
wouldn't ever thought uh lendin' nobody but you
dat much dough. Ah laks yuh an' dis is gwine tuh
be strickly private 'twix us."

"Mighty nice of you, Sugar Kid," William
acknowledged.

Slippery stepped into the room as soon as Sugar
Kid cleared the door, a broad grin wreathing his
homely red face, struggling to control his laughter
until Sugar Kid was out of hearing. He puffed an
imaginary cigar and imitated the lolling gambler.

"Gee, dat nigguh gives me uh laff, he'll keep it uh
secret. Ha, ha! He kin hardly wait to git cross
de street to spread de news but Ah'm gonna fix 'im.
Ah'm gonna git dat paper off'en him 'fo he kin say
scat an' den let him try an' collect his ole measly
thirty-five dollars," he avowed.

"You better say you reckon," William laughed,
hurrying out of the shop to pay Stevens the money

which would at least save him in that direction, and wondering what would be the next mishap to befall him.

Neither he nor Slippery dreamed how much trouble that small slip of paper would cause them both.

CHAPTER X

John Stevens was surprised when a short time later, William appeared at the store and paid over the thirty-five dollars and said in his usual blunt way.

"I hated to have to be so severe with you, William, about my money, but business is business, and right now it's as bad as it can be, and I need money to carry on. You people are easy going. You jes' live today with no thought of tomorrow, and have to be shaken up to get anything out 'er you."

"That's all right, Mr. Stevens. I'm glad to get it off my mind. I ain't making much money now in my shop, that's why I haven't paid it before," William replied.

"You know I can't see why you don't stay home and help your Ma and Jim with the farming, William?"

"I'm attending school here. That's why, Mr. Stevens."

"Didn't you go to school in Byron? Yo' Pa, John Carter, ain't never went to high school, and he was as good 'er farmer as there was anywhar. You young darkies make me sick, hanging round going to high school, and when youse come out all finished, all you'll do is loaf."

"I'm going to college when I finishes and I'm not going to loaf when I'm all through, neither," William answered shortly, hardly able to hide his anger.

But before he left the store, he and Stevens were laughing and talking pleasantly, and he had accepted

an offer from the merchant to ride to Byron with
him Saturday. The rest of the week he loafed
around his shop while Slippery did the little work
that had been brought in. The days were hot,
bringing thunder storms that did not help the suf-
ferers in any way except to make the streets sloppier
and the air more stifling, and bring in their wake
swarms of mosquitoes that made the long close
nights a torture.

The streets were filled with strangers, their dirty,
sweaty overalls sticking to their bodies, as they
loitered around Broad street, filling up on white
mule, playing pool and Georgia skin or dancing in
Daddy Jenks' back room to rancorous tinpanny
music.

Sure-Foot-Jack, a six foot policeman, who had
been so nick-named because of the fact his foot
never failed to connect with the part of the anatomy
at which it was aimed, was kept on the alert hunt-
ing out vagrants.

William felt sick of the whole thing. Even Slip-
pery's coughing and spitting around the shop, wher-
ever it suited him, got on his nerves, and Sugar Kid
whose greatest fear was the Law, had taken to sit-
ting around the shop almost all day, much to his
displeasure. So he spent most of his time in Ethel's
room laying half clad on the rusty iron bed, pushed
close to the window, while Ethel, happy to have him
around, brought his meals up to him from one of the
many dingy little restaurants.

Saturday came at last and William rode home in
Stevens' car late in the afternoon. His mother and
Ruth were seated on the front porch when he
stepped out of the car.

"Lawd heah's my boy," Sara Lou exclaimed happily, running to the gate as fast as her rheumatic legs could carry her.

"Yea, the prodigal is here," William remarked.

"You ain't no prodigal, son. Kaise yuh ain't done nothin' wrong," his mother laughed. "You jes' comin' home to yo' ole Ma whut loves yuh.

"Howde Mr. Stevens. Ah clean forgot my manners, bein' so glad to see dis heah boy."

"Jes' fine, Aunt Sara. Thought while I was coming out, I'd jes' as well give William a lift."

"An' Ah'se sho thankin' you for it, Mr. Stevens. 'Member me to de misses, when you gits home. Lawd don't look lak Ah helped to nurse her, time done pass so fast."

"No, it don't, Aunt Sara, not with all the six young uns she's got hanging round her skirt tail now. How's your cotton comin' on?" John Stevens asked, looking towards the field in the distance.

"Jes' fine. Jim says dis gointer be de best crop we's had!"

"Wal, I'll be moving on Aunt Sara. You ain't heard nothing from Gordon, is you?" he asked, as he turned the car in the direction of his place two miles further.

"No suh, not uh word since way lass month. Guess he'll be gone a spell." Sara Lou called, to which William added his thanks for the ride.

"Mighty fine uh Mr. Stevens bringin' yuh home, Willyum," Sara Lou said, looking after the fast disappearing car.

"Sure was, Ma," William replied, seating himself on the edge of the porch at Ruth's feet.

"Come on in an' git yo' supper, son, we done

eat but Ah put yuh uns whar it ud keep hot," Sara
Lou said, playfully pulling William to his feet.

"Ah'se gotta 'sprize for yuh," she said later as
she set a generous portion of ginger bread before
him.

"I've got a mind to eat it first," William threat-
ened.

"Dar yuh go jes' lak when yuh was uh little boy,
wantin' to eat yo' dessert fust. Mind out or Ah'll
take it way from yuh," his mother teased reaching
for the plate.

"Ah'll be good Ma, 'clare to goodness I will.
See, cross my heart and Ah'll give you a big kiss to
boot," William teased, as he caught the hand that
held the plate and drawing her to him, smacked a
kiss on her cheek.

"Lawd boy, you'se de beatinest for makin' a
body do whut you wants done," his mother laughed.

As he ate, his gaze rested on Jim and Ruth, whom
he could see through the window, their heads close
together, tying a vine that had broken and lay
across the path. He could not help a pang of hot
jealous anger that gripped his heart. He had been
a fool to think that Ruth did not care more for Jim
than she did for him. There was a look in her eyes,
as she looked up into his face that told plainly that
she did.

He felt ashamed of the murderous thoughts the
knowledge brought him and wondered could he give
up the hope of winning her. One thing he was sure
of, he had never liked Jim and at that moment he
hated him, and would like to have swept him from
his path, no matter how.

He was slowly finishing his meal, absorbed by his

jealous thoughts when his mother sat at the table opposite him.

"You think yuh gointer finish school dis year, William?" she was asking.

With a start he brought his thoughts back to the present, answering, "I'm sure of it, Ma. It won't be hard for me to make two terms when I get started."

"Dat's fine, son, an' Ah'm goin'ter lay by a little money from de cotton dis year for when yuh starts in de preachin' school. Ah jes' knows you goin'ter be de finest preacher dere ever was, Willyum. Ah'se wearin' out my knees prayin' for dat one thing an' Ah gointer keep rite on prayin', an' Ah knows dat God gonna answer my prayers."

"Thank you Ma. I'm going to do my best."

"Dat's all we kin do, our best all de time an' not git too proud an' puffed up kaise God don't want us to be too proud."

"I know Ma but sometimes I don't feel like I really know what I wants and I tries so hard to make myself satisfied with what blessing I have but, oh, I don't know, Ma, it just seems like a lots of different devils fighting inside of me, making me want to do wrong and makin' me not able to do what I really wants to do. Ah! Don't mind me, Ma. I'm kind'er talking crazy now, ain't I?"

Sara Lou, tears filling her eyes, reached over and patted her favorite on the shoulder.

"My pore boy," she murmured. "Ah knows jes' whut yuh means. Dere's lots uh things William dat Ah'se allers prayin' you'll escape. Maybe Ah should tell 'yuh 'bout' 'em, but Ah ain't got de courage."

Tears of remembrance filled Sara Lou's eyes as

her mind traveled back over a past that was filled with things she would have loved to forget. William caught and squeezed her hand, and rising quickly, walked around the table and placed his arm around her shoulder.

"Don't Ma," he whispered huskily.

"Don't mind me, Willyum. Ah'm gittin' ole an' Ah guess sometimes Ah does git crazy ideas. Ah'll jes' set dese things 'way an we'll go an' sit on de porch an' sing some hymns. Dat'll cheer us up. Dere ain't nothin' lak singin' God's praises to cheer a body up," she whispered, closer to William than she had ever been, even in the days she had cuddled his brown curly head on her breast and tried to figure out what the future would hold for her illegitimate child, who would always walk in the middle of the road, not being able to get a firm footing on either side.

"Yes I guess when you sings you ain't got no time to think about the things that worries you," William said thoughtfully, but there was no enthusiasm in his voice and his mother looked at him inquiringly.

"Whut's troublin' yuh, Willyum?" she asked, placing her hand on his shoulder tenderly.

" 'Tain't nothin' much, Ma. Nothing that you can help," looking beyond her searching eyes.

"But maybe Ah kin help. Tell me son."

"Well for one thing, Ah needs some money. The shop ain't been doing so well lately and I owe a debt I've got to pay right'er way. If you could let me have the money, I'll pay it back as soon as I start making money."

" 'Course Ah'll let you have de money. Ah ain't been botherin' wid lookin' atter things 'round heah

uh late.   Ah'se jes' left it all to Jim an' Ah don't
know dat he's got any money left atter de Spring
seed buyin' but Ah knows we'll have some jes' soon
as we sells dis cotton crop."

"But I needs it the first of next month, Ma."

"Den Ah'll find out whut Jim's got.   Ah could
allers go to Mr. Gordon when he was heah."

"There ain't much chance of me getting it then
if you expects to get it from Jim," William replied
hopelessly.

"Ah don't know why you two boys is allers 'gainst
one 'nother.   It's jes' plum pass understandin', Will-
yum.   Sometime Ah wonder ef'fen yuh loves one
'nother uh tall lak brudders aught to."

"It ain't my fault, Ma.   Jim is just so set against
me stayin' in Macon and tryin' to get an education.
Jes' because he don't care for school, he can't see
why anyone else should, and thinks I'm throwing
away lots of money when the fact is I don't have
none to throw away."

"Don't blame him too much, son.   He jes' lak his
Pa was, hard-workin' an' no frills but he got uh
good heart an' you is jes' lak Ah was 'fore you was
born, cravin' atter learnin' and wantin' to be some-
body.   Yuh two is far uh part as de east an' west
but Ah sho wish you'ud try an' git long together,"
Sara Lou sighed.

"I do try, Ma, but Jim is stubborn and don't seem
to even like me," William complained.

Sara Lou shook her head slowly and led the way
to the front porch, where Jim and Ruth were seated
on the steps.   Jim turned and looked at his mother
and William as they came out of the house.   He
could see from his mother's troubled expression that

something was wrong and wondered what William could have been saying that disturbed her. He had not seen William since he came home an hour earlier and although he was glad to have him home, he never made a fuss over his visits and now calmly helloed in his slow, undemonstrative way.

Ruth sat in a low rocker at Sara Lou's side, and William seated himself on the step she had just vacated beside Jim.

The early twilight brought a breath of coolness after a day that had been hot and sultry. The heavy odor of honeysuckles that clung to the porch was sweet with fragrance. Sara Lou, rocking back and forth, started singing one of her favorite spirituals. Ruth's soft soprano mingled with the deeper melody of the two boys as song after song floated upon the air.

William's thoughts drifted in comparison to the noisy music of Daddy Jenks' dance hall with its sordid crowd shouting discordant blues. The quiet peace of his home engulfed him with a mood of spiritual longing. He hated Macon fiercely for all of the corruption it had brought into his life during that brief spell of emotion. He wondered how he had been able to stand it so long. New resolutions formed in his heart.

His mother's plaintive singing smote his heart. "Go find my sheep," her voice crooned soft and effectively, bringing hot tears to his eyes. He felt relieved when she rose and announced it was time to go in and have their usual evening prayer.

Lighting the kerosene lamp that stood on the little marble topped table in the parlor, Sara Lou opened the bible to the twenty-third psalm, and passed it to William to read.

"William, you lead us in prayer dis evening. You ain't home much an' Ah laks to hear yo' voice in prayer. It kin'er gives me mo' stren'th to carry on," she said when he lay the book on the table at the end of the reading.

William knelt obediently. He knew what his religion meant to his mother and although he did not feel like praying, after he started, he poured out his soul to God, tears of repentance flowing down his face. Sara Lou rose from her knees feeling better than she had during the two weeks he had not come home.

"Come on, Ruth chile, less us go on upstairs, an' leave dese boys to dey seffs. Maybe dey want'uh talk wid one 'nother widout us womens hangin' 'round," Sara Lou remarked, playfully pushing Ruth up the narrow stairway before her.

William and Jim talked for a while about the cotton and the Gordon peaches that Jim was busy picking with Luke Brown and Slack Henderson assisting him.

"What are they bringing, Jim?" William asked interested.

"Twenty-five cents uh bushel an' it looks lak Ah'm goin' to have 'bout five hundred bushels," Jim replied proudly.

"We ain't gonna have no peaches this year to amount to anything I notice," William remarked.

"No Ah jes' set dem trees out lass year an' Ah didn't 'speck much ud dem dis soon but next year dey gonna be loaded."

"How 'bout the watermelons and canteloupes?"

William asked, turning the leaves of a book that lay on the table.

"Not so bad but dere ain't gointer be no money but de cotton money dis year an' when we gits uh few things dat we needs to fix up de place, dat'll be all gone. Ah'm doin' all Ah kin dis year so as next year we'll uh have some spare money. Ma's so set on you goin' to Atlanta to dat preachin' school," Jim said, trying hard to keep out of his voice the trace of impatience he felt towards his brother's ambition.

William did not answer. He knew that school was a sore spot with Jim, and he did not want to start an argument, not just now when he needed a favor anyway.

"I'm sleepy. Guess I'll go to bed so that I can get a little rest. Got to be in church all day to-morrow," he said instead.

"You laks bein' in church all day, William but Ah jes' hates to sit dere an' heah dem ole sisters uh moanin' an' de preacher gittin' all het up an' spittin' 'round. Ah don't mind de singin' and prayin' but dey keeps at it too long to suit me," Jim complained.

"Why Jim, anybody to hear you wouldn't think you was brought up in a Christian home an' by a mother like Ma."

"You mean dey'd be sprized to see dat Ah kin tell de truth. Most uh dese folks 'roun' heah would say de same thing ef'fen dey wasn't scared uh whut de others 'ud say ef'fen dey heard 'em, but Ah ain't. Ah'ud heap ruther be home hoein' cotton or somethin'. Ah b'lieves in God same as everybody else does, but Ah knows dat most uh dat loud preachin' is jes' uh bluff to cover up de fact dey don't know nothin' 'tall 'bout de bible an' it makes me sick.''

"But don't you ever let Ma hear you talk like that. It would make her sick in bed," William cautioned, adding: "And I don't like to hear you talk like that myself cause some day I intends to be a preacher."

"An' when you gits to be uh preacher, effen yuh ever does, you gointer be plenty learnt an' yuh ain't gointer preach long for fear de folks'll forgit to put plenty in de collection plate," Jim laughed.

William felt a wave of anger rising within him but he hid it with a smile, as he said.

"Never mind, Jim, jes' wait till you get religion. Then we'll see how you feel about it. I bet you'll want 'er be sittin' in church all day."

"Ah'll be jes' lak Ah is now, plain an' strait. Religion or nuthin' ain't gointer change me, an' ef'fen dey ever makes me uh deacon, de fust thing Ah'se gointer do is vote dat ole brudder Thomas don't never be lowed to preach agin long as he lives," Jim declared.

"What has poor brother Thomas done now that you're ready to shut him up forever and break his poor old asthmatic heart?" William asked, laughing heartily at Jim's serious mien.

"He ain't done nothin' but git up lass Sunday an' preach for two solid hours."

"How did they ever stop him?"

"Some uh de folks jes' got to singin' an' he couldn't talk louder den dey could sing so he jes' shut up. Boy it sho was funny."

William could not help joining in the laugh Jim

was enjoying. He could imagine he saw Brother Thomas gasping for breath and preaching on and on.

"But William dat ain't nothin' to de one dey calls de Swamp Angel dat preached lass Sunday night," Jim went on and William listened again to a lengthy description of that preacher.

"Honest Jim, it's a sin to make fun of God's messengers like you do," he said at the end of his recital.

"Ah ain't makin' fun uh dem. Ah b'lieves in dem when dey preach good sound gospel but jes' jumpin' 'roun' makin' lots uh noise don't mean nothin'."

"Well anyhow, we'd better be getting to bed," William said, leading the way. Jim closed the front door and followed.

They undressed in silence. It had been rather pleasant to laugh and talk together without ending in an argument, Jim's thoughts ran. He loved his handsome wayward brother and did not even surmise that deep down in William's heart, he disliked him and always had. He had played his cards well and managed to keep cool for a point and long after Jim had fallen asleep, William lay planning how he would try and get a loan out of Jim by playing up to him pleasantly.

CHAPTER XI

Sunday morning's radiant sunshine brought an exultant feeling to Sara Lou, as she stood in her kitchen door throwing handfuls of corn to the chicken cackling noisily at her feet.

"Ah sho got plenty to be thankful for," she mused, as ripples of laughter reached her from the barn where Ruth and Jim were busy milking. As she hurriedly prepared breakfast, her eyes traveled to the old-fashioned clock on the mantel over the table.

William was still upstairs. She would have to wake him for breakfast. She climbed the stairs slowly, and stood for a moment looking down on him with an indulgent smile upon her face.

"Wake up, lazy bones. You sho is de limit heah sleepin' while Jim an' Ruth an' me does all de work," she said playfully poking him in the side. "Git up an' hurry on down to yo' breakfuss." Hurrying back downstairs, she called Ruth and Jim.

"Ah'll race yuh to de house, Ruth," Jim challenged as her voice reached them from the kitchen.

"Awrite but you gotta give me a little head kaise yo' legs longer den mine," Ruth consented.

Jim reached the house a few paces ahead of Ruth and William found them seated on the back steps, laughing about their race. A few moments later when he came downstairs, he could not suppress the tide of anger and jealousy that swept over him at the sight of Jim and Ruth's happiness but hid well his real feeling when he asked pleasantly.

"Who won the race?"

"Jim 'course. His legs is longer den mine an' he jes' wouldn't gimme uh head start," Ruth laughed.

"I'll race you sometime Ruth an' give you a whole yard on me," William promised.

"Don't yuh b'lieve dat, Ruth," Jim laughed, as they seated themselves at the table. "Don't yuh never b'lieve dat Willyum goin' uh leave anybody beat him at nothin'; 'member when we'all was kids how he use 'ter win all de marbles 'roun' heah an' whut uh time Ma had tryin' to make him give 'em back?"

"Does Ah 'member? Why William even had our ole teacher Miss Jimerson scared to look in her desk after de time he put uh frog in it," Ruth laughed.

"Ha, Ha! She sho did let out one yell an' ain't never stop runnin' ontell she was heah tellin' Ma," Jim added.

"I wanted to get out early that afternoon to go fishin' an' I sure got out," William smiled.

"An' yuh got de terriblest tannin' uh yo' life," his mother ended, placing the plate of hot bread on the table, chuckling at the remembrances of William's early tendencies of having his own way at any cost.

"Now yuh'll jes' quit yo' carryin' on an' git yo' minds on church. Dis is de Lawd's day," she reminded them, bowing her head for William to pray.

William prayed fervently and her eyes filled with tears, as he thanked God for having given him such a wonderful mother.   Even Jim felt a catch in his throat as the words poured from his lips.

"Oh Lawd, make me worthy of your blessings and keep my feet in the path of righteousness," he ended.

His mother flashed him a grateful smile when she raised her head.

An hour later, the happy family was seated in church which was filled to its capacity, every inch of the long, backless benches taken.   It was going to be an important day—a new preacher had to be called, and a candidate was on hand to preach a sermon for their approval.

The long morning service was over at last and the congregation gathered around the building in bunches to discuss his merit.

The day that had dawned so fair became suddenly over-shadowed with black scurrying clouds. Loud claps of thunder rent the air and a heavy deluge of rain sent them scurrying for shelter.   Sara Lou's home, the nearest to the church, became a haven for many of them from the fury of the storm that lasted all afternoon.

Jim, worrying over what the storm might do to the cotton, went back and forth in the rain all afternoon and Sara Lou later that evening, made him take off his wet clothes and go to bed, pouring several cups of scalding herb tea down his unwilling throat.

Services were neglected that night.   Most of the farmers hurried home as soon as the storm abated. William prevailed upon his mother to stay home and he and Ruth went to church alone.   The business of calling the preacher to pastor their church took up most of the evening and to Ruth's relief, William walked almost the distance home before he said the things she had been praying he would not say.

"Some day when my dreams come true, Ruth," he began, "I wants you to be my wife. Will you promise?"

It was all she could do to keep from telling him that she and Jim were engaged but they had planned to keep it a secret, and she would not tell even William although it would perhaps keep him from forcing his attentions on her. Instead she answered simply.

"Ah can't say whut Ah'll do dat far off, William."

"It don't have to be far off. We can marry now an' while I'm away in Atlanta, you can jes' go on livin' with Ma," William persisted.

"But Ah don't love you dat uh way, William. Ah jes' feels toward you lak uh sister."

"Do you feel the same towards Jim?" William asked, determined to have his answer or know whether Jim was the cause of her evasiveness.

"Let's don't talk uh 'bout it," Ruth evaded, as some of the church members caught up with them.

Martha Green and Sally Ann Peck dropped back beside them to talk about the new preacher.

"Ah b'lieves we all gointer like de new Preacher," Sally was saying. "He don't preach all night lak some uh dem does an' whut he says is de gospel truth."

"Yeah, dat jes' suits you, Sally," Martha broke in. "You don't lak to sit church 'long nohow. As for my part, Ah don't know as Ah'm gonna lak him uh tall. He puts on too much airs."

And the battle was on as usual. Ruth thought of

what her father had had to contend with, how these same people had fought him when he first came to their church and wondered why it should always be so with every new preacher.

William ended the discussion by letting them know he was going to back the new preacher in every way, and Martha, not wanting to oppose any one Brudder William was for, fell to finding many good points in the sermon and decided after all, the new Reverend Hooper was all right.

Sally Ann laughed heartily at her sudden change of heart and they were again off on one of their usual arguments.

"Ruth, think over what I asked you," William said when they were again alone after bidding the two women good-bye.

She did not answer, but quickening her steps, passed into the house and ran lightly up to her room.

* * *

Monday morning Jim realized his fears had been well-founded although the storm had done no serious harm to the cotton except to beat some of it down a bit, which could be fixed by filling in the rows with the dirt that had been washed away. But other damage had been done. The cotton house-roof had been partly blown away and the posts that held the long rails that made the fence around the field were in many places down and needed immediate repairing.

William rose early and helped Jim and Ruth with their work, deciding to stay a few days and help with the repairs, which surprised and pleased Jim.

"Ah'll be mighty glad to have yuh helpin' me, William," he said warmly.

And Sara Lou, always alert to the best in her beloved son, remarked happily.

"Dat'll be jes' fine, Willyum. Ah sho will be happy to have both my boys 'roun' workin' together an' me an' Ruth cookin' hot dinners for yo' hungry mouths. Lawd, it'll mind me uh times when yore pa was livin' an' you an' Jim was helpin' him wid de farmin'."

"An' Ah'll help too. Dere's lots Ah kin do," Ruth added.

"Lawd chile, you can't do nothin' to suit dem two men 'side cook an' wait on 'em," Sara Lou laughed.

"We'll see 'bout that, Ruth. You may be useful in keeping me an' Jim from fightin' before the week is over," William remarked.

"Now don't you two go an' git in no fight kaise ef'fen you does, Ah'll jes' switch yuh both," their mother warned.

They all laughed heartily at the mental picture of her switching them and started the day merrily, working first on the cotton house roof. Sara Lou hummed happily as she worked around the house, a contented smile wreathing her round face.

"Come heah, Ruth an' take dis bucket uh grub an' some milk over to Julie for de new baby she got," she called when the dishes had been washed and dried.

"Ah'se ready An' Sara," Ruth answered, taking the pails.

"You hurry back, Ruth. Ah clean forgot Julie. Her breast done dried up an' dere ain't a blessed thing for dat pore little mite to nurse on. Dat husban' uh hearn is too lazy for anything. Jes' sittin' 'roun' waitin' for cotton pickin' stead 'er gittin' out pickin' up uh nickle or two. Pore Julie is smart uh nouff when she ain't got uh new baby to keep 'er in bed."

"An' dat ain't often she ain't," Ruth said, as she hurried away.

William and Jim worked steadily all morning and returned to their job after the noon day dinner.

That night they sat out on the porch after supper to get a breath of fresh air and Sara Lou laughed and talked and led in hymns until time to retire.

Several times during the next day William tried to get up courage to ask Jim to let him have some money. He felt sure there was none on hand to be had but Jim stood well with everybody around Byron, and could borrow money any time he needed it. Besides he knew he had received some money for the peaches he had already delivered to Mr. Carmicheil, who ran the general store and shipped crates of fruit to northern markets. The money was Owen Gordon's but Jim could lend him some of it if he cared to, and as Gordon would not be home until after the cotton was picked and sold, it certainly could be replaced.

Every now and then William glanced at Jim working a short distance away. They were working in the Gordon orchard stripping the peach trees of their last remaining luscious fruit.

Late that afternoon, William unaccustomed to working so steadily, complained of being tired.

"Go on up to de house an' rest uh spell," Jim advised. "An' close de windows an' lock up while you'se dere," he called, as William walked away.

After closing the windows that had been opened to air the house out and locking the door, William stretched himself out on the back porch to rest and in a few moments was drifting drowsily into a light sleep. Ruth's voice calling Jim from the back gate awakened him.

"Come on in Ruth. Jim's in the orchard," he called to her, sitting up.

"It's really you Ah wants. Ah got uh letter for you, William," she smiled, handing him the letter.

William glanced quickly at the envelope. It was from Macon and looked like Slippery's writing. What on earth could have made him write, he wondered. Certainly nothing that would make him happy, he decided before tearing the seal.

Ruth was looking toward the peach orchard, where the outlines of Jim's figure could be seen moving to and fro among the shadows of the trees.

"Ah'm gointer run over dere an' scare Jim," she laughed starting towards the orchard.

William read the letter carefully and tore it into small bits, kicking them under the sand with his toes. The letter was worse than he had expected. Creditors hounding the shop and Sugar Kid hanging around bragging to the boys that in a few weeks he would be running the shop. His heart filled with anger towards Jim. How easy it would be for him to help him out. He realized he had made quite a few mistakes but if Jim would only let him have enough money to square himself he would not be a fool again, he promised himself.

He could see Jim and Ruth talking under the trees. Jim was handing her a large yellow peach from one of the crates. She was smiling her thanks prettily. Fierce hatred filled his heart. He resented everything about the homely, ignorant, cool-headed Jim, who although his inferior in looks and learning, possessed the power to make him feel small with his calm, clear vision and busy useful life.

Ruth waved a cheery goodbye as she passed through the yard, and he waved back to her listlessly, and sat for a few moments trying to calm the emotions that filled his heart. When he walked over to where Jim was busy sorting peaches, he was coolly smiling.

"Did yuh rest any?" Jim asked.

"Yes, a little but I just received a letter that made me feel more tired than I was before."

"Bad news?"

"Yes, it sure was bad news and I want to ask you to do me a favor."

"Whut is de favor, William?"

"I wants you to loan me some money."

"How much an' whut for, William?" Jim asked, looking for the first time at William.

"Well as much as I dislike asking a favor, Jim, I'm behind in the rent of my shop an' last month I borrowed some money to pay it when it was due and now I've gotta pay the money I borrowed back an' the rent again too. I ain't been makin' nothin' and I gave a fellow a note on the place, and I know it'ud worry Ma if I lose the shop."

"How much money does yuh need?"

"Fifty dollars would square everything and I'd pay you back as soon as I make some money."

"Ah haven't got fifty dollars, Willyum an' besides Ah knows dat you'se lyin'. You borrowed money to pay Mr. Stevens wid at'ter me givin' yuh de

money to pay for de things lass Spring," Jim spoke
calmly.

William's face turned a dull red, as his temper
flared but he bit his lips and tried to control him-
self.

Jim went on in his same maddening, calm way.

"Mr. Stevens tole Mr. Carmicheil all 'bout you
owing him so long an' he havin' to jump on yuh for
his money, an' when Ah went to de store yistiddy,
Mr. Carmicheil tole me he knows whut yuh done.
Yuh gambled de money 'way. Cotton Eye tole me
dat when he was heah lass week to see Aunt Sofia."

"It's all a pack of lies, dirty lies!" William al-
most shouted. "An' I don't b'lieve nobody tole you
nothing."

"Have it yo' own way but you got yo'self in dis
mess, an' you'll have to git yo'self out. Ah ain't
got no money nohow," Jim replied, stooping to raise
the crate of peaches to his shoulder.

"You'll have that much an' more when you deliver
all these peaches."

Jim placed the crate upon the ground again as he
said slowly. "Dat'll be Mr. Gordon's money. You
ain't askin' me to steal, is yuh, William?"

"It won't be stealin' and besides you can replace
it before Mr. Gordon gets back."

"Well, Ah ain't gointer do it. Ah wouldn't
touch uh penny uh dis money lessen Ma was low
sick, Willyum."

"Then I'll ask Ma to borrow it from somebody
else for me," William answered, turning away but
Jim's next words brought him around again angrily.

"Ef'fen you ask Ma for one penny, Ah'll tell 'er

all 'bout yuh gamblin' in Macon an' everything Ah knows 'bout yo' doin',' Jim threatened.

"And if you do, I'll smash your ugly black face in, you stingy good-for-nothing fool," William hissed, and, completely losing control of himself in face of what he realized was failure to get his aim, he struck Jim full on the mouth, taking him by surprise, but not for long.

Jim's fist shot out catching him on the point of the chin, and William reeled, almost falling to the ground. The fight was on. Back and forth blows rained. They fought like mad beasts until a hard blow from Jim, the stronger of the two, sent William to the ground. Jim stood over him for a moment undecided whether to pull him to his feet and knock him down again or to walk away and leave him where he had fallen, but as William lay still, realization dawned upon him that he was not faking but unconscious. Quicky drawing water from the well nearby, he bathed his face and lifting him to his shoulder, carried him to the Gordon porch, where he worked over him until he regained consciousness and was able to stand. Jim felt sick and ashamed of what had happened and tried to tell William how sorry he was but William gave him no answer, as he carefully brushed the sand from his clothes, and walked out of the gate, his head high, hate and anger raging in his heart. All the pent-up feelings he had had against Jim for years filled his heart. He would make him pay for beating him that afternoon. There were several ways. He knew them all. He had taken over the farm which was as much his and his mother's and ran it, spending the money as he saw fit. He would put an end to that, he vowed.

Jim sat where William had left him. His head bowed in his hands. It was the first real fight they had had since they had grown to manhood and although William had struck him first, he blamed himself for losing his temper to the extent he had. It had been so pleasant the last two days working and talking together.

It was a relief to them both when Ruth told them on reaching home that their mother had gone over to Sally Brown's cabin, as Sally was sick and alone.

"She sayd for yuh to bring me over dere soon as supper's over, Jim," she said.

And as soon as the dishes were washed and put away, Jim and Ruth went over to Sally's, leaving William sulking at home.

Sara Lou looked up as they entered, a wave of disappointment passing over her face.

"Whar's Willyum?" she asked anxiously.

"You didn't say for him to come so he stayed to home," Ruth answered, sensing something had happened between the brothers.

"No. Ah ain't sayd but Ah thou't him hearin' dis pore chile was so low sick, he'ud want to pray wid her."

"He's jes' tired, Ma. You know Willyum ain't use'ter workin' hard all day lak we'uns," Jim excused.

The long, hot night passed slowly. Jim sat with his mother while Ruth dozed in a chair nearby. Neighbors dropped in from time to time, and Sara Lou cared for the sick woman and prayed for her recovery but deep in her heart, she was worried.

Something had gone wrong at home. She felt it, but said nothing.

Martha Green and Sally Ann Peck came during the early dawn and relieved the others, and Sara Lou, Ruth and Jim hurried home, but William had gone, leaving a note for his mother that he would be home early Saturday afternoon.

fill up on bad moonshine while their hard-earned money disappeared over the gambling tables.

Sugar Kid profited nightly by their losses and strutted around days, his bead-like eyes shining, as his hands jingled the silver that lined his pockets, very much pleased with himself, but frightened at the interest the law was taking in his and other gambling places. A general cleaning up was in progress and his place might be raided at any time but he made up his mind to get his while the getting was good.

Every time William entered the club room, he patted his pocket affectionately, and felt an exultant joy in the fact that in another week the thirty-five dollars William owed him would be due. He would either have to pay it or pass over his little shop. But William, apparently not aware of his presence, was coolly aloof and indifferent.

Sugar Kid's arrogant attitude nor Ethel's amorous advances interested him in the least. In fact, Ethel made him sick and he frankly told her so, and proceeded to ignore her entirely.

Ethel, more in love with him than ever, tried every known trick imaginable to win him back but in vain.

Sugar Kid watched the little drama with a keen feeling of satisfaction. He liked Ethel for himself and told her so and she laughed in his face, but he felt that sooner or later she would realize that William would have no more to do with her and turn to him.

"See yo' high yaller is givin' yuh de gate, gal," he taunted, as they danced around Daddy's back room.

CHAPTER XII

During the next few days William sulked around the shop planning in his mind some way of hurting Jim severely for his imagined wrongs. His two years in Macon had changed his entire outlook on life and brought out all of the worst there was in his twisted make-up. At first he had enjoyed spending most of the Summer on his mother's farm, not that he helped any with the work if he could get around it, and contrived most of the time to get around it, leaving it entirely to Jim, while he lay under some tall leafy tree on the smooth green grass and read or dozed in the welcome coolness of its shade.

But each year he found excuses to stay more and more in town, where the lights and laughter suited him better, and the convention of the staid farmers could not reach him. Even if the hot mid-summer days with sudden drenching thunder storms did depress and madden him, as he sat around his little windowless shop playing cards with the boys, there was always Daddy Jenks' place, where there was music, cold soda pop, cards and dice and an occasional game of pool to liven things up.

During July and August, the city was filled with riff-raff that drifted in to prey upon the farmers, who drove in daily from nearby farms to sell their products. With their small proceeds they would make straight for some place of amusement, and

"Whut's dat to you, ole fat head," Ethel snapped back.

"It ain't nuthin' to me but it jes' goes to prove whut Ah done tole yuh. He thinks he's too good for de sun to shine on. 'Roun' heah puttin' on airs, goin' to school, jes' kaise his mammy's got little cotton growin' an' is fool 'nough to let him lay 'roun' wid his lazy seff."

"Huh. De pot's callin' de kettle black," Ethel laughed. "You ain't done uh day's work in yo' life, Sugar Kid."

"But Ah ain't puttin' on no airs an' makin' out how great Ah am when all de time Ah'm jes' uh gambler."

"Dat's kaise you ain't got no education. As for gamblin', Ah don't see no harm in William playin' cards ef'fen he wants to. He don't smoke nor drink."

"But he hangs out wid you an' dat's bad 'nough," Sugar Kid sneered.

"It sho is kaise he ou'ter stop it an' give you uh chance," Ethel came back.

"Aw well, Ah ain't doin' no worryin'. He done borrowed money from me an' ef'fen he don't pay me back, Ah'm goin' uh take dat shop uh his or collect my money from dat dotin' ma uh his'n," Sugar Kid said, walking away.

Sugar Kid's remark about William owing him money worried Ethel. She knew that William would not want his mother to know about his having to borrow money or losing his shop. A little later she decided to go over to the shop and offer to help William pay off the debt. It would be a good excuse to have a talk with him and if she did him a favor, it would also win him back to her.

The front door of the shop was open and she walked in and started through to the back room, where she could hear William and Slippery talking. She stopped for a moment at the door. She could not catch their softly spoken conversation. William was talking rapidly and Slippery was saying little but agreeing to what William was saying. A chair creaked across the floor as one of them stood up and not wanting them to find her trying to eavesdrop, she slipped out of the front door and across the street again.

"Say gal, why don't yuh git wise to yoseff an' stay on dis side uh de street," Sugar Kid grinned, as she reached the other side.

"Shut up an' mind yo' own black business," she retorted with spirit.

"Come on in an' have a drink on me," Sugar Kid invited, and seating themselves at a table with a pint of corn before them, they were soon laughing and talking, the best of friends.

Later when William went to his room out at Sissy's. Slippery dropped into Daddy's to play a game of pool. Ethel's pent-up anger for William, inflamed by bad liquor, flared up at the sight of the little sickly red man.

"Come on over heah, William's lakey, an' have a drink wid decent folks," she called.

Slippery ignored her remark but sat down at the table gulping down a big drink as a bracer. As the liquor began to take effect Sugar Kid became very talkative and bragged about having lent William thirty-five dollars, pulling out the note William had given him to prove it. Waving it in Ethel's and Slippery's faces, they were compelled to read and reread it to please him. Fumbling he pushed it back into his pocket and continued pouring drink after drink down his throat. The night wore on. Slippery left them and Sugar Kid staggered upstairs to his room.

The next day when he looked for the note it was gone. Vaguely he remembered taking it out of his pocket the night before to show it to Ethel and Slippery. Slippery had stolen it, no doubt to protect William, he decided, and would give himself away, and then he would be justified in beating him up for picking his pocket.

But that night fresh disaster came to the gambler. His place filled with players was raided. Few escaped but most of them were taken to jail and released the next morning with light fines.

He, himself, did not fare so well and was held without bail for running a gambling house.

"Dey liable to keep dat nigguh in jail all Summer," Slippery remarked, when William returned to Macon and they talked of the luck that had made them two of the few that had not been caught in the police net.

"That sure will be a break for me," William declared.

"An' Ah b'lieves yuh gointer git dat break kaise dat ole judge don't care much for 'im kaise he don't b'long in Macon and de way he done looked at dat darky was lak he'ud jes' soon keep 'im in jail forever."

"I know Daddy Jenks is glad. Now he'll have his clubroom back agin."

"You know, William since Ah comes to think 'bout it, Ah b'lieves Daddy done put de white folks on dat nigguh anyhow kaise dey tells me dat Daddy was upstairs in de club room an' as soon as he went downstairs, de white folks rushed in," Slippery said with conviction. He had meant to tell William that he had stolen his note from Sugar Kid the night before but decided, as William had outlined a plan by which they both could profit, he would not mention the note, as William might get cold feet and abandon their plan so William, with no knowledge of Sugar Kid's being helpless to harm him, rejoiced that at least the day of reckoning was delayed.

Things were once more normal over at Daddy Jenks', who again took over the club room and ran it full sway.

Ethel, peeved over William's indifference, went on a wild spree, keeping the dance hall lively with her songs and squirming dances, but gradually the old passion she had awakened in William flared into life again and he was once more spending his nights in her room.

Two weeks had passed since he and Jim's fight. William had not been home. He dreaded facing Jim, and stayed away. Saturday came again. William rose early and helped Slippery finish what work there was on hand, determined he would go home, Jim or no Jim and he would take Slippery with him, as he had done several times during their acquaintance.

Saturday night he and Slippery rode to Byron with a farmer, who was returning home.

His mother welcomed Slippery, and tried in every way to make him feel at home but Jim, who had never liked him, could not entirely hide his resentment and Ruth kept out of his way as politely as possible.

Sunday was by no means a pleasant day for anyone and William, who felt the hostility, appealed to his mother.

"Ma, I'd think you'd teach Jim to be at least civil to folks," he began.

"Lawd, son, whut Jim gone an' done now?" she asked in alarm.

"Well, I invited Slippery out here so he could attend church seeing he won't in Macon an' Jim acts like he's afraid he'll steal the doors off the house."

"Ah thought Jim was treatin' 'im real nice, seein' dat he don't lak him," his mother replied.

William said no more but when the time came for them to go to evening services, the strain of watching and praying all day that Jim in his outspoken way would say nothing that would start an argument, proved too great for her and instead of going to church, she went to bed with a severe headache.

All day Monday after William and Slippery had gone, she bustled around in a state of excitement and by evening she was worn out and again ill.

"It sho is uh shame how Willyum does things to upset Ma, bringing dat no count Slippery out heah," Jim complained.

"Ah don't b'lieve he means to upset her. He's jes' tryin' to be kind to Slippery seein' he's uh stranger an' sick," Ruth defended.

"Ah guess he got you fooled lak everybody else,

Ruth, but as for me, Ah don't b'lieve dere's no good in him," Jim replied.

"Why Jim, Ah'm 'sprized at you, speakin' lak dat 'bout yo' own brother," Ruth exclaimed, looking at Jim, who stood calmly regarding his feet.

"Ah can't help it, Ruth, and brother or no brother, yuh gointer find out Willyum is uh bad lot, someday."

"When we gointer start pickin' cotton?" Ruth asked, anxious to change the subject which she realized was embarrassing to Jim.

"Nex' week, Ah got lots dis year an' Ah gotta start early kaise Ah ain't able to hire nobody but Luke to help. Ma's so determined to let William have some money to put side for his schoolin' in Atlanta."

"Ah'm gointer help you Jim, an' Ah kin pick uh lot an' you don't need to pay me nothin'," Ruth said, putting her arms around Jim's neck and laying her cheek against his.

"Ah sho'll need yo' help, Ruth, but Ah hate to have you pickin' cotton in de hot sun."

"Shame on you, Jim. Ah'm useter pickin'. Ah done picked for pay since Ah was eight years ole. How is it gointer hurt me?"

"Awrite, we ain't gointer augue 'bout it honey."

"Is William comin' heah to pick any, Jim?"

"Lawd no, he jes' goin'ter sit an' wait ontell us gits it ginned an' sold an' den hold out his purtty yaller hands for his share."

Ruth laughed heartily. "Jim," she said, "Ah know whut's de matter wid you. Youse jes' jealous uh William kaise he so light-skinned and you ain't."

"No, Ah ain't but he's so biggity an' stuck up. Ma's fair as he is an' look how sweet she is."

Ruth gave him a poke between the ribs, and ran away to do some unfinished work in the house. Jim turned to his garden that needed his care and worked until dark with it. Work and routine meant everything to him.

Friday he received the balance of the money for the peaches. He felt proud and happy knowing he had done better than even Owen Gordon had expected. His mother was surprised when he gave her the twenty dollars he had taken out for his labor but Ruth refused his offer to buy her a dress. Later that evening Sara Lou trudged down to the village general store and bought it for her anyway.

"An' Sara, you'all shouldn't uh done dat. Ah'se 'nough expense as it is to y'all," Ruth pleaded.

"Chile, you does 'nough work 'roun' heah to pay for uh little ole calico frock," Sara Lou assured her.

The week passed happily. Even with the many duties that filled each day, Jim and Ruth found time several afternoons when the sun disappeared beyond the western horizon to wander hand in hand over the flat fragrant woodland, saying little, content and ready to burst into childish laughter at the little nothings that amused them.

Most of these excursions ended at the old hickory nut tree, where with a few strands of hair they had become engaged. Sitting there, they would plan their future and return home swinging hands and singing songs.

Monday proved an ideal day to start picking cotton. Bright with cloudless skies, long before sunrise, Jim was in the field, his long sack slung across his shoulders.

The cotton seemed ready to burst from its bowls. Sara Lou busied herself with cooking and household duties but late that afternoon she shouldered her sack and laughingly teased.

"Lawdy, you youngsters is slow. Heah Ah done filled my sack in no time."

"Dis my fourth, An' Sara an' Jim not wantin' me to pick," Ruth smiled proudly.

"Well at dis rate we'all 'ull be through 'fo' de rest uh de folks 'roun' heah gits started," Jim bragged.

All around busy people were laughing and working. Bits of song floated upon the air. Wagons of cotton passed down the red clay road on their way to the gin. Happy children picked at their parents' sides. At night men gathered at the general store to discuss how many sacks they had picked during the day. Everybody was busy and happy.

Sara Lou's home was the happiest of them all for this year there would be more money than there had been since John Carter's death. She breathed a prayer of thankfulness for her many blessings, and smiled as she remembered how even Marshall Bailey had complimented her on having two such fine sons.

Saturday came round again and Sara Lou having finished her Sunday cooking, stood on the front porch waiting for a glimpse of her darling boy, her face brightened with a smile. But she was doomed to be disappointed. A farmer returning from Macon handed her a letter sent by William explaining he would not be home this week-end as his cousin Sissy had been seriously injured and he would have to stay in Macon with her.

"Huh, dat's jes' lak Willyum, takin' on everybody's troubles," she remarked when later she showed the letter to Jim.

CHAPTER XIII

August passed swiftly. Soft fluffy cotton held the attention of the farmers, who worked from sun-up until darkness gathered, making their task impossible.

Sara Lou's little cotton house was fast being filled but William did not come home, not even for the usual week-end. Jim said nothing, as his mother querulously complained about his absence.

To his mind the excuse William gave in the letters his mother received from him, of having to stay with Sissy, were just lies. But for once William was telling the truth. He had gone to his room late one night and found Sissy lying on the floor bleeding profusely from several long gashes inflicted by one of her latest men friends, a strapling six-footer. William had hurriedly summoned a doctor and for weeks the wounded woman had hovered between life and death.

She had few friends in the dismal little alley she made her home. Most of the women hated her because she kept to herself. The few, who had wormed their way into her home, remembered her sharp tongue and ready fists, and stayed away henceforth. When William appealed to some of the women to come to his assistance in caring for her, they laughed in his face.

"Let some uh dem injun folks she done bragged 'bout she comed from look at'ter her," one fat, jet-black woman taunted, remembering how Sissy had bragged about her long straight hair and copper colored skin having come from Indian ancestry.

"Yeah, yuh bettuh ask ole chief squattin' in de corner to sit wid 'er," another chimed in and William turned away disgusted to start what proved a trying four weeks at Sissy's bedside, relieved at times by Ethel, who on hearing the news of his cousin's injury, rushed to his aid.

But even the nearness of death did not soften William's heart towards Jim. Instead he had plenty of time while sitting idle through the long nights to conjure up the smallest grievances of his childhood when their father, John Carter, had taken Jim's part against him. He brooded over imaginary and real wrongs until his heart filled with hate and seemed almost bursting with longing for revenge, but no one, who saw him daily, would have believed beneath his suave smiling personality, a tumult of rage and hate burned fiercely.

To Sissy he was perfection. "Lawd, William, Ah jes' kain't figure how come you is so diffunt from the rest uh yo' folks," she said, as she and William ate breakfast the first morning she was able to be up.

"Ma offered to come an' see you, Sissy, but I begged her not to, cause they pickin' cotton an' Jim needs her home," William said.

"Yeah, An' Sara is kind lak you is. Ah kin'er glad she didn't com' to see me in de fix Ah was in."

"Now that you're better, Sissy, I'm gonna ask Ethel to stay with you while I run out home Saturday."

"Sho William, you go see 'bout An' Sara, but

don't bother askin' Ethel.   Ah kin take care uh myseff now."

So William wrote his mother he would be home Saturday and all day Friday he and Slippery worked steadily finishing up the work that had been left in the shop.   Late that evening Slippery donned the one good suit he possessed, and slipping his well-oiled, shiny pistol in his pocket, departed for a visit to a nearby village, where as he put it, "De gamblin' was good."

Saturday afternoon William closed the shop, and took a late afternoon train for Byron.

Sara Lou saw him, as he came swinging down the road, smiling brightly.   Throwing his bag on the porch, he caught her in his arms and kissed her affectionately, and holding her at arms' length looked at her admiringly.

"Go 'lon' boy, whut yuh doin' 'zamin' yo' ole Ma to see if she done growd uglier?" she asked, chuckling happily.

"Uglier?   Why, you're the prettiest girl in the world to me, Ma," he answered, hugging her close.

"Lawd, William, Ah sho don't see how any gal in de world kin resist you, effen yuh makes love to dem lak yuh does to me."

"I ain't tried it out on any gal yet, Ma.   Ah'm practising on you first," William laughed.

"Well, you is purtty nigh purfect," she smiled, as she hurried in to complete preparations for his supper.

William walked out on the back porch just as Ruth came up with an armful of kindling.

"Hey William, how'se you feelin' after yo' sick nursin' job all dese weeks?" she greeted.

"Fine an' how's the old cotton picker gettin' on?" he replied.

"Back's nigh 'bout broke but outsid-er dat, Ah'm on de up and up," she laughed. But more seriously —"Ain't you glad Sissy didn't go an' git hurt after yo' school had started?"

"I sure am, cause I've got to make two terms in one this year."

"Ah wish Ah could go to high school," Ruth sighed, dropping the kindling into the wood box at the kitchen door.

"Why, Ruth, I never thought you wanted to go back to school. Maybe I could help you," William replied, taking her hand and looking fondly into her upturned face.

Ruth slowly withdrew her hand and hurried into the kitchen. Jim was standing on the steps and William realizing what had caused Ruth to hurry away, burned with quick, hot anger.

Sunday Sara Lou was happy. William was in Church sitting on the little rostrum, where she could look at him, while the neighbors paid him the homage she felt was his due. William beamed on them all, and accepted their tribute as his rightful due.

"Us don't never git de scripture read so as we'all kin understand it ontill you'se heah, Brudder Will-yum," Martha Green commented after the service, as they all walked home together.

"Well, Brudder Simms does de best he knows how an' dat's always 'ceptible in de sight uh God. Everybody ain't edercated lak Brudder William," Sally Ann remarked.

And she and Martha entered one of their usual

arguments in the midst of which William and his Mother left them at their gate.

The day passed uneventfully but pleasantly. When time for the evening service came, Jim complaining of being tired, stayed home.

"Dere's uh 'Vangelist preacher gonna preach tonight, Jim. Ah sho wanted you to heah 'im kaise it's high time you try gittin' some religion," his mother remarked, hoping to change his mind.

But changing Jim's mind was no small task and to her pleading, he simply answered: "Ah jes' don't feel good an' Ah don't want 'er sit up half de night when Ah'se got so much work to do early in de mornin'."

And she, William and Ruth departed without him. In Ruth's mind there was a doubt as to Jim's not wanting to attend the service. She was sure he had overheard the conversation between William and herself when she had expressed a desire to attend high school, and the knowledge that she was not entirely satisfied had disturbed him. She heartily wished she had not said anything about school. After all she was content as things were. It was just William's presence that brought it to her mind. William's presence always disturbed their quiet peace, she remembered.

Jim sat for a while on the front porch thinking of Ruth, William and the future. He had never dreamed that she was not contented to just become a farmer's wife. The bit of conversation he had overheard, disturbed him. She was young. Perhaps after they married, she would rebel against the monotony of the only life she had ever known. William would be preaching, going from place to place. Wouldn't a life of that kind suit her better, he asked himself over and over. He would rather die than see her unhappy.

Slowly he rose and walked down the narrow path that led to the big road.

The skies were clear and starlit. A gentle breeze fanned his cheeks. A good long walk alone would do him good, he decided, as his feet struck the hard clay road, and from force of habit, propelled him towards the Gordon place, a mile away.

"Lawd, Ah jes' goes dere so much ontell my feets jes' natu'ly turn dat uh way when Ah ain't thinkin'," he laughed. It would be a good chance to make sure that the place was well locked up and secure, he thought, his mind on the tracks he had seen around the back of the house when he went over to do some work earlier in the week.

The moon shining brightly through the long branches of trees threw ghostly shadows across the road. Firebugs flew close to his face. Now and then he caught one in his hand, turning it loose later to watch it flicker through the air like the tail light of a small machine and disappear in the distance.

He was within a few feet of the house when a sudden cracking of dry leaves in the thick growth of young trees frightened him for a moment, but as he drew nearer, the cause of his agitation caused him to laugh heartily.

"Lawd, dat's jes' Marshall Bailey's old mare an' heah Ah was scared stiff. Come heah Josie," he coaxed softly, holding out his hand as if offering some tid-bit to the animal who shied away and bounded to the back of the place.

Thinking of the harm she had once done to the place, he tried to catch her but failed.

"Ef'fen she's still 'roun' heah when Ah goes home, Ah'll catch de critter an' take 'er home to de Marshall. Ah bet he's huntin' every whar for dat crazy onery fool dis minute," he thought, going through the back gate.

The house, built several yards back from the low picket fence, looked like some deserted castle, its large, colonial pillars gleaming white against the dark foliage of oleander bushes. Vine covered, its veranda extended the length of two sides of the house. The dining room at the back with its numerous long, green blinds added to the ghostly aspect of the place.

Jim walked around the kitchen. Suddenly he stopped and could have declared he saw a dim light moving about in the dining room, but tried to dismiss the idea as only imagination.

"Huh!" he grunted, "De next thing ah'll be b'lievin' in ghosts," trying to shake off the uneasy feeling that possessed him.

There it was again. He was sure this time. Someone was moving around in the room. He could see the light, first on one side, then on the other. For a moment, he stood stark still, watching the window, fascinated. His first feeling of fright soon passed, and gliding up to the porch cautiously, he picked up an old lantern, he had left there, lighted it, and moved noiselessly to the back door, slipping the key he always carried into the lock. He turned it slowly. A rasping sound came from within. Someone had gone out through the side window that opened on the veranda.

Rushing quickly into the now empty room, holding his lantern high, he dashed for the window, which the intruder had left open. There was no one there. The oleander bushes obstructed his view beyond when he tried to pierce the darkness of the grounds.

Giving up the effort as fruitless, he re-entered the room. Something white near the window caught his eye. Stooping he picked it up. Just a small piece of soiled paper, he decided, and started to throw it away. A jumble of figures were written across its creased surface. Nine stood out clearly, followed by the word right. Another number that looked like five. He spelt out the word—left.

There was something strangely familiar about the writing. His heart almost stopped beating. It was the combination of the safe in William's handwriting. He had seen it all his life, and had copied pages of words and figures he had written in an effort to help him learn.

Walking over to the safe he noticed for the first time that it was standing wide open. He ran his hand into its depths. The money he had so recently put there, was gone! He remembered William had wanted that money. He had copied that combination and gave it to someone to steal it for him. He could easily guess who—Slippery. Well, they would not get away with it. Brother or no brother, he would have them arrested. He decided—but even as he made the decision, thoughts of his mother filled his mind. William was her idol. She would never survive the blow. It would break her heart, and William was not worth it. Hastily before he had a chance to change his mind, he tore the paper into small bits. He would just have to replace the money and not let her know anything about it. Of course, William would have to answer to him for this night's work. He would not be as easy on him as he had been when they last had an encounter.

Suddenly he thought about the small bag of antique jewelry that Owen Gordon kept in a secret drawer in the safe. If that was gone, it would be a different story.

Reaching again into the safe, he felt for and pressed a small spring. Trembling he pulled out a small shammy bag that contained nearly one hundred pieces of old jewelry, heirlooms of several generations. Breathing a sigh of relief, he dropped it into his coat pocket, and stood so absorbed with his thoughts that he did not hear soft footsteps, as someone entered the room.

Marshall Bailey and his wife returning home from Macon where they had spent the day, saw their old mare grazing at Owen Gordon's back gate. The marshall got out, intent on trying to coax her home. He noticed the figure of a man emerge through the window, look around, and enter the house again. Cautiously he slipped to the porch and peeped through the blinds. He was amazed to see Jim take something from the safe and slip it into his pocket. Slipping into the room, he faced the startled boy.

"Jim, will you tell me whut you's doin' snoopin' 'roun' Gordon's house this time 'er night?" he asked sternly.

"Why, Mr. Bailey, Ah jes' happened to walk over heah an' while Ah was heah, Ah thought Ah'd see dat everything was locked up good, an' den Ah seed uh light in dis room so Ah comed on in, but whoever it was in heah dey had done got out 'er dat window," Jim replied, indicating the window through which the Marshall had just stepped. An incredulous look in the Marshall's eyes brought to his realization the seriousness of the situation.

"Well, go on! Whut else happened?" the Marshall asked testily.

"Nothin', but Ah ain't seed uh livin' soul an' when Ah looked in de safe, Mr. Gordon's money dat Ah put in dere from de sale uh his peaches was gone."

"How was the safe opened?"

"Wid de combination, Mr. Bailey."

"Who knew the combination?"

"Nobody but me an' Mr. Gordon. He done tole me to put his money in dere an' mine too in case Ah had any."

"Are you sho nobody knew it but you two?"

"Dead sho. Ma ain't even knowed it."

"So you thought you'd come heah and take the money out tonight and pretend it was stolen, is that it?"

"Ah 'clare 'fo de Lawd Ah didn't take de money, Mr. Bailey," Jim answered, almost sobbing.

"Was that all that was in the safe, Jim?"

"Yes suh," Jim answered, forgetting in his agitation the bag of jewelry he had slipped into his pocket.

"A likely story," the Marshall said, his voice hard with disbelief. "But Ah been watching you ever since you came in here from the porch, where you no doubt went to make sure there was no one around." Walking over to Jim, he ran his hand quickly into his coat pocket and drew out the bag of jewelry. Opening it on the table, he poured out its glittering contents.

"Huh, larceny after trust is whut Ah calls it," he said, sweeping the jewelry back into the bag and catching Jim by the arm, he pushed him through the door before him.

CHAPTER XIV

Jim's arrest was the biggest shock the little settlement had ever had. For months nothing else was talked of. Cotton and even church receded far into the background, as the farmers discussed the surprise of it and the outcome of the trial set for early November.

Sara Lou engaged one of Macon's best lawyers, John Hayden, a former partner of Owen Gordon's, to defend Jim, who through the lawyer's efforts, had been released on bail the Wednesday following his arrest.

There had been a very tearful scene at the Carter home when his mother, William and Ruth had returned from Church and found him in Marshall Bailey's custody. The Marshall had been waiting to question them, but there was nothing they could say that would help Jim, and amidst his mother's tears and prayers and Ruth's pitiful sobs, he had been taken away. Ruth had torn aside the secrecy of their engagement and begged to be taken to jail with him. Marshall Bailey had been glad when it was over, and Jim was landed safely in the little leanto jail.

But Lawyer Hayden was hopeful. The evidence to his mind was too flimsy to win a conviction. He also felt sure that Jim, although not guilty, knew who had committed the robbery, and was trying to shield the guilty party. But as time passed, he found that getting him to talk would be a harder job than he had anticipated.

Jim refused to talk, persisting that he knew nothing but the bare facts he had already stated to the marshall.

"Is there anyone who visits your home that you have reason to suspect?" the lawyer asked him.

"No, suh, not uh soul," Jim answered positively.

"Could anyone except yourself have at any time seen that combination without your knowledge?"

"No, suh. Ah kept it hid all de time an' Ah ain't never recollecked it bein' missin'."

"Did your brother know you had that combination?" the lawyer asked, looking straight into Jim's eyes to see the effect his question would have on him. But if Jim was taken by surprise he did not show it, as he calmly answered.

"Yes, Mr. Hayden, William knowed Ah had it, but he ain't never seed it."

"Well, Jim, ain't that slick nigger that works 'round his shop in Macon been visiting your home?"

"Yes, suh. He done been dere lots uh times, but Ah watched him an' he ain't never been upstairs whar Ah keeped de combination," Jim answered, without batting an eye. After a moment he continued: "Anyhow, he was in Spring Valley, William tole me, dat Sunday night."

"Yes, I know he has a trip to Spring Valley as an alibi, but I'm investigating its authenticity," Lawyer Hayden said, rising to indicate the interview was over.

Jim realized, as he rode back to Macon that he was throwing away the only chance he had of clearing himself, and would perhaps have to suffer for a crime he had not even thought of committing, but it was the only way to save his mother from a lifetime of suffering. She knew that he was not guilty, but if he told what he knew, William could easily be proven the culprit, and break her adoring heart.

His blood boiled to think that even now, William was again in school posing as a martyr to the students, who sympathized with him for having a brother under suspicion of robbery.

Through the remaining days of October, Jim worked doggedly up and down the rows of cotton, cleaning up the last fragments. Ruth worked tearfully at his side, blaming herself for the tragedy. Had it not been for her remarks to William about school which Jim had overheard, and worried about, he would have been in church with them that night. He had stayed home because he felt angry and hurt.

One evening she sobbed out her self accusation to Sara Lou, as she helped with supper.

"Don't you feel dat'uh way chile. Dey would 'er 'cused Jim anyhow, ef'fen he had uh been in church jes' kaise he's de only pusson dat knows dat ole combination," Sara Lou comforted, tears filling her eyes. "Anyhow, dese white folks is mad 'roun' heah kaise Mr. Gordon done left Jim in charge uh his place, but don't you worry, honey, he gointer come out uh it 'thout uh bit uh trouble."

But Ruth did worry, and as days passed into weeks, she became just a shadow of herself. Black circles appeared under her eyes. Her shoulders drooped and she grew years older. And Sara Lou for all her assurance of the outcome of Jim's trial being acquittal, worried herself sick in bed. The once happy home became sad and silent. No more songs floated out upon the still night air. The family retired almost at dusk, to lay and restlessly toss throughout the long night. Neighbors, who loved them, not wanting to see the sorrow that had befallen them, stayed away as much as possible.

William, conscience-stricken, did not come home Saturday, making excuses of having to study hard to keep up with his school work; while in Macon he and Slippery spent sparingly the fruits of their crime for fear of detection.

As the time for the trial drew near, speculation as to its outcome was rife among the farmers. Sally Ann Peck and Martha Green nearly came to blows because of their difference of opinion. Martha had said as they walked home from church:

"Lawd, Ah jes' kain't see how Jim kin be so innocent uh dat robbin' when don't nobody else know dat combination but him."

"You shut yo wide mouth up 'oman. Dey ain't nobody found out whut went wid de church money you was keepin'. You is de lass one whut aught'er go layin' blame on folks," Sally came back hotly.

"Is you 'sinuatin' dat Ah ain't tole de truth when Ah said dat de money was stole out 'uh my house," Martha asked threateningly, shaking her fist under Sally's nose.

"Ah ain't 'sinuatin' 'nothin' but Ah is sayin' dat folks whut lives in glass houses gotta watch out when dey throws stones."

"Yeah, you is somebody to talk. You ain't got no husban' uh yo' own an' you'se allers sneakin' 'roun' at'ter somebody else's. Folks is talkin' 'bout running you out'er Byron right now," Martha snorted.

"Ah sho ain't sneakin' at'ter yo's, Martha, kaise he done left you years ago 'bout dat Jones boy an' you readin' de Bible down by de branch in de moonlight," Sally laughed.

"Ah gotta good mind to wring yo' neck for dat remark, Sally Ann Peck," Martha retorted beside herself with rage.

"Don't let yo' wooden God an' cornstalk Jesus fool yuh, 'oman nor yo' good mind, neither, no matter how good it is," Sally retorted.

Martha gritted her teeth and walked away, throwing over her shoulder. "Don't you never speak to me agin long as yuh lives."

And although the two shared the same two room log cabin, Jim's trial was over before they spoke to each other again.

Jim, the subject of all their discussions, worked on silently, as the days swiftly passed. There was no malice in his heart for the brother who had wantonly placed him in the shadow of the chain gang— only pity for his weakness and for his mother, trying so hard to hide her real anguish from him.

Bright sunshine, warm and cheering, the morning of the trial, mocked the anguish within the hearts of Sara Lou, Ruth and Jim, as they rode the ten miles to the county seat of Peach County. William, silent and making a fine effort of grieved concern, rode beside Jim on the front seat of the wagon while Sara Lou and Ruth sat behind on a board laid across its body.

Sara Lou's cousin, Ella, Jerimah and their six children drove in their team behind them and almost of the entire population of Byron greeted them when they rode up to the one story frame court-house.

When the doors were opened at nine o'clock, the building was soon packed, and the trial started by Lawyer Hayden's insisting that a jury be impanelled instead of the customary judge presiding and deciding the case. After many objections and discussions, a jury of twelve sturdy farmers was selected, and the case proceeded.

William, the first witness called, could tell nothing except he and his mother and Ruth were in church the night of the robbery. He knew nothing of the money paid Jim for the peaches and had never seen the combination of the safe. His mother, next called, proved a difficult witness. Her testimony collaborated with William's exactly, but the judge and lawyer had a hard time keeping her to the point, as she insisted on telling how Mr. Gordon trusted Jim and how she had brought him up in the fear of God.

"We ain't askin' you aller that, An' Sara. We'all knows that Gordon done gone off and left a parsel'er you niggers running over his place instead'er a good, honest, white man and this is what has come of him doing it," Judge Graham, a former resident of Byron and a friend of Owen Gordon's informed her.

Sara Lou's sobs became louder and louder, until the Judge dismissed her from the witness stand and asked that she be taken from the court-room.

Ruth was next called. She proved the most damaging witness of the trio. The judge determined to establish a reason for the usually trust-

worthy Jim turning thief, questioned her relent-
lessly.

"Didn't Jim always take you to church?" she was
asked.

"Yes, suh," the answer came soft and quivering.

"Were you two in love with each other?"

"Yes, suh. We is."

"Were you engaged to be married?"

"Yes, suh, we is."

"Didn't he promise to buy you pretty clothes?"

Ruth raised her eyes and looked around the
court-room as if seeking someone to aid her, and
the Judge had to repeat the question.

"We jes' looked in uh catalogue an' was admirin'
uh dress," came hesitatingly.

"And he promised to buy it for you, eh?"

"Not zackly, suh, he sayd it'ud look mighty nice
on me."

"What else did he say?"

"Dat some day Ah might wear it."

"That's just the same as promising it to you,
ain't it?"

"Yes, suh. Ah mean, no suh," Ruth sobbed dis-
tractedly.

"Well at any rate, there was a reason for Jim
wanting this money desperately," her persecutor
announced.

And Ruth, realizing that her testimony had been
unknowingly damaging to Jim, burst into a torrent
of uncontrollable weeping.

Lawyer Hayden was on his feet, his face red, his
eyes blazing. "Judge, your honor," he shouted.
"This is no love affair. This Jim Carter is on trial
for robbery not for being in love."

"All right, Attorney," the Judge replied, looking over his glasses. "Proceed with the case! Call the next witness!"

Marshall Bailey told without interruption his story of finding Jim in the Gordon dining-room, where the safe stood empty and of finding Owen Gordon's jewelry in his pocket, and all the incidents leading up to his going in to investigate.

" 'Bout what time was that, Bailey?" he was asked.

" 'Round ten o'clock," the answer came promptly.

After a few more pointed questions, the Marshall was dismissed, and Jim called to the stand in his own defence. He told how he happened to walk over to the Gordon place but could tell nothing about the robbery but what he had told the Marshall. He admitted he alone knew the combination of the safe, but could give no excuse for having the jewelry in his pocket, except that he was so glad it had not been taken. He slipped it there, and forgot all about it in the excitement of the Marshall's appearing on the scene which the persecution claimed was a sure sign he planned to steal it.

After a torrid examination, his testimony ended. Lawyer Hayden used every argument he knew in his summary to try and clear the frightened boy. The hour then being late, court was adjourned until the next morning at nine o'clock.

All through Jim's testimony, William sat, his eyes averted, avoiding his brother's haunted face. It was a joy and relief when they were again on their way home.

CHAPTER XV

On the evening of the next day Sara Lou sat in her bare, clean dining room. Her cane bottom rocker swayed back and forth in even rhythm with her sobs. Her friends, Sally Ann, Martha, Ella, Sally Brown, Reverend Hooper, and a few others sat grim-faced and sympathetic trying to console her. They had just returned from the County seat, where Jim had been convicted and sentenced to five years in the chain-gang.

Reverend Hooper rose and bade them kneel while he carried Jim's case to a greater judge than Judge Graham. For almost an hour he prayed, and as they rose from their knees, Martha Green sang softly, helped by the others. "Ah'm leanin' on de Lawd."

"Dat's jes' whut Ah'm doin'," Sara Lou declared, as the song ended.

"He's uh good one to lean on, An' Sara, but ef'fen yuh could 'ford to git dat Lawyer Hayden to git uh 'nother trial for Jim an' have it in Macon, it might help de leanin'," Sally Ann remarked earnestly.

"Lan' sakes, Sally Ann, you don't trust de Lawd for nothin'," Martha chided.

"Course Ah trusts him but sometimes he kind 'er slow to act. Lak de time my ole man Joe was 'cused uh stealin' in Macon. Ef'fen Ah hadn't been workin' for dat big lawyer man dat took up Joe's case, he'ud been in de gang till now."

All eyes were turned on Sally Ann in horror but, undaunted, she continued. "To tell de truth, Ah should 'er let 'im gone to de gang kaise Ah had to work uh whole year to pay de lawyer an' 'fo Ah was throu' payin' 'im, Joe he ups an' runs off wid uh trifflin' gal dat was stayin' wid us."

"Huh, served yuh right," Martha grunted, and to avoid further discussion of the matter, Sally Brown started another song.

William, who had been walking around to get away from the sight of his mother's suffering, came into the room and hinted that his mother needed rest, and they bade goodnight and hurried away. William assisted his mother up to her room, where Ruth, who had been preparing the evening meal, served her, and for the first time in Sara Lou's busy life she was unable to leave her room for a week. As strength came back to her during the week that followed, her first concern was William.

"You must git back to yo' school, son," she said, as they sat around downstairs for the first time since Jim had been sent away.

"I will, Ma, soon as you feels all right again, but I'm in no mood for study," he replied obediently.

"You jes' git in de mood. Dere ain't nuthin' heah to do an' us jes' kain't give up. We jes' gotta trust in de Lawd. He's gointer make everything all right an' bring de guilty to judgment."

"Ah sho wish Ah could b'lieve lak dat, An' Sara," Ruth remarked sadly. "But things lak dis makes me b'lieve sometime dat de Lawd ain't much bothered 'bout whut comes to us folks."

"Why, Ruth, dat ain't no way for you to talk!"
Sara Lou exclaimed in surprise.

"It sure ain't no way for a Christian to talk.
Maybe if Jim had got religion instead of making
fun of preachers and the church, this might not
have happened to him," William said with an air
of pious dignity.

"Religion ain't got nothin' to do wid it. Ole
Judge Graham is uh deacon in his church an' Ah
ain't never seed nobody act any more unfair den
he did tryin' Jim," Ruth exploded angrily.

"When is you seen them act fair when there's
one uh us on trial?" William asked quietly.

"Dey jes' takes it for granted dat we'se guilty
'fo we'se tried, but Ah thank God dey ain't de
judge when it comes to gittin' to heaven," Sara
Lou smiled, happy with the prospect of that far off
reward.

Ruth's reply filled with defiance shocked them
both. "Shucks, Ah ain't wantin' to have to wait
ontill Ah gits to heaven to have uh little happi-
ness," she said, walking out of the room.

Later that evening some of Sara Lou's neigh-
bors dropped in to see if there was anything they
could do for her, and for a while they all sat
around talking, trying to forget the tragedy that
had befallen them.

"William, Ah want yuh to write Mr. Gordon a
letter an' tell him whut done happened," Sara Lou
said when she, William and Ruth were again alone.

"All right, Ma. That's a good idea! Do you
know his address?"

"Ah jes' know dat he done write Jim from a
place called London. Ah got de letter heah so

send it dere," handing the letter to William, who wrote the long, rambling letter his mother dictated, telling Owen Gordon the details of the robbery and begging him not to believe Jim guilty.

"I'll mail it first thing in the morning, Ma," William promised, sealing the missive.

"Awrite son, an' tomorrow is Tuesday, you go back to school."

"I will, Ma," William promised, glad to get away from home, where everything reminded him of the crime he had committed. Things had turned out far different from what he had planned. He had had Slippery take the money because he needed it to pay the debts he owed and to spite Jim, whom he knew would have to replace it, but he had not dreamed that the outcome would be as it was. In fact, he blamed Jim for going to Gordon's house that night when he might have been in church, and wondered why Fate had sent Marshall Bailey by just at that time. But now that it had happened, he could not find one spark of pity in his heart for Jim. If it had not been for the suffering the whole thing caused his mother, he would have been happier than he had been in years.

"Ah wonder ef'fen Lawyer Hayden could git my boy uh new trial?" his mother's voice brought him back to the present.

"Maybe so, Ma, but it'ud cost a lot of money," he answered without enthusiasm.

"Lawd, Ah'd sell de roof from over my head to git Jim out'uh dat prison!" Sara Lou declared.

"Let's wait a while and see what Mr. Gordon says when he writes," William suggested.

"Ah sho' hopes he answers right 'er way," **Ruth**
breathed hopefully.

Sara Lou rose reluctantly and stretched her arms
above her head. She had been sleepy and on the
verge of going to bed for some time, but the pros-
pects of lying awake thinking until far into the night
had kept her putting it off.

"Ah'm goin'ter carry my ole bones to bed, chil-
lun," she said, moving towards the stairs.

"Ah'm goin' too, An' Sara," Ruth said, rising.

William caught her hand and pleaded. "Please
don't go, Ruth. I've got a new book I want to tell
you about and it's only eight o'clock anyhow."

Ruth reluctantly resumed her seat. She did not
want to hurt William's feelings but would rather
have been anywhere than alone with him in her
present state of mind.

"Why didn't you tell me you and Jim was en-
gaged?" his first question brought an uneasy flush
to her face.

" 'Cause Jim an' me promised to keep it uh secret
an' we wasn't goin'ter marry nohow ontill Ah was
out uh mourning."

"Now that Jim's in prison for five years, you
ain't aiming to wait for him that long, are you?"

"Sho' Ah am! Ah'ud wait twenty years for Jim."

"But you're young and I loves you, Ruth. Would
you rather sacrifice five years waiting for him than
marry me?"

"Please William, don't talk lak dat. It ain't fair
to yo' brother when you knows dat Ah done prom-
ised him, an' anyhow Ah ain't goin' to listen to yuh,"
Ruth answered, rising.

"Jim ain't selfish enough to want you to wait that long for him nohow, Ruth."

"Leave go my hand, William," Ruth begged, trying to free herself from the grasp William had on her hand. "Ah want to go to bed anyhow. Ah'm sleepy," she pleaded.

"Let me kiss you good night. I ain't kissed you since we were children," William begged, drawing her to him.

Ruth shrank as far away as possible, but William drew her struggling into his arms. She placed her hand over her mouth but William gently removed it and held her close, pressing his lips to hers in a long passionate kiss. Again and again his lips pressed hers, despite her desperate struggles to free herself from his embrace. When she finally pushed him aside and ran to the stairway, her limbs were trembling so violently, they could hardly carry her weight.

CHAPTER XVI

The next morning, William left Byron to return to his studies. He tried to get a chance to speak to Ruth alone before leaving, but she steadfastly avoided him and greatly disappointed, he left to catch his train.

He had lost considerable time; but it would mean nothing. Studies had never even been an effort to his alert brain, and before the week was over, he had caught up with his classes, and was again spending his leisure time over at Daddy Jenks' with Ethel.

For long hours she would sit beside the bed and watch him as he lay stretched full length upon it, his eyes closed, one arm thrown carelessly above his head, letting her fingers linger for a moment upon his face as they glided on through his soft curly hair. As she waited for him to open his eyes or in some way respond to her caresses, she loved him with all the love of her starved warped soul.

William stirred uneasily and pushing her hand aside, sat up on the side of the bed.

"Whut's de matter, William, did Ah wake you up?" Ethel asked softly.

"No."

"Are you angry wid me, honey?"

"No."

"Well den, Ah got something Ah wants to talk to yuh 'bout," she persisted, sitting on the side of the bed beside him. "Ah been thinkin' long time, William, dis ain't no place for you. Why don't you come on up north wid me whar you kin 'mount to somethin' some day. You kain't ever be nothin' heah. You may finish school an' become uh stomp knockin' preacher, but dat ain't no good for you when you could do so much better."

"I'm not leaving Georgia, Ethel, now or no time! I belong here, and I'm gonna stay here. I guess you think because I hangs out 'round you, I ain't never gonna be no good. Well, I'll show you, I'll stay away!" William retorted sharply and dashed angrily from the room.

Ethel's harsh laughter followed him until he was out of hearing.

Once again he swore he would keep away from Daddy Jenks' gang and Ethel. He loved Ruth madly. Her clean, sweet beauty, fascinated him. With her as his wife he would be safe from himself, his weakness and passion; and able to make of himself the great man his mother wanted him to be.

He went straight to his room and was thankful that Sissy was out. For several hours he studied and read, and before getting into bed, knelt and prayed that God would give him strength to do the things he wanted to do.

But getting rid of Ethel was no small task. She hung around his shop night and day, sometimes sober, but more often drunk and in an ugly mood.

"Yuh think you kin ditch me jes' lak dat?" she said—snapping her finger under William's nose the next afternoon.

"Ethel, I've got to study and I've got lots of responsibility and can't be bothered," William explained.

"Aw, yeah? Well, you gonna be worried uh

hell'eva lot an' before Ah'm through, Ah won't be de only one botherin' yuh, neither," she returned, rushing out of the shop.

But William continued to stay away and she drank more and more, and tore things up in general.

Jim had been in prison two weeks when William got sufficient courage to visit him. He hated the trip. The chain gang held a horror for him that made his visit a torture, but his mother had asked him to go, and he could not refuse.

Jim had intended telling him what he had found in the Gordon dining room, the night of the robbery, and make him promise by holding the knowledge of his criminality over his head, to stop being a hypocrite and live right for their mother's sake, but the presence of the guards prevented him from doing so, and he treated William civil in their presence—not because he wanted to.

It was almost time for him to leave when he said casually: "It sure is a shame the way Ruth is worrying, Jim."

"Whut's she worryin' 'bout more den usual?"

"Well, she's young and realizes five years is a long time to be engaged."

"Did she say dat?"

"No, she wouldn't say it for the world, but she thinks it, and she did say something like that to me when I was home last."

"Ah don't want 'er to wait five years for me, William. It jes' wouldn't be fair nohow."

"Well, don't be too hasty, Jim, in tellin' her that you don't. Mr. Gordon may come home, if he gets

Ma's letter. And get worried 'bout his place, and he may get you out."

"Less don't talk uh 'bout it."

"Just as you say, Jim," William answered, uneasy because of the look he saw in Jim's eyes.

He felt he was treading on dangerous ground and bidding Jim goodbye, left the prison. Later when he told his mother the events of his trip she said:

"Me an' Ruth jes' dyin' to see de boy an' we goin'ter take him lots uh vittels when we goes out dere, ain't we honey?" turning to Ruth.

"We sho is, An' Sara, an' we goin'ter be jes' dat cheerful, dat he goin'ter be laughin' 'fo we leaves."

Ruth was all excitement as the holidays drew near—the time she and Sara Lou were to visit the chain gang. Jim had scribbled a few short letters and every morning she ran down to the post office to see if there was anything for her or Sara Lou.

Two days before Christmas Eve she returned, her steps lagging as if they were lead. In her hand she held a letter tightly clutched. Sara Lou heard her enter the house and start upstairs and called her into the kitchen, where she was putting away a cake she had baked for Jim.

"Lawd chile, whut's de matter wid you? Is yuh seen uh ghost?" she exclaimed when she saw Ruth's drawn face.

For answer Ruth handed her the letter she had received from Jim. Sara Lou spelt out the few lines carefully.

"Dear Ruth:

   Dis is jes' to tell yuh dat Ah ain't holdin' yuh
to our engagement kaise five years is too long to
ask you to wait.   Jim."

"Shucks, Ruth, dat boy is crazy!   Don't yuh pay
dis no' 'tention," Sara Lou said, drawing Ruth into
her arms.

"Ah don't know whut maked him write me lak
dat, An' Sara," Ruth sobbed.

"He jes' scared he gointer have to stay in dat
place five years sho' 'nough an' dat's worryin' him,"
Sara Lou consoled.   "When we goes out dere, he
goin'ter take dat all back."

"Ah don't know ef'fen Ah'm goin' out dere, An'
Sara, not rite uh way nohow.   Ah knows Jim well
'nough to know he don't never joke.   Ef'fen he
say our engagement is broke, he means it, an' Ah
ain't gointer worry him 'bout it, kaise he got 'nough
to worry 'bout as it is."

Ruth spent the rest of the afternoon wandering
in the woods that surrounded the farm.   For a long
time she stood looking at her and Jim's hickory nut
tree, where their hair had been buried years back.
When she returned home she found William, who
had come home as usual to spend Sunday, sitting
with his mother.   He had brought her a new book,
and a box of candy for his mother to share with her.
His witty jokes soon had them both laughing and in
a measure feeling better than earlier in the after-
noon when Jim's letter had so cruelly hurt her.

William was diplomatic and took sides with Jim,
excusing his action with the hopelessness of facing

years in the terrible confinement of prison. After Ruth had gone to bed, he and his mother sat for a while talking.

"Ah goin'ter bring dat boy to his senses when Ah goes out to dat prison," she declared.

"If I was you, Ma, I'd let them settle it themselves. You know how stubborn Jim is. He might not like you interfering."

"Dat's rite, son," Sara Lou agreed. "Ah won't say uh livin' word, less'n he mentions it hisseff."

William went to sleep that night relieved and pleased with the progress he had made in breaking up Jim's engagement. He was now removed as a rival, and with time and the many ways he would use to win Ruth, everything would be in his favor. He had feared more than anything else his mother's asking Jim why he had written that letter, and Jim, in turn, telling her and Ruth what he had said during his visit.

CHAPTER XVII

The Christmas holidays passed quickly, but not happily for the Carter household. A gloom hovered over the house that the visit to the chain gang seemed to intensify; instead of dispel. At the time of year when many people visited their friends and relatives in prison and extra care was taken to guard the place, Ruth had had no chance to say the things to Jim she had wanted to, and returned home sadder and more hopeless than ever.

William was glad when time came for him to return to school, and spent more time than usual studying. He saw little of Ethel or the boys, but Sugar Kid's release from prison caused him many sleepless nights, as he worried him daily for his thirty-five dollars.

January and February passed and he had not paid the debt because Sugar Kid had failed to produce the note. It was Saturday afternoon early in March, and William was helping Slippery to finish the work in the shop when Sugar Kid walked in.

"Say, listen heah, William," he began.

"I knows just whut you're going to say, Sugar Kid," William interrupted. "That you want yo' money, and I'm going to say what I've told you before—that you can have it when you give me back the note I gave you so save yo' breath, if you ain't got the note with you."

"Yeah, Ah gonna say jes' dat an' Ah'm goin'ter say something else. Ef'fen yuh don't give me my money right now, Ah'm goin'ter scatter you all over de state uh Georgy," Sugar Kid retorted angrily.

"Not so fast!" Slippery spoke up, reaching for his gun that he kept in a drawer nearby, and walking over to the door where Sugar Kid was standing, he continued: "You is one snake, Sugar Kid dat Ah's jes' dyin' to step on an' flatten out, so yuh better git out uh heah an' stay out 'fo' Ah does jes' dat!"

Sugar Kid backed out of the door quickly, and walked across the street cursing the two of them roundly under his breath, his mind made up to get even with Slippery, if it was the last thing he ever did.

"Ah guess dat's de last uh dat snake, askin' for dat thirty-five bucks," Slippery laughed.

"I don't know about that, Slippery. Sometimes I feels that I aught'er give him that money. It might cause lots of trouble yet," William replied, thoughtfully.

"Aw you'se jes' uh tender, William. Ah knows how to handle dese darkies 'roun' heah. Dey don't scare me."

" 'Course I'm in my rights. He insisted on me writing a note that I owed him the money and if I pay him without getting it back, he can produce it later and make me pay him again."

"Well, whut yuh worryin' 'bout den? Jes' forgit it!" Slippery advised.

"Gee, whut's all de commotion over at Daddy Jenks'?" Slippery exclaimed a moment later, when a loud scream carried him to the door.

A large crowd had congregated in front of Daddy's place and several policemen were struggling with someone as they dragged them towards the patrol wagons standing near the sidewalk. William and Slippery looking on from their door, tried to make out who the struggling culprit was. Slippery no longer able to control his curiosity, crossed the street, returning in a short time with the news of the fracas.

Ethel, who had gone on a drunken rampage, had been the unwilling struggling prisoner. Daddy Jenks had tried to keep her quiet and had almost succeeded when Sugar Kid came in and started raving about what he was going to do to William and she had broken loose again, and grabbing Daddy's ice pick, had gone for Sugar Kid. The police had to be called, finally, to keep her from committing murder.

"Ef'fen dat gal ain't careful she goin'ter git runned out'uh dis town! She done been in court four Mondays hand running," Slippery remarked.

"She sure can raise Cain, all right. I don't see how she gets away with it," William said, worried over the outcome of the trial, when mention of him might get him into an unpleasant situation.

"Well, she stands in wid de deputy sheriff. Dat's how she gits way wid it. Ef'fen yuh don't know," Slippery was glad to inform him, hoping it might keep him away from Ethel henceforth.

But William ignored the remark and turned the subject to other things. Later that evening, he left the shop to catch a train home remarking laughingly to Slippery, as he went out of the door.

"See you Monday. Be careful of Sugar Kid. Don't let him get the drop on you."

"Don't worry. Ah been wantin' to bump dat

bird off long time an eff'en he starts anythin' dat'll jes' be my chance," Slippery called cheerfully.

Late customers started dropping in to get their clothes and Slippery had his hands too full to think further of Sugar Kid. Cotton Eye, among the last to call, was in a particularly talkative mood, when he flopped down on a box to wait while Slippery put the finishing touches to his one and only suit.

"Gee boy," he said between mouthfuls of peanuts, he crammed into his mouth from his overall pockets. "Dere sho is been some tall doin's 'roun' heah today. Dey tells me dat Ethel done gone to jail an' dat Sugar Kid is raisin' hell over at Daddy Jenks."

"Whut's he raisin' hell 'bout?" Slippery asked.

"Well, for one thing, he swears dat he goin'ter plug you full uh holes de fust time yuh steps foot in Daddy's place, an' dat's got Daddy all hot an' bothered kaise he don't lak nobody startin' nothin' in his joint."

"Daddy needn't be kaise Ah ain't scared uh Sugar Kid. Ah'm goin' in de place any time Ah gits good an' ready. Ain't nothin' to dat bag uh wind nohow."

"All Ah gotta say, Slippery, is jes' watch yo' step!"

"Ah kin take care'uh myself. Don't you worry."

"Ah ain't gonna, but Ah jes' hopes Ah be dere when de fun start. Ah wouldn't miss it for nothin'," Cotton Eye grinned, handing Slippery the money for his suit.

It was almost eleven o'clock when Slippery closed the shop for the night and walked slowly over to Daddy Jenks. A tremor of excitement passed over the crowd standing around when he entered the door. Sugar Kid, his back towards the door, was not aware of his presence until he called for a drink. Everybody expected a fight or even gun play when the two men faced each other. A sigh of relief and disappointment went around the room when instead, Sugar Kid walked over to Slippery and said casually.

"How's de boy, Slippery?"

"Ah ain't so bad off, Sugar Kid. How's you?" Slippery replied, his eyes on Sugar Kid's hand fumbling in his pockets.

"Ah awrite. Now dat Ah'se kind'er cooled off, less have uh drink. Daddy sit up uh bottle," Sugar Kid answered.

Bottle after bottle was placed on the counter, and Sugar Kid and Slippery drank. It was near midnight when Slippery walking somewhat unsteadily, followed Sugar Kid and the boys upstairs to gamble. For all the liquor he had consumed, he played carefully and in fairly good luck. Someone suggested they put the cards aside and shoot dice instead and he readily consented.

As the game progressed, Sugar Kid became quarrelsome and the boys realized he was trying to pick a fight with Slippery. One by one they dropped out of the game, leaving him and Slippery facing each other. Slippery had won several passes when Sugar Kid suddenly reached for the dice.

"Why, yuh dirty crook!" he shouted. "Whut yuh mean puttin' dese crooked dice in de game?"

Slippery looked on in surprise as Sugar Kid threw the dice to one of the boys standing near.

"Look at 'em! Ain't dey loaded?" Sugar Kid demanded.

"Sho is!" the reply came, as the dice went down the line from hand to hand.

"Ah didn't put 'em in, Sugar Kid, an' you know it!" Slippery denied hotly, realizing he was being accused of a deed that was considered the lowest among gamblers.

"Yuh did an' Ah'm goin'ter git yuh for it, tryin' to rob me right 'fo' eve'ybody," Sugar Kid snarled, making a dash for him.

"Git back dere," Slippery warned, reaching for his hip pocket, but Sugar Kid came on slowly advancing around the table towards him, shaking his arm. Slippery saw something shiny drop from his sleeve and backed away until he was against the opposite wall. Still Sugar Kid advanced slowly like a cat ready to spring, his gums drawn back from his teeth in an ugly snarl.

"Git back, Sugar Kid!" Slippery begged, trying in vain to slide beyond his reach, one large hand reached out, almost touching his throat.

Slippery wiggled along the wall; shouted again to the advancing man to keep away. Suddenly his hand came out of his pocket. In it his pistol was tightly grasped.

"Look out—he's got a gun!" someone yelled.

But Sugar Kid gave one lunge and as Slippery jumped aside, his hand ripped the collar from his shirt. A shot rang out, found its mark. Sugar Kid paused for a second, his hand clutching at the weapon, his eyes wide and bulging as he swayed dizzily; his knees sagged and carried him crashing to the floor.

Slippery leaped over his prostrate body and before anyone could recover sufficiently to stop him, was gone.

Pandemonium reigned. Men fought to get out and soon the club room was as clean as if no one had been there. Sugar Kid lay still upon the floor, killed by a single bullet from Slippery's gun.

* * *

William, just seventeen miles away from the tragedy, slept peacefully through the night. He had set up late with his mother, who was almost overcome with the joy of having received a letter from Owen Gordon, who had just reached London, and found her letter awaiting him.

"Jes' to think, Willyum, Mr. Gordon goin'ter be home soon, an' he goin'ter git my Jim right out'er dat chain gang," she had said, her eyes filled with tears of joy.

"Don't get yo' hopes too high, Ma, cause after all, maybe Mr. Gordon won't be able to get Jim out, and maybe he won't want to nohow. After all, he's white, and he might believe like the other white folks, that Jim did steal his money," William replied, avoiding his mother's happy face.

"'Deed he ain't goin'ter think dat Jim did no stealin' an' 'nother thin', he ain't lak no other white folks. He's jes' Mr. Gordon lak hisseff an' de smartest lawyer dere ever was an' he laks Jim an' he goin'ter git him out, yuh'll see."

"I hope so," William assented, bidding his mother good-night. Until after midnight he lay wondering whether Owen Gordon's home-coming would in any way affect his secret of the robbery which he felt was safe between Slippery and himself.

Ruth, who had gone to Ella's to help care for one of her boys, who had been taken suddenly very ill, returned early Sunday morning. The child was worse and Ella wanted Sara Lou to come and see what she could do for him.

"Land sakes, why don't dey git uh doctor? Ah ain't no doctor!" Sara Lou grumbled, putting on her clean white Sunday apron to go to Ella. "You chillun jes' go on to church. Dinner's cooked an' ef'fen Ah don't git back by night, William you bring Ruth over to Ella's at'ter de night services."

"Ah may come over dere 'fo' dat An' Sara," Ruth replied anxiously, as she did not like being left at home alone with William all day.

Sara Lou was on her way happily trudging the distance between her and Ella's home, her thoughts on the end of her trouble being near. Snatches of happy songs burst from her lips every now and then. Between the prayers of thankfulness she murmured:

"My boy gonna soon be home. I kno it Lawd."

Later William and Ruth, after attending morning services, stopped by to see Deacon Simmons, who had been sick for several weeks and then came home to have their dinner.

"Lord, William, it jes' beats me how dese pore igno'ant folks 'roun' heah kin lay sick an' not git de doctor—jes' leavin' An' Salisbury stew up roots for dem an' makin' 'em think dey's conjured," Ruth remarked, as they cleared the table.

"Yes, Ruth, it is a shame. You know sometimes I get so tired of this place, I can hardly stand it. I'd like to go up north some place where things are different and our people gets somewhere. Wouldn't you like to live where our folks are educated and livin' like white folks."

"Ah don't know, William. Sometimes Ah dream uh livin' in uh big city an' enjoyin' life but Ah'ud be so scared an' lonely," Ruth answered thoughtfully.

"You wouldn't be if you was my wife. Some day I'm going to have a big church and folks would just worship you, Ruth, as their preacher's wife. You are so pretty and refined," William said softly, placing his arm around her shoulder and trying to lift her head so that he could look into her eyes but Ruth moved away quietly, as she said evasively:

"Yuh know Ah ain't promised to marry you yet, William. Ah still loves Jim an ef'fen Mr. Gordon gits him out, we's goin'ter marry yet."

"But he's broke your engagement. What you goin'ter do—beg him to take you back?"

"Ah won't have to beg him, William. He still loves me. It's jes' dat ole prison dat made him write whut he did."

"But, Ruth, honey, I loves you, loves you 'till it makes me hurt all over. Marry me. I'll make you so happy. I needs you, Ruth. Jim don't."

Ruth sank into a chair. William, who had stood, his arms around her, could feel her body trembling violently as he pressed her unwillingly to him. Dropping to his knees beside her, he continued pleading softly, tears gathering in his eyes. He lay his head in her lap, sobs shaking his frame, as he told her how weak he was, and how much he needed her to strengthen and encourage him.

There was something about him that fascinated her. She felt unable to resist his pleading. As she looked down upon his bowed head, she wondered if it was love that made her feel so sorry for him. She didn't want to promise him anything but when he rose and sat beside her and gently drew her to his lap, she did not resist but lay pensively in his arms. As he covered her face with kisses she felt dizzy and weak and afraid to stand, fearing her limbs would not support her.

"Honey, you do love me," he whispered close to her ear.

Trying to release herself, she pleaded feebly. "Oh, Ah don't know, William. Ah want to think. Please let me go!"

Gently assisting her to stand, he watched her as she staggered haltingly upstairs to her room, where she fell upon her knees before her bed, trying to close her eyes and shut out the memory of his face but she could not. She could still hear his soft pleading voice whispering in her ears. She did like the way he took her into his arms. His passionate kisses still smarted her lips. A thrill crept deliciously over her body, as she remembered the way he held her close.

Suddenly her thoughts frightened her. She was just a wicked sinner and out of wickedness could come nothing but sorrow and disgrace. Clasping her hands she prayed for guidance, tears flowing down her cheeks, as she silently rocked herself back and forth in agony and repentance.

CHAPTER XVIII

William walked back and forth in the room down-stairs, where Ruth had left him. In the grip of alternating hope and despair, his passionate love for Ruth and the desire to have her for his wife so filled his mind, he did not hear the light taps on the back door until they were repeated several times. Mechanically he passed through the short hall, opened the back door and started as if he had seen a ghost, as Slippery ducked quietly by him into the room and sank into the nearest chair.

"What on earth are you doing here?" William whispered, looking around the room as if expecting to see someone spring out from behind the furniture.

"Keep yo' shirt on, bo, an' Ah'll tell yuh," Slippery answered shortly. "Ah'm in trouble an' wants you to help me git 'way."

"What kind'er trouble—been raided for gambling?"

"God. Ah wish it was jes' dat. No William, it's serious dis time. Ah killed Sugar Kid."

"My God, Slippery, that's awful!" William exclaimed paling.

"Yuh tellin' me? But Ah'll git out uh dis. Ah been in tighter places den dis an' got out," Slippery bragged.

"But spose the marshall sees you coming out'er my house? Don't you see what a mess you'll get me in?" William asked, taking a cautious peep from the half-opened door.

"Dat's all you ever think of—yo' own yaller skin. Ain't Ah in uh worse mess an' whose de cause uh it all? You, if yuh ask me—helpin' you out. Dat's what got me in dis spot and yuh know it. Wasn't for you, Sugar Kid wouldn't uh picked on me," Slippery rattled off, for the first time in his life angry with William.

"How come you to kill Sugar Kid is all I wants to know and it ain't no need'er you getting mad because I'm worried 'bout the outcome," William replied, frightened at the attitude Slippery had taken.

"He picked uh fuss wid me in uh crap game. Ah begged him to keep way but he comed on an' Ah saw uh razor drop from his sleeve. He put de crooked dice in jes' to git uh chance to cut me. Ah didn't want to shoot him. Ah swear Ah didn't but Ah had to. Ah jes' had to. It was his life or mine. You know why he was mad wid me? 'Twas 'bout dat money you owed him an' Ah had to shoot." Slippery whimpered on and on almost breaking under the strain of fear.

"Well, it's done and here's all the money I've got," William interrupted, handing him a small roll of bills and assisting him to his feet. "Suppose they catch you, Slippery?" he asked when they reached the door.

"Effen dey do, put dis down in yo' little red book. Ah won't bring you into it even if dey string me. Ah swear it, William. Heah," he added, as he stood in the doorway, handing William the note he had stolen from Sugar Kid's pocket.

"When did you get this?" William asked, looking hard at the crumbled piece of paper.

"Ah took it of'fen Sugar Kid sometime ago."

"Why didn't you tell me you had it, Slippery?"

"Ah didn't want to, not den," Slippery answered, slipping out the door and sliding around the house towards the back fence. William tore the note into small bits and turned to go back into the parlor but drew back. Ruth was standing in the hall door.

"You scared me Ruth. How long have you been there?" he asked.

"Soon after Slippery came in," she answered calmly.

"Then you heard?"

"Yes every word Slippery and you said. Ah didn't want to eavesdrop yuh'all but Ah jes' couldn't help it, William," she answered wearily.

"Poor fellow, he's in trouble, Ruth."

"Yes, because of something you've done. He's uh murderer an' you'se jes' as bad."

"Why Ruth!" William started.

"Keep still, William. You'se jes' uh mean, low hypocrite gittin' people into trouble. Dat's whut you is."

"Ruth, you don't know what you're sayin'."

"Aw yes, Ah do. Ah heard Slippery promise yuh not to tell on yuh, no matter whut happens. He must know something dat you'se scared stiff he'll tell. Ah see through you now William. Dat's why Ah was al'lers scared uh you an' to think Ah almost made myself b'lieve Ah loved you," Ruth cried almost in tears.

"But you do love me, Ruth. I'm not as bad as you think," William pleaded, trying to take her hand.

"Don't yuh touch me, William Carter," she screamed, shrinking from his touch.

"I'm going to touch you," William said slowly through clenched teeth. "I love you and I'm gonna make you love me and even if you don't, you'll be glad to marry me."

Ruth, frightened by the look she saw in his eyes, backed away, her hands before her face. William pulled her into his arms and pinning her hands behind her back, kissed her lips, her neck, her shoulders, pressing her to him in a close suffocating embrace, his breath coming in short quick gasps, as his hand slid over her throat and down the neck of her dress until they touched her round full breast, the touch of her warm flesh firing the passion of his body until he trembled violently from head to foot. His usual calm was gone. In its place a savage passion swept all else aside. Ruth, weak and exhausted, felt her strength failing her, as she fought to free herself.

"William! Aunt Sara!" a loud voice called from the gate.

William came to his senses with a start. His arms dropped to his side, as he straightened himself and ran his hand over his rumpled hair, trying to collect his scattered wits and finally stumbling to the door. He faced Kenneth Bailey, the marshall.

"See you been sleep, William. Sorry to disturb yuh but has you seen dat fellow dat works in that shop in Macon with you, this afternoon?" the marshall greeted.

"Why no, Mr. Bailey," William answered slowly, almost afraid to hear the sound of his own voice.

"Wal, he done killed 'er nigger in Macon an' I thought maybe seeing he worked for you dere, he might'er come to you for help," the marshall said, eyeing William uncertainly.

"I'm sorry to hear he's got himself in trouble, Mr. Bailey, but I'd be the last one he'd expect to harbor him," William said firmly, unaware of the fact that Ruth had stepped into the doorway behind him. Her voice came like an electric shock to him when she said:

"Mr. Bailey, Ah b'lieve Ah done seed de man you lookin' for."

William looked straight before him. He was sure Ruth was going to tell all she knew about Slippery's recent visit to the marshall which would put him in a desperate spot.

"Gee, I'm glad you can help out, Ruth. Where did you see him?" the marshall asked eagerly.

Ruth hesitated a moment. A vision of Aunt Sara's face rose before her. If she told all she knew about the afternoon visit it might cause William's arrest and a world of sorrow to his mother. William had treated her shamefully but he was not worth the sorrow his mother would suffer. No, she could not do it, she decided as she said:

"He was sneaking down de road back uh de barn. Ah was lookin' after de cows when he looked over de fence at me, den sneaked on down de road in de direction uh de ole school house."

"Thanks, Ruth. Ah got'er man station over dat'er way. Ah guess he was tryin' to see you, William, an' seeing Ruth scared him 'way."

The marshall hurried away and William too relieved to speak, walked over to Ruth and held out his hand which she ignored.

"Thank you Ruth," he stammered brokenly.

Ruth turned to enter the house and at the door, turned and faced him leaning heavily against the wall.

"Ah didn't lie to save yo' skin. Ah did it because of An' Sara. She loves an' trusts you. It's all she lives for. You're her wooden God an' Ah couldn't even to save my own life hurt her."

"But Ruth, I want to beg you to forgive me," William pleaded, following her into the room. "Please forgive me. I wasn't myself this afternoon. I wants to be good. I swear I do but sometimes there's something inside'er me, I jes' can't control. I wants to be a Christian and do all the great things Ma expects of me but I don't know why. There's so many different parts of me. I can't understand myself. I swear I wish I was different."

Tears were running down his cheeks as he dropped into a chair and covered his face with his hands. She could not help a feeling of pity that filled her heart.

"Ah'm going to church. Ah don't know whar from dere," she said simply turning away to go upstairs.

"Now, I've lost you forever, Ruth. I can't go on livin' knowin' that. Before God I can't," William's voice sounded so hopeless and desperate it frightened her, as she walked up the stairs. When she returned to the room a moment later, Marshall Bailey was again at the gate talking to William, who sat on the steps of the porch. As she came out, he was saying:

"Yas siree. We caught that fellow slick as grease over dar by the school house. My man's

done took 'im to jail and locked him up by now till
they can send from Macon to fetch 'im.   Thanks
to you, Ruth," he added, smiling at the stunned girl
standing in the door.

She had not meant to tell the marshall where
Slippery really was and had just said the old school
house at random but he would have been caught any-
way, she reassured herself for Bailey had stationed
a man over there before he came to the house.

To William the news was a blow.   More than
anything else he wanted Slippery to escape and never
to come back to Macon again.   Ruth walked past
him and out of the gate but he scarcely saw her.
Fear of what might happen next clutched his heart.

CHAPTER XIX

Several hours later Sara Lou came home, after making Ella's boy comfortable and leaving instructions for his care during the night. When she lighted a lamp in the darkened dining room, an exclamation of surprise fell from her lips, as a ray of light fell upon William crouched down in a large horse-hair rocking chair.

"Lan' sakes, William, you sho did scare me. Whut's de matter wid you, sittin' dere in de dark lak you done lost yo' lass friend?" she asked.

"Nothing, Ma," William replied, straightening himself up.

"Yes, dere is. You can't fool yo' ole Ma. Youse worried." Seating herself beside him, she drew his head to her shoulder and patted it tenderly.

His eyes filled with tears. He would have given his life to have been able to tell her everything but he was afraid. She would not understand and he would thereby cause her sorrow and anxiety. Instead he answered, gaining a small amount of his usual cool composure.

"It ain't nuthin' much Ma, only Slippery's got hisself in trouble. He killed a man in Macon and they've got him in jail."

"De Lawd!" his mother whispered shocked.

"I guess I'm jes' sap' enough to feel sorry for him—seeing he worked for me in the shop."

"Dat's jes' de Christian spirit in you, William. You jes' kaint help feelin' bad for de pore sinner but uh murderer is bad kaise God says, 'Thou shall

not kill,' so don't you worry 'bout no sinner kaise
dey ain't worth yo' tears."

"That's right, Ma."

"Whar's Ruth?" she asked, looking around the
room.

"She's gone to church. I didn't feel like goin'
after what happened to Slippery."

"Ah guess Ah better go fetch'er home," Sara Lou
decided and hurried in the direction of the church.
As she came in sight of it, she could see the wor-
shippers standing around outside, gossiping. The
services were over. They all greeted her warmly
and inquired why William had not attended the
service. Sara Lou made excuses for him and hur-
ried to where Ruth stood, talking with Aunt Salis-
bury, who had whispered to her during the meet-
ing that she wanted to speak to her outside.

"Heah, Ruth," she had whispered when Ruth
joined her, holding out a small red flannel bag.
"Dis uh good luck charm. Pin it inside yo' dress."

And Ruth had obediently pinned the bag to her
dress and listened while Aunt Salisbury instructed
her to wet it in vinegar every morning. She and
Sara Lou walked home together discussing the
plight Slippery had gotten himself into, Sara Lou
bewailing the fact that it had worried her William
so he couldn't attend church. Ruth listened and
wondered when would she wake up to find her
idol fallen and demolished, and breathed a silent
prayer that it would never happen.

When they reached home, William had gone,
leaving a note that he had caught a late train for
Macon to be there early Monday for school. But
he had really gone to Macon to be on hand when

Slippery was brought in.   He wanted to satisfy himself once more by hearing it from Slippery's lips that he would not be involved.

Monday afternoon he visited the jail and offered to get a lawyer for him but Slippery flatly refused to let him and went on trial a few days later undefended, except for defense given him by the State. He flatly refused to tell anything of his former life, and at the start was handicapped.   The State was bitterly arrayed against the stranger who came from God knows where, to commit a crime within its bounds.   There were many witnesses to the crime, but none could swear Sugar Kid had a weapon.   The razor found near his body went unidentified and could have belonged to any of the two dozen men who were in the room at the time. It did not take long for Slippery to be found guilty of manslaughter and the judge in sentencing him to twenty years in the chain gang, lectured him on how lucky he was not to have drawn a first degree murder sentence.

Ethel Myers, who had been arrested for drunkenness and disorderly conduct, fared better and was let off with a suspended sentence and ordered to leave town at once.

At one stroke William found himself rid of the two people he feared most and made up his mind henceforth to settle down to school and business and live a better life.   For the rest of the term he made greater strides in his studies than ever.

*   *   *

Life in Byron had also taken on greater interest. Sara Lou's outlook on life had changed now that Mr. Gordon was coming home, and she hoped he was going to get Jim out of prison. She was again happy and cheerful as of old, working around the place with a song on her lips and a bright smile on her face.

Ruth had also been made happier than she had been since her father's death by going to work for Mrs. Carmicheil, the wife of the proprietor of the general store. She helped with the housework and cooking each week-end when the four grown daughters of the family came home from Macon, where they attended high school, with a bevy of young friends.

Ruth wanted to divide the dollar and a half she received for her work each week with Sara Lou, but she would not accept it.

"No chile, you buy yuh some clothes," she advised.

Ruth made up her mind she would buy her a present. She could not refuse to accept that. She felt happy and relieved that she would now be away while William visited his mother, returning home every Monday afternoon when he had gone to school.

"Lawd honey, Ah sho does miss you an' Ah hates to think'er you dere slavin' all day Sunday sted'uh tending de services wid me an' William," Sara Lou greeted her when she came over to visit.

"Ah don't mind An' Sara 'sides it's 'bout time Ah earned my keep stead'uh livin' on you," Ruth smiled.

It wouldn't last long anyway, she thought, and tried to plan some way she could try and get work that would last all summer.

The Spring was with them at last. The green blooming things around them made them feel in accord with the joys of the season. Ruth's steps regained some of the elasticity they had lost.

The first week of April passed and the Monday for the Church Aid meeting that had been so sadly neglected, came around again.

Ruth was busy setting the chairs around in the dining room while Sara Lou supervised Luke's work in the field when looking up she saw Aunt Salisbury standing in the door.

"Lawd yuh sho scared me," she exclaimed laughing. "It was jes' as quiet an' heah Ah looks up an' you'se standin' dere lak uh ghost."

"Dis ain't no time for sounds nor words nuther, Ruth," Aunt Salisbury said grimly. "Ah done had uh bad dream las' night—on dat means death to dis house so Ah done fetched yuh dis charm to keep bad dreams from comin' true." And Aunt Salisbury solemnly held out the little bag which Ruth took grimly and promised to bury it under the front steps as directed. The shriveled-up old woman hobbled away grumbling to herself, her once tall, bony figure bent almost double, her jet-black face hardly visible beneath the numerous bandannas wrapped around her head.

The church aid sisters arrived early, anxious to hear if An' Sara had any news of interest to tell them, and were soon laughing and gossiping like a group of children. Sara Lou laughed and joked as she had before the dark days of Jim's imprisonment.

"Chillun," she said, "we jes' gotta live closer to de Lawd den we'se been livin'. Ah jes' keeps uh prayin' dat my boy'll git out uh dat prison an' Ah'm sho God goin'ter answer my prayer in his own time."

"Well, An' Sara, wid faith lak youse, God jes' gotta heah yuh," Sally Ann agreed.

"An it'ud pay us all to have mo' faith den we'se got," Martha Green said, casting a meaning look in Sally's direction.

"Dere yuh go, Martha, sweepin' fo' somebody else's door when de dirt is knee deep 'fo yo' own," Sally came back hotly.

"Now den sisters, less don't have no cross words," Sara Lou begged.

"You sho is right, An' Sara," Sadie Smith approved, looking with disgust at the two women, who could never be together long without a battle of words.

Ella Brown read the minutes of the last meeting and plans were discussed for the coming big camp meeting to be held at Calvary Church in which Sara Lou was again taking an active part. Long after the meeting was over and the women had gone home to attend to their many duties, Sara Lou sat alone thinking, wondering whether Owen Gordon's homecoming would really mean her boy's release from prison. He had been very good to her in the past years, sharing with her a secret she had never divulged to any other living soul. Through all the years of her life he had befriended her but after all, time and his trip might have changed him. At any rate, she made up her mind she would pray and hope and wait, and let the future take care of itself.

CHAPTER XX

All day Monday in Macon a steady downpour of misty rain had fallen. By afternoon the streets were covered with soft sticky mud. The air was close and murky.

William had spent a restless night and felt nervous and doubtful of the outcome of his examinations that were to begin that day. Contrary to his usual custom, he was bewildered and confused on the very subjects that during the term he had been so sure of. The buzz of voices irritated him and kept his mind wandering from his books. He had tried to study at home but his mother's information about Owen Gordon's return had upset him. School would be closing soon, and if Jim really was pardoned and returned to the farm, all the humiliation he felt he had endured before, would be heaped upon him again. He longed to get away from it all to some place where he could live his life like he pleased and not with his mother's expectant eyes upon him. He didn't want to be a preacher anyway, he decided. Thoughts of Slippery in the same prison with Jim and Ruth's reproachful eyes kept annoying him.

The teacher called his name several times before he realized he was again holding up the class, but at last the long April day was over. School was dismissed. He passed out of the room hardly seeing the smiling faces around him. Their cheery goodbyes were answered with an absent grunt.

He wanted to be alone. He hurried to the shop, forgetting that on the Saturday before he left for Byron, Cotton Eye had said:

"William, yuh don't know much 'bout dis kind 'uh work. An' even if yuh did, youse too busy in school to do it so why don't yuh leave me help you? Ah ain't got no job an' no place to stay an' if yuh lemme stay heah an' gimme 'nough to feed me, Ah'll take care uh dis place for yuh. Whut yuh say?"

And thinking it a good idea, he had consented, glad to be rid of the work he disliked.

Cotton Eye moved in and with him most of the gang from over at Daddy Jenks' whose place the law had closed because of Sugar Kid's murder. His back room had immediately been turned into a gambling joint. He profited by the few pennies cut from the games but he had promised himself he would not play. Gambling had already cost him too much trouble.

For several weeks things had been bad for him. Very little work came to the shop, and at home it was even worse. The money received from the cotton crop had been spent. The place had become run down and fences needed fixing. Nothing was the same as when Jim was there. His mother had not complained, but he knew by the scarcity of food she placed on the table, things were almost desperate.

As he stepped into the open door of the shop, his hat pulled low upon his eyes, the odor of frying bacon reminded him that he had not eaten all day.

"Come on in, boy, yuh jes' in time for dinner," Cotton Eye called.

He stood in the door uncertain.

"Stick yo' feet under de table an' try some uh dese taters an' fried bacon."

"I don't b'lieve I want anything to eat, Cotton Eye," he answered, not wanting Cotton Eye to know how hungry and miserable he felt.

"Say whut's de mattuh wid you anyhow, William? Yuh sho is in de dumps."

"There's nothing wrong with me. I'm just anxious about my examinations."

"Yeah, dat's whut comes uh folks tryin' to learn all dere is in books. It jes' causes yuh double worry. Look'er me. Ah jes' takes things easy. Ain't got uh care in de world. Jes' come day—go day."

"I wish I was like that, Cotton, but there's always something insider me planning and planning. I jes' can't help it."

"Well folks don't git nowhar plannin'. De plans allers goes wrong. Ah'm jes' gointer take it easy an' let life take care uh me. Come on sit down an' eat. Whut yuh needs is vittels."

William drew a box to the table and ate the hot food with relish, washing it down with a strong cup of black coffee. After the meal, the dirty dishes were stuck away in a pan and a game of cards started, as the gang one by one dropped in and sprawled around on boxes and broken chairs, smoking and talking.

For a while William looked on. Then put on his coat and left the shop, saying to Cotton Eye, as he walked out of the door:

"I won't be back today. I've got some studying to do at home."

"Sho is too bad dat boy ain't white. It beats all

how he kin put on airs when he gits ready," Red Shirt commented, as he walked away.

"Dat's de trouble.   He ain't nuther one thing nor de other an' he's always 'twix' an' between in his mind.   Jes' studyin' an' plannin' to 'stonish de world some day wid his learnin' an' sometime wantin' to give it all up an' jes' be nacherel.   Dat's how he 'pears to me," Snake declared with a shake of his bullet-shaped head.

Cotton Eye looked up from the hand he was laboriously trying to make win him a few pennies.   He was proud of the fact that he was the only one of the boys that knew William's history and said:

"It's dat boy's Ma dat keeps him all upsot wantin' him to be uh preacher an' him not wantin' to be kaise it jes' ain't in 'im but dat's de way wid de whole family.   Dey allers wanted to be somethin' dey wasn't.   Den at'ter dey all had done borned half white bastards, dey'd marry some preacher man an' put on mo' airs den de law allows.   His grandma done it an' den his ma followed suit.   Dey's uh mess."

"Who's dis man Gordon whut William's brother Jim is in de gang for robbin'?" Snake asked.

"He's de finest white man whut ever lived.   He sho is done lots for An' Sara, William's Ma. 'Course de folks says dat his son was William's Pa. Ah don't know nothin' 'bout dat but Ah does know he mighty good to her," Cotton Eye explained.

"Dere's somethin' funny 'bout de whole thing," Snake remarked.

Cotton Eye turned to look up and down at Snake, who was seated behind him before he replied: "You bet yo' life dere is.   But don't yuh try to figure it out kaise it's way over us nigguh's heads an' al'lers will be."

Conversation turned to other subjects as the boys played on, and William sat at Sissy's house trying to work out some of his most difficult problems. It was near midnight when Sissy and her latest man friend came home much the worse for moonshine. Entering she spied William deeply absorbed in his studies.

"See dere, whut smart folks Ah'se got," she said turning to her companion.

"Dere ain't nothin' smart 'bout folks worryin' dey heads night an' day wid uh pile uh books. Ah calls dat dumb. When deys smart dey does lak Ah does—leave dem books for de white folks to worry over," he grinned.

William laughed and began gathering up his books. Sissy's men were a joke with him. They lasted as long as they pleased her fancy. When she tired of them, they were kicked out and she was free to choose another. As she often remarked, "They fit like a loose garment." William looked at her standing in the door unsteadily, her tall angular form filling the doorway, her straight features and high cheek bones set in a face of rich brown, her straight long black hair wound in a knot at the nape of her neck, making her look more Indian than negress which fitted her heathen and utter disregard for principle.

Swaying over to his side, she placed her hand affectionately on his arm, and asked:

"Does yuh want me to fix yuh some vittels, William?"

"No, Sissy. I think I'll go to bed. I'm not hungry," he answered, starting to his room.

"Dat's right, boy. Stop bustin' yo' head open wid dem books," her man advised.

"Thanks I will," William replied, closing the door behind him.

Until late that night he could hear Sissy and her man arguing about his learning. Finally all was quiet, and he slept.

When he awoke Sissy had cooked breakfast and was waiting for him to come to eat. As they were seated at the table, she talked of the good time she had had the night before.

"Lawd, dat man sho is de limit when it comes to makin' uh body laugh," she chuckled.

"He's a brand new one, ain't he, Sissy?" William asked.

"He's kind uh new. Ah had him 'bout three weeks now but Ah b'lieve he's awrite. Ah might settle down to jes' him ef'fen he does good as he been doin'," she answered thoughtfully.

"That will be big news," William laughed.

"Sho will but ef'fen he carries on any, dere's mo' whar he comed from an' Ah'm de gal whut'll send him on his way."

"Well, let's hope you won't have to," William said, rising and hurrying off to school, feeling better than he had for several days.

The examinations did not prove such a problem after all and William hurried to the shop after school, feeling that his papers would bring good marks. Cotton Eye met him outside the door of the shop, where he had been eagerly watching for him.

"William, ole man Hopkins from out Byron done been heah lookin' for yuh. He say yo' folks done say for you to come home at once," he greeted.

"How come?" William asked anxiously.

"Ah don't know. He gone to de store to git some seed and say for yuh to be ready byance de time he gits back."

"How long ago was he here?"

"Not so long. While you'se waitin' come on in an' eat."

"No thanks. I'm too worried now for anything. Ma may be sick."

"Don't git all excited. It ain't nothin' serious. Ah don't b'lieve. Dere he comes now," Cotton Eye exclaimed, as a wagon with a bent form came in sight.

Old man Hopkins, his dried up brown face looking more like a mummy than a human being, stopped at the curb and William rushed forward.

"Is dere anything wrong with Ma?" he asked eagerly.

"Well, dere is an' den agin, dere ain't. Dat is 'cordin' to how yuh looks at it."

"Why does she want me to come home, Uncle Hiram?" William persisted.

"Yuh bettuh come on out dere an' see. Git in. My ole 'oman done tole me to fetch her uh box uh railroad snuff. Ah'm gonna git it, den Ah'll be ready," Hiram Hopkins stated, starting to climb down from the wagon.

"Wait'er minute. I'll get it for you," William interposed quickly. "You'll take too long," and William bought the snuff in the little dingy grocery store near his shop and climbed into the wagon.

All the way to Byron he tried to get information
from Hiram as to why he had been sent for so hur-
riedly but each time he evaded the subject, and Wil-
liam bade him goodbye at his gate as much in the
dark as when he left Macon.

William rushed into the house. There was no
one downstairs but at the head of the stairs he was
met by Ruth coming out of his mother's room, her
eyes red with weeping. He grasped her arm
anxiously.

"What's the matter with Ma?" he asked, a fright-
ened sob catching in his throat.

She drew him into his room and closed the door
softly before answering.

"An' Sara is mighty sick, William. Doctor
Clarke jes' left an' he say he gonna be back toreck-
ly," she explained between sobs.

"What's the matter with her, Ruth?"

"Well, day 'fore yistiddy she was out tryin' to fix
de fence 'round back uh de field an' she gits all tired
an' worn out. Den she 'sides she'ud walk down to
de post office to see if dere was any mo' mail from
Mr. Gordon. Ah begged her not to go kaise uh
storm was comin' up but she went anyhow, an'
comin' back, she got wringin' wet. Ah tried to git
her to take off her wet clothes but right den some-
body comed by an' sayd dat Deacon Simmons was
dyin', an' she lites right out an' stays wid him on-
tell almost midnight in dem wet clothes, an' when
she comed home, de chills set in an' dis morning she
was out'er her head wid fever."

"Oh Lawd!" William groaned.

"Doctor Clarke sayd if she was strong lak she

use'ter be, dere wouldn't be much danger but she done grieved so inside an' ain't eat right in so long, he 'fraid it's serious. She's restin' right now. He gived her something to keep her quiet."

But William was gone. He stood looking down on his mother, who in her delirium, tossed and called his name. All through the long night he sat motionless, moving only when some of the neighbors asked him to so that they could attend the sick woman.

Doctor Clarke had returned and found her worse, her fever rising rapidly, and held out scant hope to the distracted man who, as he sat and watched at his mother's bedside, blamed himself for her illness. His lies and sins had brought about her illness and might cause her death. Remorse ate at his heart. He had sent Jim away to prison—Jim, who slaved about the place, saving her steps and worry. A battle raged within him. A silent prayer trembled upon his lips, asking God to spare her life. Repentance filled his soul, as he pleaded with the Lord for a chance to right the wrong he had done. He felt sick and ashamed of the past. If she lived, he would tell her all and on his knees beg forgiveness—he promised himself. Quietly he slipped from the room just after midnight, and wandered into the dark, silent woods beyond the farm. Driven relentlessly on and on by the tumult of black despair that engulfed his wretched soul.

Early the next morning Ella's husband, Jerimah and the minister found him on his knees, his body bent double until his head rested upon the damp ground, moaning and praying, as tears streamed down his cheeks. They lifted him to his feet and led him back to the house, up to his room, where he lay all morning. The soft voices of the church aid sisters' songs finally brought soothing sleep to his tortured brain.

CHAPTER XXI

Six months of long, hard, drab days of toil in sun and rain passed slowly for Jim, shut away from the things he had always loved.

May, the most beautiful month of the year, brought little cheer to the boy, who had lived the happy-go-lucky outdoor life of the farm. Watching flowers, birds and green things grow and breathing in the fresh fragrant air of the flat fertile fields had been his very life. Came times when he felt he could not endure another day, the torture of the close smelly prison, the grumbling, grouchy companions that surrounded him, but each morning found him in his usual place ready to start another day of work and struggle.

Slippery's incarceration had not surprised him. He wondered how he had escaped as long as he had. He had never liked Slippery and had resented his visits to his home, and the thought of having to work day by day beside the man he felt sure was the cause of his imprisonment, maddened him. Not that he altogether blamed Slippery. William had taken him in, sick and penniless, for just the purpose he had later used him for.

As day after day they worked along the road, a feeling of pity filled his heart for the man, who was dying with consumption. Sometimes he was hardly able to move from place to place, but was driven on by the guards who disliked his stubborn, sullen ways.

Jim tried to ease over to him and help in some way to lighten his work but the guard checked him and sent him to the further side of the road.

"Hey, you lazy red nigger, get to work and quit stalling," Jim heard the guard call to Slippery as he moved away. Looking back, he saw Slippery knocked to the ground.

"Now Carter, you kin get him 'way from heah," the guard called.

A half hour later, Slippery opened his eyes. Jim was kneeling beside him, bathing his head. He looked up stunned.

"How's yuh feelin' now, Slippery?" Jim asked kindly.

"Ah'm awrite," he answered gruffly turning his head away.

That night Jim lay awake thinking of the day of horror that had just passed. It made his blood boil to think anyone could so cruelly strike a dying man. He was puzzled as to why Slippery had taken the attitude he had towards him. He seemed friendly with all the other prisoners, but he scarcely spoke to him and tried to avoid him at every turn. He fell asleep thinking of his mother and Ruth and dreamed that Slippery and William with long whips, one on each arm, were chasing him towards a deep ravine filled with long, wriggling snakes. He awoke, weak and perspiring.

It was Sunday and many visitors would visit the prison. Almost everyone would have a relative or friend who would call except Slippery. No one during the few months he had been in prison had come to see him. William had made one joint visit to him and Jim—but that was all. Slippery did not seem to care, and as he often expressed himself, "Ah'se glad dere ain't nobody to come heah moanin' over me.   Dey'd make me sick'er den Ah ez."

"But ain't you got no folks uh tall?" someone had asked.

"None dat knows whar Ah is or would miss me if Ah was planted," he answered with no trace of regret in his voice.

Jim wondered as he glanced at him, lying on his bunk gasping for breath whether there had ever been anyone who had cared for him.   The guard brought his reveries to an end.   His visitors had arrived.   He rose quickly and followed him to the room where they were waiting.   He noted with a sinking heart that his mother was not with Ruth and the preacher, Reverend Hooper.

"Ah'm sorry, Jim, but An' Sara ain't comin'. She ain't feelin' so well," Ruth explained. "William done stayed home wid'er so de Rev. heah comed 'long wid me."

"Howdee Jim," Reverend Hooper greeted cheerily.

"Ah'm all right, Rev.   It was mighty good 'er you to come out heah wid Ruth but Ah hopes Ma ain't serious," he continued, turning to Ruth, who avoided his eyes as she answered.

"No, she's jes' feelin' kind uh down, but Ah got good news for yuh, Jim.   She done hearn from Mr. Gordon an' he'll be home soon an' goin'ter git you out uh heah."

"Dat's good news, sho 'nough.   Ef'fen he jes' don't b'lieve Ah stole dat money an' tried to steal his jewelry," Jim remarked hopelessly.

"You knows Mr. Gordon knows you bettah den

dat an' he's de smartest lawyer dat ever was.   An'
Sara says dat he kin git yuh right out," Ruth replied
earnestly.

"Now ain't dat somethin' to be thankful for,
Jim?" Reverend Hooper asked.

"Yeah, it sho' is, but Ah ain't gointer git too
thankful ontell it done happens," Jim insisted.

For the rest of the visit Ruth talked cheerfully
about the farm and related the gossip of the settle-
ment, careful to make no mention of William. Ella
had a new baby girl, and one of the Jones' girls had
gotten into trouble, and the man had refused to
marry her.

They laughed heartily, at the picture she vividly
portrayed of the girl's father roaming around with
his double barrel shot gun under his arm, looking
for the guilty man to make him marry her.

Sally Ann had married the Reverend Hanson,
who pastored a church in a small village a few
miles from Byron and had gone there to live, re-
turning every few days to visit Martha Green and
have their usual verbal battle.

For the first time since his imprisonment Jim
laughed and talked unrestrainedly, and enjoyed
their visit which came to an end too soon. Ruth
was gone before he realized it. He had had no op-
portunity to ask her how she and William were get-
ting along or if she had wanted to break off their
engagement, as William had led him to think.

William had always gotten what he wanted in
the past, he thought bitterly, and there was no doubt
he had succeeded in getting Ruth's consent to marry
him.

A short time later, as he sat on the side of his

bunk thinking of the happy times he and Ruth had
enjoyed at home, one of the guards called him to
assist in moving Slippery, who had grown worse, to
another part of the camp. After they had made
him comfortable and Jim turned to go, Slippery
stirred and opened his eyes. He asked in a voice
scarcely louder than a whisper.

"Will you pray for me, Jim?"

"Ef'fen Mr. Myers say Ah kin. Ah'll do my
best," Jim replied, turning to the guard standing
nearby.

"Go uh head, Jim. Prayers ain't goin'ter hurt
him nohow, Ah reckon," the guard consented.

And Jim, frightened and bewildered, knelt be-
side the cot, and for the first time in his life, prayed
aloud. The guard had walked to the other side of
the room, and stood waiting to take Jim back to
his side of the prison. As he started to rise, Slip-
pery touched his arm and Jim leaned closer to hear
what he wanted to say.

"Ah'm goin'ter git you out 'uh heah, Jim. Me
an' William done dat stealin' an' Ah'm goin'ter tell
'um so," he whispered.

"For God's sake, don't do it, Slippery. It'ud
kill Ma. Promise me yuh won't never tell," Jim
pleaded, glancing fugitively to where the guard
stood looking out of the window.

Slippery looked up at him unable to understand
his wanting to turn down a chance of getting out of
prison. Slowly, with great effort, he tried to raise
himself. He would call the guard and tell him any-
way. He opened his mouth to speak, but a long
stream of blood gushed forth. He fell back, weak
and exhausted.

Jim was hustled quickly back to his place, and through the long night he lay awake, his heart filled with the fear of Slippery's reviving and telling the guard the story of his brother's guilt—the revelation of which would bring new sorrow to his mother.

* * *

Sara Lou was again able to come downstairs and watch Luke work in the field, planting and caring for the farm, but for two weeks she had hung between life and death. William, his ambitions and struggles forgotten, had scarcely left her bedside, turning over in his mind plans of the many ways he intended telling her the sins he had committed, which had brought sorrow to their home and begging her forgiveness so that he could start all over with a clear conscience to live a better life. As days went by, he put it off until she was entirely recovered.

Sara Lou's thoughts were as usual for his welfare.

"Lawd, William, yuh ain't goin'ter finish school dis year effen yuh don't git back to Macon," she moaned.

"I ain't worryin' 'bout school, Ma, long as you needs me," he assured her, patting her shoulder tenderly.

Several days later he left for Macon, determined when he next visited home, he would without hesitation tell her everything. During the few weeks before commencement, he worked hard, and seldom went near Daddy Jenks' or saw the old gang. Each week, he received a letter from Ethel, but they went unanswered. He was through with all of that! She was out of his life forever, he told himself.

But in that particular, he was mistaken, for Ethel's return to Chicago had been met with little enthusiasm from her brother, a lawyer and one of the city's most respected citizens. Ethel had disgraced him in the past, and he did not try to hide his annoyance at her return to disgrace him again, and told her so in no gentle manner. For a while, the girl was on her guard and tried to do right but years of wild living and her love for liquor soon drew her back to her old South side haunts and before a month had passed, she was in jail again. Her brother paid her fine and demanded that she leave Chicago but Ethel, older and wiser, made her demands also that he send her money each week, if he wanted her to stay away from Chicago. In the end, he agreed and Ethel boarded a train for Atlanta deciding that after all, her trip had done some good. William had not written her, but she was determined that being in Atlanta where he would be attending school during the next winter, she would make him renew his friendship with her.

On reaching Atlanta, she wrote him again, but receiving no answer from her letter, she became blue and disappointed, and went on one of her prolonged sprees, laying for days in a drunken stupor. A thought formed in her mind. It would be good to steal into Macon and demand a show down with him, and she boarded a train immediately for Macon.

Daddy Jenks, who was again running his place

at full swing, was surprised when she swaggered in
that night.

"Look'er heah gal, yuh sho' is doing uh danger-
ous thing comin' back heah when de white folks done
tole yuh to stay 'way," he said.

"But dey ain't goin'ter know Ah'se back less'en
some uh you nigguhs tell 'em," Ethel sneered.

"Far as Ah'm concerned, dey ain't goin'ter know
but Ah kain't swear for de rest uh de boys dat hangs
out heah," Daddy assured her.

But she got her old room back and her meals sent
to her room each day. William heard of her return
with grave misgivings. He had sincerely hoped she
had passed out of his life forever. Her return
threatened to again ensnare him into the life he was
trying to put behind him.

He stayed away from Daddy Jenks, and even his
own shop, but Ethel, who had been good to Sissy
when she was laid up badly cut, became a welcome
visitor at her home and little by little wormed her
way back into William's life.

As soon as school closed, he hurried to Byron,
promising to run into town to see her often—a
promise he failed to keep so Ethel ranted to Daddy
Jenks of how she would get even with William for
all she had suffered through their sordid love affair.

"Gal, why don't yuh leave dat boy uh alone? He
don't want to be mixed up wid you, nohow," was all
the consolation he gave her.

"He done took uh mighty long time to find dat
out," Ethel would reply, and for days would drink,
brood and plan.

William had not graduated, as he had hoped.
Due to the many weeks he missed from his studies,

he would have to spend another winter in Macon, but he made up his mind that for the present he would just be a farmer and show his mother he could take care of the place, with Luke's help. He threw himself into caring for and building up the farm, which had become a wreck since Jim's imprisonment.

Everybody was busy and more contented than they had been for months. The garden was again doing nicely. Jim's flowers of myriad colors were again blooming and filling the air with their sweet fragrance. Even his old dog Towser showed an agility in accordance with the Spring lightness which belied his eight years of dog life.

Byron was beautiful with its velvet-like green grass in which nestled wild pansies and violets. The smell of young pines filled the air with a clean sweetness, as the busy farmers tilled their soil, stopping in the heat of the day to sprawl beneath the welcome shade of trees.

Sara Lou, a hopeful smile illuminating her face, moved about, her favorite song on her lips. Owen Gordon's expectant return was a ray of light in her troubled life. To her mind, he had only to say the word and Jim would walk out of the chain gang free.

Ruth was again smiling and cheerful and working around the house and in the field from sun up to dusk. Even William's presence did not upset her as it had. She had become accustomed to having him to talk with evenings. When the work was done at night the family sat out on the front porch to blow a spell and sing spirituals again.

A month had passed since Mr. Gordon had written and at times Sara Lou would think with a

sinking heart that perhaps after all, he had decided
to prolong his stay abroad. On occasions when she
passed his plantation, the sight of its dilapidated
condition made her heart sick. The house had been
nailed up, but grass and weeds over-ran the place.

"Po' Mr. Gordon," she would mumble. "He sot
so much store by his orchard. Now look at it—
weeds an' eve'ythin' jes' chokin' dem trees."

Tears would burn her eyes, as she remembered
how her husband, John, and later her son, Jim, had
worked so hard to make his the finest orchard
around the country.

"My Jim would'uh been heah now keepin' dat
place spick an' span ef'fen some low life skunkin'
thief didn't git 'im in prison."

Trudging on, the many kind deeds Owen Gordon
had done for her family and herself would fill her
mind, and her confidence thus restored in his help-
ing Jim to freedom, would make her happy and
content to wait.

She had wanted to visit Jim, but her illness had
left her weak and emaciated. She did not want him
to see her that way as she felt sure it would worry
and upset him. Ruth's trips to the prison always
brought her the news of Jim's cheerfulness, and
with that she had to be content.

William had accompanied Ruth on her last visit
there and had returned home silent and morose.
His mother wondered what had happened to worry
him, but William had told her nothing. He had
long ago made up his mind that his confessing
to her the many slips he had made, during his
two years in Macon could not do any good, and
would only worry her. The information he re-

ceived at the prison concerning Slippery's condition frightened him. For days the sick man had laid in a coma, but if at any time he revived, William felt sure he would tell the truth about the robbery and he would be made to suffer for his deed after all. He fervently prayed that Slippery would die before regaining consciousness and trembled every time he saw Marshall Bailey approaching the house. His mother noticed his agitation, but said nothing, trying in every way to dispell whatever there was worrying him with thoughtful kindness, which like coals of fire, burned into his soul.

CHAPTER XXII

It was a beautiful morning early in June when Owen Gordon stepped from the pullman car to the station platform in Macon. Macon had not changed much during the year he had spent abroad. After all, it was good to be home again.

He removed his light felt hat and ran his hand slowly over his fast, thinning gray hair that had once been a luxuriant dark brown. His face round and smooth, showed little signs of his sixty odd years.

An anxious porter ran forward to assist him with his bags. Yes, it was the same old darky, who had carried his bags when he went away. With a merry twinkle in his eyes he pressed a dollar bill into his wrinkled black hand. Old Sam nearly dropped the bags when he saw the bill and looking up to see who the liberal white man was, who could afford to give him a whole dollar, he recognized Owen Gordon.

"Lawdy mussy, if it ain't Mr. Gordon hisseff!" he exclaimed. "Ah sho is glad to see yuh, boss."

"Glad to see me or the bill, Sam?"

"No, suh! Ah's dat glad to see yuh—ah 'clare Ah is."

"All right, Sam. See how quickly you can get me a taxi then," Gordon smiled.

"Yess suh. Thank yuh, suh. Ah gits one 'fo yuh kin say scat," Sam replied, gesticulating wildly to a passing taxi.

Owen Gordon leaned back meditatively, as he rode to one of the Macon's prominent hotels. There was business he would have to attend to before going out to Byron.

The year he had spent in Europe passed pleasantly through his mind. He had been sick and almost hopeless during the few days he had spent in New York consulting specialists about the ailment that had worried him for years. They had advised a trip abroad and complete rest, and he had continued his journey. His sojourn in London had lasted only long enough to attend to business, and to leave strict orders with his solicitors that no mail from the United States be forwarded to him. He wanted to be free to wander and rest. He smiled as he thought of the peaceful weeks spent in Northern France followed by a month in Switzerland—happy weeks near the Alps, and the ideal spot he had finally found in Southern Italy, where the climate and quiet peace had restored his health and peace of mind. He had spent the greater part of the year there, eating plain, wholesome food, dressing simply and spending most of his time out-of-doors.

His physician had finally pronounced him cured, and he had taken the first boat home, glad to be back in the quiet of his Byron home, where his plans to live peacefully with Sara Lou to take care of his house and Jim Carter to look after his orchard, stretched before him pleasantly.

On reaching London, Sara Lou's letter had given him quite a shock. There was no doubt in his mind of Jim's innocence and that he had been made the victim of some smart criminal. He made up his mind that Jim would at least get another chance to prove his innocence, as he would do all he could to have the guilty party brought to justice.

At his hotel he unexpectedly ran into Richard Hayden, an old friend and associate.

"Gordon, you're the very man I've been wanting to see. When did you get in town?" the lawyer asked in greeting.

"Just arrived this morning, Hayden."

"I guess you've heard about the little affair out at your place?"

"Yes, Sara Lou wrote me. Her boy's in prison."

"That's what I want to talk with you about, Owen. That boy got the rawest deal I've ever seen. I defended him and Judge Graham convicted him in his mind before a witness was heard. Why, the boy knows no more about that money being stolen than I do. I thought at first he was trying to shield somebody but I found out I was wrong. He's been railroaded to the chain gang simply because you left him in charge of your place when some of those Byron crackers thought they should have had the job."

Owen Gordon listened attentively to the lawyer's long explanation, his eyes studying the point of his shoes, but his mind drawing a mental picture of the trial that had sent Jim away for five years' hard labor. When he spoke, he had made up his mind as to what would be the best move to make under the circumstances.

"Think I'll be calling on Graham day after tomorrow," he said simply.

Richard Hayden told him all the details of the trial adding his belief that the thief could be found if a plan he had worked out came through as he expected, and before they parted, a meeting a few days later had been arranged.

Owen spent several days quietly at home in Byron. Sara Lou had her hands full trying to set the house to rights as she expressed it, and preparing his meals. They talked a great deal about Jim and Owen made a few round about inquiries concerning William's activities during the past winter. Sara Lou glowed with pleasure, as she told him how hard he had studied, what a wonderful son he was, and her plans for his future.

Then one afternoon, he visited Judge Graham. It was not until after they had dined and talked of old times that Owen mentioned Jim's case and explained his belief of the boy's innocence.

"Innocent, bosh! A jury of twelve men found him guilty, didn't they? And Ah knows he's guilty. It's jes' in niggers to steal," the Judge exploded hotly.

"That's just it, Graham. You tried the boy only looking at it from the standpoint of his color, but I know him. He's as honest as any white man alive! His father before him worked for me twenty years and was as straight as a string. His grandmother, his mother and the whole mess of 'em have always been around my house and they are all honest. I'm gonna get that boy out of the chain gang. He'd never been there had I been home," Owen ended convincingly.

"And if you'd left a decent white man in charge'er your place, there wouldn't have been a robbery," the Judge declared.

"It's my business who I leave in charge of my

place, but I'm gonna find out what you failed to find—who really robbed my safe."

"Go 'er head! Personally, I'm not interested. I ain't no nigger lover an' it don't matter to me what becomes of 'em."

Owen Gordon's eyes flashed angrily, as he turned to the Judge.

"Now you listen to me, Graham, your father and I were partners. He died a real Southern gentleman and out of respect for him, I'll take what you're insinuating, but don't you forget that I am every inch a white man, the same as you are, but unlike you, I want to see everybody get justice. Even if Jim was found in my house with my jewelry in his pocket, the money taken from my safe he had put there, and had he wanted to, he could have kept it. He knew that, and as for that old jewelry, he had had every opportunity to take it for the past four years, had he wanted to. I've owned more niggers than anyone else around here, but I've never been accused of being unjust to 'em or of loving 'em either."

"I'm sorry, Gordon. Maybe I have been too hasty in my words," the Judge apologized.

Memories of indiscretions of his own youth which had somehow never been discovered, passed through his mind and shamed his declarations of hatred of negroes. They parted good friends and he decided that although he would do nothing to help him get Jim pardoned, he would do nothing to hinder it.

A few days later when Gordon again conferred with Hayden he was surprised to find how closely the lawyer had checked up on William's activities right after the robbery.

"You don't suspect William, do you Hayden?" he asked looking at him quickly, a startled expression in his eyes.

Something in his voice brought back to the lawyer's mind bits of gossip he had heard concerning Gordon's son Franklyn at William's birth. He answered cautiously.

"Well no, but a nigger called Slippery that worked around his shop, has since been sent up for murder and I've been checking up on his movements. The night of the robbery he could have easily slipped out to Byron from Spring Valley between the time he was seen in a game there, and returned."

"Maybe you're right, but who is he in the meantime?"

"An all around bad character. He visited the Carter home several times, and I've got a fellow over at the shop now trying to find out something about his past.'

"Who've you got there?"

"They call him Cotton Eye."

"Yes, I know him. He's a slick thief—will steal anything he can lay hands on, was born and raised in Byron. Have him here tomorrow morning and we'll question him," Gordon said in parting.

Early the next morning a frightened Cotton Eye was ushered into the office where Owen Gordon and Hayden sat.

"There ain't nothing against you this time, Cotton Eye. Mr. Hayden and I want some information about this fellow Slippery," Gordon greeted to put him at ease.

"Ah ain't found out nothin' 'bout him 'ceptin' dat he comed from Chicago an' dat his fust name is

Jessie.   A gal named Ethel Myers done tole me
dat," Cotton Eye answered sheepishly.

"That's good.   I've got a friend in Chicago who's
one of the best detectives in the country.   I'll get
him on the wire and in a few days we'll know all
there is to know about this Slippery," Gordon com-
mented.

"By the way, Cotton Eye, where is this Ethel
Myers you spoke of, now?" Lawyer Hayden asked,
turning to Cotton Eye, who was edging towards the
door eager to get away, before Owen Gordon re-
membered.   His last encounter with him had been
in court where he was being tried for stealing one
of his best hogs.

"She puttin' up at Daddy Jenks' when she heah,"
he answered hastily.

"You can go now, Cotton Eye.   Keep your eyes
open and if you find out anything else, let Hayden
or I know," Gordon said dismissing him and press-
ing a five dollar bill into his hand.   He pocketed the
bill and backed, grinning, out of the door.

Their call to Chicago brought plenty of informa-
tion concerning Slippery's checkered past and Law-
yer Hayden and Owen Gordon pinned their hope
of getting Jim out of prison on Slippery's forced
confession, if he really did do the robbery.

A few days later with the information in their
briefcases, they visited the chain gang for an inter-
view with their suspect.   But on arrival, to their
disappointment, they found they were a day too
late.   Slippery had died during the night without
making a statement of any kind that would in any
way help their case.

CHAPTER XXIII

Although Owen Gordon and Lawyer Hayden tried in every way to get Jim's case before the Board of Pardons during the next few months, it was never brought up, and Jim, always a model prisoner, resigned himself to serve his alloted time.

Sara Lou aged rapidly when the realization that Owen Gordon, the best and smartest man on earth to her mind, was powerless before the merciless men who held Jim's freedom in their hands.

William finished school that winter and came home happily displaying his diploma. Sara Lou was happy and to add to her good fortune, Owen Gordon finally got the board to consider Jim's case.

She would not allow herself to hope too much for fear of again being disappointed but went about her work with a constant prayer on her lips for Jim's eventual release.

The Winter had been made miserable for Ruth. William's constant pleas and protestations of love had worried the tenderhearted girl.

Sara Lou had also unwittingly added to her dilemna as afternoons when they sat sewing, she too had added her plea for William.

"Yuh know, Ruth," she had said one evening, "Ah ain't never said nuthin' to you, 'bout my boys seein' dey both loves yuh and Ah loves yuh too, but Ah kind uh scared for my William goin' to dat Atlanta. If he'd up an' marry de wrong kind uh woman it 'ud ruin his life kaise he allers is been kind uh restless an' it'ud break my heart. You is de only purson dat kin save him kaise wid you for his wife, he'ud be settled an' happy."

Ruth had made no answer. Sara Lou's tired eyes filled with tears had touched her heart as William's pleas had never done. She loved her and could not bear the thought of the sorrow that would come into her life if William disappointed her.

That evening she had slipped away to sit under her hickory nut tree and prayed for strength to do the right thing, but as the weeks wore on, her resistance had become weaker until finally to please and comfort his mother, she had promised to marry William before he entered college.

And now with the knowledge of Jim, perhaps being pardoned, and at home again; she wondered how she would ever be able to face him now that she was engaged to William.

But none of their problems worried William. His first scare of Owen Gordon's finding out he had his safe robbed over, he had become his old confident self, had learned much about farming, even taking over Jim's work in the Gordon Orchard, becoming very friendly with—Owen Gordon whom he had always thought disliked him. There had been times when his restless nature had cried out against the monotony of the dull drab life of the farm and times when he had longed for the soft, sensual caresses Ethel had lavished so freely. But he had fought hard against his passions and prayed for strength to overcome them, spending most of his time in church. He had become a senior Deacon, and in the pastor's absence, conducted the services.

It was a late afternoon in June. Sara Lou wiped

her hands on her apron, as she hurried around the house in answer to Gordon's call from the gate.

"I just got a letter from Hayden, Sara," he greeted, "and he says the Board has signed Jim's pardon."

"Lawdy, Mr. Gordon, my prayers done been answered! Oh my Lawd!" she cried, tears of joy running down her cheeks.

"Well, you can look for him any day now," he called; riding away quickly, keenly touched by her overwhelming joy.

The news spread over Byron by night causing much joy among Sara Lou's friends. A special meeting of thanksgiving at the Calvary Church was called for Sunday, and everybody in the little village turned out to show their sympathy for the best loved family among them—singing, praying and shouting the whole afternoon.

"We sho' is got tuh thank God, for dis blessing," Martha Green commented as she and Sally Ann, who was visiting her, walked home from the meeting.

"Yeah, an' we got to thank dat Mr. Gordon some too," Sally Ann remarked dryly.

"Dat's jes' lak yuh, Sally Ann, tryin' to take some uh de credit from de Lawd," Martha retorted.

"Ah ain't tryin' to take de credit from God, but dat's uh white man and de way he done worked to git Jim out, yuh'uh thought he was his blood kin," Sally came back.

"You aught'er know kaise God ain't had nothin' to do wid you gittin' dat Reverend Hanson for yo' husband. Dat was An' Salisbury's mojo' dat you used on him," Martha laughed.

"Ah ain't used no mojo but whut God gine me. It's too bad you don't try usin' some to git Slack Henderson dat's been hangin' 'roun' yuh for de lass six years," Sally hinted.

Aunt Salisbury's overtaking them, ended what would have been a heated argument and the conversation turned to other things, for they all feared Aunt Salisbury whose charms were supposed to make snakes and lizards crawl about under the skin of her victims often causing their death.

Ruth still loved Jim and realized it would be difficult for her to face him. She was unhappy as the days passed, watching Sara Lou working around the house preparing little things for Jim's return. She realized her only escape from the situation she found herself facing would be to run away. Mrs. Carmicheil had asked her to go with the family to Valdosta. She would go. It would only be for a few months, but it would afford her time to think clearly away from the overwhelming influence of William's love-making.

But trouble was brewing for William from another source. Ethel, who had seen him seldom since his graduation, had not given up hopes of having him again as her lover. She was now living in Atlanta and had managed trips to Macon where he had at times joined her for a few days. It was on one of these trips he told her of his approaching marriage and firmly dismissed her from his life, but it was not her idea to let it remain so. She wrote him again and again, begging him to come to Macon,

but her letters remained unanswered. He did not
show up.

After a night of hard drinking, she borrowed
Daddy Jenks' car and with Kongo driving, set out
for Byron. During the seventeen miles ride, she
drank frequently from the flask of corn whiskey she
carried, plying Kongo with big drinks at intervals.
Late that afternoon the car was parked at the back
of the Carter cotton field.

William's mother and Ruth had gone to spend
the afternoon with Ella and William, left alone,
planned a quiet few hours' reading. Comfortably
seating himself in a large chair with his book rest-
ing on his knees, his thoughts drifted to the events
of the past few years.

His mother standing at the fork of the road, as
if uncertain about leaving him alone, brought an
indulgent smile to his lips.

"Poor Ma. She makes me feel like a baby the
way she worries and fusses over me," he mused
sinking into the depths of his chair and brushing an
inquisitive fly away from his face.

The cool afternoon breeze enveloped him like a
curtain. Far out in the field he could hear the faint
droning of bees and a bird's shrill call. The tall
stalks of corn growing near the house waved to him
lazily. A drowsy feeling stole over him, his eyelids
felt like iron pressing down—down. His hands re-
laxed and the book slid to the floor as he dozed.
He had slept almost an hour when a hand shaking
him and a persistent voice calling his name, awak-
ened him. He opened his eyes slowly and rubbed
them in an effort to dispel the drowsiness that clung

to them, making it hard to realize that Ethel, who stood looking down upon him, was not an unpleasant dream.

"Yeah, it's me in de flesh an' not uh ghost," she said stepping back unsteadily.

"What're you doin' here, Ethel?" William asked realizing that she was drunk, and would be hard to handle in that condition.

"Ah'm heah cause Ah'm fool 'nough to still love you and wanted to see you," she answered shortly.

"But I asked you never to come to my home," William said angrily.

"Ah know yuh did but ah ain't payin' dat no 'tention," Ethel laughed harshly.

"Now that you're here, what do you want?"

"Ah want you to go to Macon wid me."

"And I say I'm not going."

"Well, in dat case, Ah'll stay rite heah an' meet you' Ma an' dat country wench, you goin' ter marry an' tell 'em 'bout us an' lots'uh other things yuh might not want 'em to hear."

"You can't scare me, Ethel, into doing anything I don't want to do. You should know that so get outer here this minute," William retorted, advancing threateningly towards her.

Ethel threw her head back and laughed heartily, and when her laughter died, said coolly:

"Ah ain't goin' ter budge uh God damn step less'en you go wid me, William, an' when Ah gits through tellin' yo' folks whut Ah knows 'bout you, dey'll drive you out lak uh dog—you damn gamblin', lying, cheatin', yaller bastard."

Her voice rose higher and higher as anger and

whiskey swayed her emotions, frightening William to the extent that he would have done anything—even murder to get her away from his home. He decided there was nothing to do but go with her, if only a short distance from the house, and get rid of her and come back. Placing his hand on her arm, he said calmly:

"There's no need'er carryin' on like that, Ethel. I'll go to Macon with you. Wait till I leave a note for Ma."

A few moments later, they were seated in the car speeding towards Macon. William seated in the back of the car, looked on in disgust as Ethel reached under the seat, drew out a pint of corn liquor, placed it to her lips, and took a big drink, leaning back crazily, passing the bottle to Kongo, who drank and grinned up at her. Then leaning low over the wheel, he let the car out to its limit—faster and faster they raced over the smoothed red clay road. The car swerving crazily from side to side, at times the wheels hung dangerously over the edge of the narrow road, threatening to topple over into the deep ditches dug on either sides.

Once they miraculously missed colliding with a passing truck, and a few yards further missed by inches running over a low stone wall on a bridge built over a narrow stream.

At each narrow escape, Ethel and Kongo laughed with glee, but William, seated in the back of the car with his eyes closed—to shut out the sight of his drunken companions and the nearness of death, breathed a prayer. His life of sin and selfishness passed in vivid clearness through his mind; as they raced on through the gathering dusk.

Once he cried out in desperation, "For God's sake, Ethel, don't let Kongo drive so fast!"

And Ethel's voice came back harsh and bitter above the noise of the motor.

"Whut de hell difference does it make? I'm bound to go to hell anyhow some day so why keep de devil waitin'?"

William remained quiet and bewildered, the rest of the journey—as the car with its three strange occupants shot like a streak through the night.

* * *

In the meanwhile, Sara Lou and Ruth had walked in the opposite direction almost to Ella's house, when the older woman stopped and stood for a moment thinking.

"Whut is it, An' Sara?" Ruth asked, noting her troubled expression.

"Ah don't know, Ruth, but Ah jes' feel lak turnin' 'roun' and goin' back. Jes' uh funny feelin' done run up an' down my spine lak dey say yuh feels when uh rabbit done jumped over yo' grave."

"Oh, tain't nothin' An' Sara. Jes' yo' nerves," Ruth assured her.

"All de same Ah'm goin' back. You jes' keep on to Ella's. Maybe me an' William'll come over dere later on to-night."

And Ruth watched her, as she turned and started back towards her home that she had just left. Then walking slowly she continued in the direction of Ella's home.

Sara Lou gathered speed as soon as she was out of sight of Ruth and stumbled along as fast as her legs would carry her, never slackening her pace until she was in sight of her home, where a car parked at her door, attracted her attention. She looked at it quizzically.

"Ah wonder whose car dat is," she murmured walking around it, as Owen Gordon and Marshall Bailey stepped into her open doorway.

"Hello, Sara!" Gordon greeted cheerfully.

"Land sakes, Mr. Gordon! My mind jes' kept tellin' me to turn 'roun' an' come on back home. Now Ah knows why, you was heah lookin' for me," she laughed, hurrying to the house.

"Wal, we thought we'ud surprise you, Sara," the Marshall chuckled, motioning to someone in the house to come out.

"An yuh sho done 'sprised me. Who dat in de house?" Sara Lou questioned, coming up on the porch and trying to look beyond them into the room.

"It's Jim, Sara. I just brought him from Macon. He's been pardoned and is home to stay." Owen Gordon smiled.

"No, Mr. Gordon, you don't mean it," Sara Lou cried, taking Jim, who had rushed from the room into her arms, laughing and crying in her excitement.

"Oh, thank de Lawd! Praise His name!" she sobbed, tears flowing down her cheeks.

"Lawd, Mr. Gordon, Ah sho thanks you wid all my heart. De Lawd knows Ah does! Ah done knowed all de time my poor boy 'ud git out uh dat awful place. Ah knowed God in His own time would make it awrite. Ah jes' kain't help cryin', Ah'se so happy." Her words rushed out in a happy jumble.

"We'll be going, Sara," Owen Gordon said, motioning to the marshall to leave them alone.

"Jim, there'll be lots of work over at my place waiting for you, as soon as you've rested up," he called back.

"Ah'll be ready to start in de morning, Ah ain't uh bit tired," Jim answered.

"Come on in, son, an' let's find Willyum," his mother said tenderly, leading the way into the house and looking out of the back door where she had left William seated on the porch.

"He ain't heah!" she exclaimed disappointed at not finding him. Raising her voice, she called loudly: "Yuh, Willyum! Willyum! Ah guess he done gone for uh walk an' 'ull be back tuhrechly," she explained, as she bustled into the kitchen to fix Jim some food. "Ah know youse jes' starved at'ter eatin' dat prison mess all dat long time. Law sakes, ain't yo' brother Willyum goin'ter be 'sprised to find you home an' Ruth de pore chile goin'ter nigh 'bout die wid happiness. She gone over to Ella's. As Ella's kind'er porely. We all goin'ter be happier den we ever was now dat our trouble is over," she rattled on happily.

Jim sat silent at the table, pleased to be home and happy to hear his mother's voice again. His hand rested on a closed book lying on the table. Taking it up, William's note fell to the floor. It was written on a small scrap of paper, and as Jim reached down to get it, William's handwriting caught his eyes.

"Heah's uh note William done rite," he called to his mother, busy in the kitchen.

At the mention of William's name she appeared promptly in the doorway.

"Whut he say, Jim?" she asked, a shade of anxiety in her voice.

"Dat he been called away on business, dat's all," Jim read.

"Well, Ah feels better knowin' whar he is," she said relieved.

The table soon resembled a feast.

"Dis heah is my Sunday dinner but you kin eat it all an' Ah'll cook more if yuh wants to," she laughed, seating herself opposite Jim who ate sparingly while she talked on and on about William, Ruth and the new preacher; how the members had begun to fight him and wanted him sent away because he had not been able to get his wife to move to Byron. Everything she could think of she related.

"Lawd, Ah jes' bout talk yuh to death, Jim," she laughed.

"Ah enjoys jes' hearin' yo' voice, Ma," Jim replied, a little tremble in his voice. He lowered his head over his plate to keep her from seeing the tears that sprang quickly to his eyes.

"Yeah, but you jes' wait ontell de neighbors heahs youse home, den dey goin'ter rush over heah an' 'tween Sally Ann Peck whut done married dat Reverend Hansom an' Martha Green an' An' Salisbury an' Ella an' de rest uh dem, dey goin'ter talk yo' head off."

The evening passed pleasantly. Ruth did not return from Ella's because a storm came up suddenly, and continued furiously until after midnight. Jim and his mother planned the work to be done around

the farm, and chatted happily, glad the rain had
kept their neighbors away.   Jim wanted to be alone
with her, his first night home, but much of the hap-
piness he had enjoyed was spoiled for him by his
mother unknowingly when she said earnestly just
before they retired:

"Jim, dere's one thing Ah wants to ask yuh to
do for me an' dat is try an' have uh little more pa-
tience wid yo' brother Willyum. He's been kind'er
restless heah uh late, an' Ah don't want him to up
an' leave home lak Ah scared he'll do, if you'all gits
to auguin' lak you did 'fo you went uh way.   Will
yuh promise me you'll try, Jim?"

Jim turned his head aside.   Fear and anger
burned in his eyes which he would not for the world
have had her see. William had sent him to prison.
He had suffered two long years and now his mother
was asking him to kiss the hand that had betrayed
him.   It hurt and crushed him, but he murmured his
promise.

"An' Jim, dere's something else, Ah want to talk
to you 'bout.   It's Ruth.   She done promised to
marry William.   That goin'ter be de best thing dat
could ever happen, kaise William loves her an' she
kin make him happy an' contented.   'Course Ah
knows you thought dat you loved Ruth when yuh'all
was chillun, but you done tole her in dat letter dat
you changed yo' mind 'bout marrying her so now dat
her an' William goin'ter git married, you ain't go-
in'ter do anything to make dem feel bad, is yuh
son?" she pleaded, laying her hand affectionately
on his arm.

Jim shook his head in the negative, not even

daring to answer in words what might expose the anguish her words had caused him. His first night at home turned out more torturous than any he had experienced, during the long, miserable years he had spent in the chain gang.

CHAPTER XXIV

When William reached Macon in spite of Ethel's entreaties that he accompany her up to her room, he went straight out to his cousin Sissy's home and to his old room. Sissy, surprised and worried over his unexpected visit and the strange strained expression on his face, tried to find out what had happened to cause his sudden appearance.

"Is anythin' happened to Cousin Sara?" she asked, as William threw himself across the rickety iron bed in a corner of the room.

"No, Ma's all right," William answered wearily.

"Is Jim done comed home? Ah heard he was to git out dis week."

"He hadn't come home when Ah left, Sissy."

"Well Ah guess Ah'll be on my way. Ah'se goin' to some kind uh shinding wid my new man. Ah sho hopes he's uh good spender caise ain't nothin' makes me as mad as uh cheap skate hangin' round showin' off."

Sissy looked at William expectantly as she talked, but for once the mention of a new man brought no kidding smile to his lips. Wrapping her snuff box in her handkerchief and shoving it into her pocket, she shook her head doubtfully as she closed the door and stood for a moment thinking.

"Dere's somethin' done happened to dat boy," she decided walking slowly away from the house.

Left alone, William lay for several hours looking

up into the rotten rafters that held the leaky roof in place, his thoughts a tumult of jumbled memories.

His wild ride from Byron to Macon with two drunken companions, his nearness to death and disaster, and association with the sordid creature, who would in time complete the wreck he was making of his life, frightened and awakened him. He saw himself as he had never seen himself before, selfish, weak, mercenary—a thief. The thought sickened him. The spoils of his crime had done him no good, but had sent his brother to prison branded for life.

A dry choking sob rose in his throat. What had Jim ever done to deserve the sin he had committed against him, he asked himself. Why had he hated him so unjustly. In his heart he could find no answer. He was just rotten, unworthy of pity or the confidence his mother had in him.

Slowly he slipped to his knees, sobs shaking his shoulders, a torrent of tears smarting and blinding his eyes as a prayer for forgiveness tumbled from his lips.

Throughout the long Spring night he prayed stripping his soul in humble repentance, putting from him all the excuses he had used in life to cover his sins.

It was almost dawn when he arose and stumbled from the house. The sight of the squalor of dirty streets and slovenly kept houses as he stumbled along, reminded him of his own life. Something within him rose in rebellion. Why should he remain shackled to the past? He would get away from it all, and prove the truth of his mother's often repeated remark.

"Son, yuh done comed from good stock, yuh jes'

different from dese folks round heah an' yuh kaint help showin' it."

He would show it—he would get away from everyone he had ever known and work out his own future without even the help of his worshipping mother.

The sun rose hot and glaring. He did not feel it as he trudged wearily on. His throat became dry and parched but he did not slacken his pace until he reached the dense woodland beyond the city limits where he sank to the grass under a tall leafy tree. Afternoon faded into twilight, and darkness with it's relieving coolness ushered in the night as plan after plan passed through his troubled brain.

It was near midnight when he retraced his steps towards the city, but his mind was made up, and a new peace filled his soul.

Early Monday morning he wrote Ruth a long letter expressing his regrets of not being able to see her before she left for Valdosta. One phrase he had written in his letter puzzled her. "It will be a long time before you see me again and when you do, it will not be the William you have always known."

She could find no meaning for his words, it sounded so different from the self-confident boasting William she knew. Of one thing she was glad —he had not asked her to answer his letter so she need not worry about hurting him, as she knew she would some day when she told him definitely she could not keep her promise to marry him.

On his way to mail Ruth's letter, he met a farmer from Byron who told him of Jim's being home. He was glad and thanked God in his heart for settling the only problem that worried him. Now he could go away feeling his mother would be well taken care of. Stopping by the pressing shop he had sold to Cotton Eye, he wrote his mother a long letter in which he told her he would not be home for several months—he was going to find himself a job, and earn enough money to pay his way through college.

Sara Lou beamed with pride when she read his letter, and later that day she showed it to Owen Gordon. "You see, Mister Gordon, Ah done told yuh Willyum was differunt from de rest uh us folks. He goin'ter be uh great preacher some uh dese days," she bragged.

"I certainly hope you're right, Sara," he commented a shade of doubt in his voice.

Jim said nothing when he read the letter but hoped for his mother's sake, William was for once telling the truth.

Later that afternoon when William saw Ethel at Daddy Jenks' place, her contrite pleading that he forgive her for coming to his home and acting as she had that Saturday afternoon, was ignored. "It's all past and forgotten," was the only answer she could get from him, and something in his demeanor frightened and repelled her, so she decided to let his anger cool off before trying to make friends with him again.

Daddy Jenks looked at William with unveiled surprise a short time later when they were seated in Daddy's little private office and he asked: "Daddy, do you know of any public work going on around here?"

"Boy, you ain't strong uh nough to do dat kind uh

work," he countered, "and furthermore you got a bad cough now dat ought'er be tended to."

"Yes, I am, Daddy, and I wants to. I've just been lazy, that's all," William replied with conviction.

"But maybe yuh could git something lak store work whut ain't so hard, Willyum."

"No, Daddy, I don't want no easy job. I wants to sweat, and work so hard, I won't have time to think," William replied earnestly.

Daddy was puzzled. It just did not sound like William. What had come over the boy, he wondered, trying to find an answer in the strange hard face before him.

"Ah don't know 'bout nothing right round heah. Ah'se got uh brother whut works at uh saw mill down in Florida, but dat's hard work an' uh long way from heah," he ventured after a moment's thought.

"I don't care how hard it is, or how far. It's the only thing that'll make a real man of me, Daddy."

"Well Ah can't help sayin' Ah lak yo' spunk. Ah allers thought it was in yuh, boy, an' ef'fen you sho' you means whut youse sayin', Ah'll give yuh uh letter to my brother an' if you ain't got nough money, Ah'll stake yuh. De mill's fifteen miles fuhm Jacksonville, jes' uh flag station but you kin git dere awrite. It's called Johnson's. Ah ust'uh go out dere to meet pay days an' dere's lots uh money in circulation out dere awrite."

"Thanks Daddy, I'll get there all right and I'll send you back your money as soon as I get started," William replied, a relieved look in his eyes. "There's just one thing more I want to ask you, don't tell any one and especially Ethel where I've gone," he added.

"Sho Ah kin keep uh secret—when you want to leave?"

"On the next train," William replied, rising.

"Dat'll be in 'bout uh hour. Ah'll write dat letter an' you kin be on yo' way." Daddy hurried away, and an hour later William was on his way to what he hoped would be a new life. He hated to leave Macon without telling his mother goodbye, but decided it would be best. She would ask questions, and no doubt would want to ask. Owen Gordon to lend her the money he could earn to pay his way through college. All of his life she had made things too easy for him. During the trip he thought of how she and Jim had worked and sacrificed so that he might sit around and take things that he had no right to accept. Her constant worship had made him selfish and robbed him of the manhood he might have had. He could not find it in his heart to blame her for the many slips he had made because of these things, but he felt he must get away and find out for himself if there was any character in his twisted make-up worth fighting for.

After a night spent in the nearby city, he arrived late Tuesday afternoon at the mill.

The double row of one and two room shacks in which the mill hands lived surrounded with tall pines, looked desolate and mean in the waning light of the setting sun, but all around them was life, pulsing and vivid; little children ran shouting to and fro, and busy women sang as they hurried about their clean kitchens getting the evening meal for their men folk.

William had never been so far from home before, it was all strange and new. He wondered if he could muster sufficient courage to face the inquisitive eyes that watched his every move.

A group of men laughing and joking came towards him, one swinging along his overalls' jumper thrown across his arm, his dark brown face streaming with perspiration that stood out like glistening drops on shiny satin, looked at him inquiringly for a moment before he asked.

"Lookin' for somebody, stranger?"

William took in his short stocky form and friendly eyes. He felt at ease. There was something likeable about him that warmed his heart as he showed him the letter Daddy Jenks had given him and explained it had been given him by the man's brother to whom it was addressed.

"Yes, Ah knows Charlie Jenkins. We all does. He ust'uh work heah awrite but he done left heah six months now," the stranger informed him, handing the letter back.

"Well, all I wants is work. Maybe you can tell me if I can get a job here," William explained disappointed at not finding Daddy's brother working at the mill.

"My name's Ben Jackson, stranger, dat is, it wuz, but de boys heah calls me B.B.," the stocky stranger informed, extending his hand.

William knew he was going to like him as he took his hand and felt the hearty welcome he wanted to convey.

"My name's William Carter," he responded warmly.

"Well, it won't be long. Dey gives everybody

round heah a nickname. Ah guess de boys'll jes' bout call you yaller," B.B. laughed. "Dese other boys heah," he indicated, taking in the group, "is Spider, Full Breaches, Tin Pan, Long John an' dis little fellow heah is Big Boy," he laughed pointing to two hundred pounds of bronzed bulk.

"I'm glad to know you all," William acknowledged cordially, looking around the group. There was not the same open friendship in their eyes that B.B.'s held and William sensed he would have no easy time making these men like him.

"Now 'bout work," B.B. continued, walking towards his shanty, William falling in step beside him. "Ah guess yuh kin git uh job round heah, as we is short uh hands right now. Most uh de boys done gone down in South Florida to work at uh new saw mill down dere in Nocotee caize de wages is bettuh den dey is heah."

"Yeah," Full Breaches put in. "De wages is bettuh an' de crackers is bigger an' bad'er," the men laughed and William joined in heartily.

"We'll see 'bout yuh gittin' on in de mornin' an' yuh kin bunk wid me ef'fen yuh wants to, yaller boy. Ah ain't married so we all kin batch together," B.B. offered.

"Thanks, I'll be glad to," William replied.

Later that evening he met Aunt Silby who cooked for B.B. and the rest of the unmarried men.

"Ah see Ah got'uh take care uh dat cough you got," she commented, as she bustled around getting the supper of collard green fat pork and corn pone on the table.

William felt at home with B.B. and the kindly old woman, and spent his first night at the mill happily dreaming of the good he could do among these people, who while they were not educated nor learned in the ways of the outside world, were honest and happy to do their job well. He wondered whether he could find the same contentment they had found, and tried to feel that he was one of them. It would be hard to curb the old feeling of superiority he had always had but he was determined to try.

Wednesday morning B.B. took him to see the "Big Boss" as Lemuel Johnson was called by his negro mill hands. He was a big man standing almost six feet tall, his ruddy face topped by a mass of red bushy hair and loud voice made him a forceful figure, but he was known throughout the state for his fair treatment of employees. His keen blue eyes seemed to look right through William, as he remarked:

"Well, you don't look like you'll make much of a millhand Carter, but I'm short so I'll give you a try."

It was settled and he was put to work piling lumber. It was hard work under blazing sun that burned through his rough work shirt into his tender skin, often there followed drenching rains that soon passed leaving him wet and sticky. But William sang with the other men and tried to forget his misery.

> "Ah got'uh gal, huh man,
> Ah loves my gal, huh man,
> Ah piles dis rail, huh man
> Throws it high, huh man
> Cause Ah loves my gal, huh man
> Till de day Ah die, huh man."

And on and on they worked and laughed and sang fitting their song to their daily task. At the end of the first week William's hands were raw and bleeding, but Monday he was at his post with thick bandages covering his wounds. At night Aunt Silby treated them, bathing them in strong salt and water and spreading goose grease on his bandages. Most of his fellow workers disliked him. He was different, they felt it. He was too fair and too well educated and was therefore compelled to think he was better. He sensed their feeling towards him, and tried to be friendly, but he realized they would not let him be a part of them. Only B.B. was different. A friendship grew between them that was sincere and lasting, but even B.B. knew nothing of his past. He told no one where he was from nor who his family was. B.B. did not ask and William volunteered no information. He spent most of his time reading an old worn bible he had found in their shanty.

During the long hot nights he prayed for strength to resist the many temptations that surrounded him in the rough and tumble mill life, where every night card and dice games were played in one of the shanties.

On pay days the games lasted until early Monday morning. On these days women flocked to the mill to reap a reward of the dollars offered by the men for their charms.

William held himself aloof from these women but it was no easy job. He was good looking and his very indifference made him more desirable.

One of the most persistent reproached him one Saturday about his apparent coolness.

"Say yaller boy, how come you allers tries to get away to yo'seff when Ah comes round? Ah could sure go for you," she coaxed.

"Don't mind me. I'm just not interested," William replied.

"Well, it ain't no sense uh you workin' yo'seff to death in de mill. You jes' don't fit round heah. Ah could be mighty nice to yuh ef'fen yuh'd come to Jacksonville an' let me," she offered.

William smilingly refused, but a few nights later he kept a rendezvous with her in the depths of the dark pine woods. He emerged feeling ashamed and disgusted. Later that night when B.B. came to the shanty from a game he found William standing knee deep in a big wooden tub of hot water scrubbing himself as if he wanted to tear the skin from his body.

"Gee, Yaller, you sho is hankerin' for bein' clean, washin' dis time uh night," he laughed.

William said nothing. He was sick at heart. After all his promises he had found himself weak and still a prey to the lust that had come near ruining his life before.

* * *

June passed, and July with its hot long days dragged slowly but came to an end eventually. During the Spring and Summer he had written his mother regularly. He had received no letter from Ruth, but his mother had taken pains to mention her in every letter he received. She was still working for the Carmicheils in Valdosta. Of Jim his mother said little but she was careful to tell him

how glad Owen Gordon was that he was trying to
earn his money for his schooling. He often won-
dered why his mother had always been so desirous
of his knowing Owen Gordon's interest in his wel-
fare and related to him every opinion he offered.

As August came in, William felt the long hot
days harder to endure. He had saved most of his
money each week and had long since sent Daddy
Jenks the money he had lent him. He was glad
the men around the mill seemed to have learned to
like him better and had stopped teasing him as he
sat reading while they played cards or dice nearby.

The woman who had lured him into the woods
had not returned to the mill the following pay day,
and when he heard that she had gotten into trouble
and was working out a sentence on the prison farm,
he could not help feeling relieved, and thanked God
fervently he had been saved from another affair
such as he had had with Ethel.

He became more reticent than ever and spent
more time reading the bible.

"Say whut yuh say fellows we make Yaller heah
de preacher uh dis outfit?" Full Breaches suggested
one night, as they played cards.

"Dat's uh good idea, den when de old Reverend
Coleman don't show up, we kin have church any-
how," B.B. agreed good-naturedly.

From then on everybody around the mill called
William, "Preacher" and on the Sundays the old
minister did not show up, he carried on the Sunday
school for the children and read and discussed the
scripture later for the mothers and fathers. He
would not let them call it preaching, but they con-
sidered it better sermons than the Reverend Cole-

man had ever preached, and William was happy—
his only worry was the dry hacking cough that had
held on through the Spring and Summer.

September with its long rainy days had almost
gone when Lemuel Johnson called William, who
was piling lumber in long even stacks under the shed
at the back of the mill.

"Say you yaller nig . . . " he started when Wil-
liam interrupted with: "I heard you the first time,
boss," turning his head to hide the angry flush that
mounted to his forehead.

"Well, I was gonna say I wants you to run this
wench machine here. Mister Casper who's been
running it, won't be round any more. I've been
noticing you, you ain't any too strong and maybe
you can handle this machine better'n you can them
logs. Nothing to do but sit and pull handles. B.B.
will show you how, course it's a white man's job,
but I guess you'll do for a spell," he finished, walk-
ing away. He had seen the flush of anger on Wil-
liam's face but somehow he liked him, and what he
had heard of his sober habits, made him like him
better.

The new job was easier and paid fifty cents more
a day and William was pleased. He had been work-
ing at the mill four months and except for one occa-
sion when he had gone to the city to buy new clothes,
he had kept his promise to give up gambling. On
that trip he had yielded to the temptation of trying
his luck in a skin game in one of the places he and
B.B. had visited, and after an hour's play, had
found himself relieved of almost a month's pay. It
had taught him a lesson he thought he had learned
back in Macon and strengthened his determination

to prove himself strong enough to resist his old weaknesses. And had done no more back-sliding.

He felt as he started on his new job, he was being rewarded for his fight against the passions that had ruled his life. Sitting all day on the wench gave him plenty of time to think and plan his future.

October ushered in more damp rainy days. His cough worried him more than usual. Even Aunt Silby's strong portions of red onion juice boiled down in syrup and lemon juice did not relieve him. He was weary when his day's work was over, and night after night he threw himself upon his bunk with a promise to write his mother the next day only to awake mornings after a restless night filled with dreams of home and Ruth, more exhausted than ever.

October was almost gone and he had not written the promised letters nor had his cough improved. He felt miserable and were he not so determined to save a certain sum of money, he would have given up his job and gone home.

It was Saturday and the last day of the month. All night William had lain awake listening to the rain that pelted down upon the shingled roof of the shanty.

The mill hands arose at four o'clock and at five-thirty the machinery started moving for the day's work.

William walked slowly towards the mill. The rain-soaked ground felt damp and cold beneath his feet in spite of the heavy shoes he wore. Clouds hung low and grey obscuring the rosy pink of the new day. Large rain drops clung to the surrounding bushes on either side of the narrow twisting path that lead to the mill. He had just seated himself on the wench and reached for the switch to start the great drum moving to and fro when Full Breaches rushed towards him, his eyes bulging with fright, his breath coming in quick little gasps.

"Wait uh minute, Preacher," he paused to catch his breath and continued, "don't yuh start dat thing dis morning caise dere is gointer be hell to pay ef'fen yuh does."

"What you talkin' 'bout, Breaches?" William asked.

"Jes' dis, dat white man, Casper Bennett, whut ust'uh run dis wench done comed back heah an' he's running mad caize Mister Johnson won't give 'im his job back an' Ah done hearn him tell de boss ef'fen he don't run dis wench, dere ain't no damn nigguh gonna run it, an' he's headed dis'uh way."

"Dat sounds serious tuh me, Preacher," B.B. added, his eyes filled with apprehension.

"I see Mister Johnson's car headed this way. Maybe he'll catch up with him 'fore he gets here," William exclaimed, pointing to the car in the distance and trying to assume a composure he did not possess.

"Boy yuh better git, Ah'm thinkin'," B.B. warned, trying to pull William to his feet.

Hot rebellion rose in William's heart. He had done nothing to have to run away for. The job had been given him openly and he had performed it well. He would allow no one but the owner of the mill to dismiss him. His old stubborn determination rose within him. He would show Casper the mere mention of a white man's name could not frighten him. With a quick jerk he freed his arm from B.B.'s grasp, and started his machine. The long arm of the wench started moving and almost instantaneous with the first throb of the machinery two shots rang out in quick succession. A sharp burning sting ran through William's left side as a bullet struck him somewhere below his shoulder blade. His body slumped to the floor of the machine and lay still, the bullet had pierced his left lung and rendered him unconscious.

Lemuel Johnson sprang quickly from his automobile. He had drove up in time to see the whole affair but not in time to avoid what had happened. Running up the steps he was at William's side and calling to the men, who had run for cover when the shots were fired, to help him lift the wounded man and carry him to his car.

"You get in the back of the car and hold him, B.B.," he ordered as they carried William's limp body to his car. B.B. got in first and the men helped to place William so that his body rested across his knees with his feet and legs on the folded small seats in front of them.

"You men get back to work," Johnson ordered to the negro workers who stood around undecided what to do.

"And Richards," he called to the white time-keeper standing near. "If there's any more trouble, you get in touch with the sheriff, have him send a posse. Better call him up anyway and tell him what's happened."

"Does you think it's safe for these men to go back to work?" Richards inquired doubtfully.

"Sure, that skunk won't start no more trouble.

I got to get this boy to the hospital. It ain't but fifteen miles and I can get him there before a doctor could get out here," he replied as the car shot down the road towards Jacksonville gathering speed at every turn of the wheel in its race with death.

CHAPTER XXV

While in Byron, Sara Lou, a little more bent and feeling many years older, stumbled along the dusty clay road daily to the village post office to inquire for mail. Every day the answer from the kindly postmaster was the same:

"Nothing yet, Aunt Sara. Soon as something comes in, I'll send it out to you."

"Thank yuh, Mr. Carmicheil," she'd smile feebly and trudged back home again slowly, her heart almost breaking with disappointment.

And long past midnight Jim would hear her praying softly:

> My Lawd an' strong God.
> Ah done bowed heah humbly at yo' feet.
> Make me yo' footstool Ah pray Thee,
> Look down in pity on my humble plea,
> Kaise Ah ain't got no other name to call
>   on but yuh, an' yuh alone.
> Ah bows heah to humbly ask yuh to send
>   my boy back to my arms
> And to de cradle uh his birth.
> If it is Thy holy will.
> Snatch him as a bran from eternal burnin'.
> And keep him from all danger,
> Seen an' unseen.
> And send him back to me 'fore my heart is
>   stilled by de hands uh death,
> And my voice is hushed to pray no more.

On and on her soft pleading voice would break the stillness of the night. Pain would clutch Jim's heart and he would join in silently with his mother's prayer for William's return.

During the Spring William's letters had come regularly and Sara Lou had been happy and proud of his independence in wanting to earn the money for his college course.

Planting and helping Jim get the place running smoothly had taken much of her time. Ruth spent the entire summer working in Valdosta and she had all of the housework to do as well as work in the field and over at the Gordon house. There had not been even time for her usual care of the neighboring sick or the church aid but they had been happy months.

Jim had fallen into his usual steady plodding from before sunrise to late at night. Owen Gordon's orchard and the garden that he insisted on planting, had taken a great deal of his time but he had gotten them all in shape and kept them going nicely.

July had passed. The cotton had claimed much of his attention, but he had kept busy trying to forget the terrible experience through which he had passed during his eighteen months in the chain gang, awaking some mornings afraid that he would find himself chained to his bunk. He had become more reticent than ever—thinking much and speaking only when he was compelled to.

August with it's hot blistering days and swarms of flies and mosquitoes brought a new interest to the Settlement. The much-talked-of Swamp Angel was to hold the big mid-summer revival meeting at their own Calvary. Saint and sinner from far and near would attend, and sing and pray to their heart's content.

The meeting, the first to be held in Byron in several years, opened on the second Sunday in August. The church grounds were strewn with long tables covered with snowy white cloths. Everything eatable from home-cooked corn bread to roast hog meat could be bought. Women in their clean gingham aprons with snowy head rags tied over their neatly wrapped hair on which sometimes perched a straw hat, sat stiff and attentive; men dressed in their Sunday best beside them. Preaching and praying was carried on continuously. The best moaners of the community grouped themselves to give concerted help to the preacher.

Outside around the tables the women committees from the different churches called their ware and tried to outdo each other in their sales.

"Rite dis'uh way for yo' hot fried fish," or "Roast polk meat over heah!" and "Git yo' hot peanuts an' roast tatters over heah!" could be heard even above the din of praying, shouting people in the church.

A little distance away in the surrounding woods boys and young men hid among the tall saplings to shoot dice or to play cards, cooling their throats occasionally with the moonshine smuggled there to cheer the sin-sick souls.

The Swamp Angel, resorting to his aisle walking with the worn old bible on his shoulder, brought many sinners to the mourners' bench but through it all Jim sat erect, tears streaming down his cheeks until candidates for baptism were asked to come to the altar. Then he arose and walked slowly down the aisle. Sara Lou ran forward and caught him in her arms but he gently disentangled himself and started telling the congregation how his soul had been saved while in prison. On and on he talked between the tears, walking up and down the aisle in his fervor. Men and women on all sides amened and shouted, as for almost an hour, the usual silent Jim swayed the congregation.

Sara Lou's cup of happiness was filled. She shouted all the way home and neighbors rejoiced with her until the little village became fired with their religious zeal.

The following Sunday she walked beside him as he was going to the River to be baptized. Somehow her thoughts kept going back to the Sunday when William had walked thus to the river. He had looked so tall and handsome and different from the others. Her heart ached for the sight of him, the touch of his hand, but she consoled herself with the thought of him some day walking at the head of his own converts, maybe a larger crowd than this.

Through the months that followed William's letters became shorter and less regular but they continued to cheer and encourage her. Then came October when they ceased entirely. She lived on each day with the hope that the next day would bring the letter she longed for. But day after day brought disappointment. Her shoulders began to sag, grief and despair showed in her eyes.

Owen Gordon stopping by to leave some orders with Jim, one day, saw the many lines that furrowed her face, the purple shadows around her eyes and with pity guessed the cause.

"When you hear from William, find out how

much that school you're so set on him attending is going to cost, Sara. I guess I can let you have the money," he said kindly, as he was leaving.

"Dat'll be fine, Mr. Gordon. Ah sho thanks yuh an' Ah'll be rite glad to tell him," she replied gratefully.

But no letter came from William. Laggingly she helped with the cotton and trudged to the post office without results.

Ruth, who now worked for and lived with Mrs. Carmicheil, who had come back to her home in Byron, visited her often but could not get up sufficient courage to talk to her about William, her heart was broken because Jim continued to avoid her. She longed to talk it over with him, and beg him to forgive her for seeming to accept William's love.

One day, as she walked out to the hickory nut tree under which the strands of their hair were buried, she saw him hurrying away. She called him and when he did not answer, ran and overtook him.

"Listen Jim," she began anxiously, "Ah been tryin' to git uh chance to talk to you but you jes' keeps out 'uh my way. Why do you do dat?"

"Jes' kaise yuh done promised to marry William," he answered, walking on.

"Ah ain't never goin'ter marry William. Ah loves you Jim 'fo' God Ah does," she pleaded.

"Yeah, maybe yuh thinks dat now dat William ain't heah but Ah ain't so sho," he quickened his steps.

"Ah ain't never loved William, Jim," Ruth almost sobbed.

"How come yuh promised to marry him den?"
Jim asked.

"Ah ain't never promised to marry him. He jes'
talked me into sayin' Ah guess Ah would. Please,
Jim, don't think Ah ever loved William kaise Ah
ain't. Dere was times Ah b'lieved Ah hated him
but he jes' kept pesterin' me and you had wrote me
we wasn't engaged no more."

Jim walked a few paces ahead in silence as Ruth,
trying to keep up with him, pleaded.

"Less us make up Jim an' marry."

"Not till William comes back and tells me wid his
own mouth you an' him is broke up," Jim answered
firmly.

And Ruth realized it would do no good to argue
with him further. Jim had always been stubborn
and set in his ways.

With the cotton all picked and ready to be ginned
and sold, Jim had more time to himself and spent
most of it in a manner Sara Lou had never known
him to before. Several times she walked up on him
hidden behind the barn, his bible across his knee,
studying it laboriously.

"Whut's yuh doin' readin' de bible so much uh
late, son?" she smiled.

"Oh nothin' Ma. Ah jes' lookin' up de sermon
de Rev. preached lass Sunday," closing the book.

"You ain't thinkin' on bein' uh preacher, is yuh,
Jim?" she asked seriously.

"Maybe Ma. Rite now since dey done made me
uh deacon, Ah might be called on to say somethin'
some time an' Ah laks to be sho uh whut Ah says,"
he answered.

Sara Lou smiled happily. Jim's conversion had

for years been her daily prayer. If William was only home or if he would only write and say he was all right, she would be very happy. But as October drew to a close and November passed slowly, her sorrow became almost desperation. Ruth now seldom came to see them. Mrs. Carmicheil was kind and had given her a nice room but there was lots of work which kept her busy.

Sara Lou, her tall form becoming more bent each day, found a strange consolation in her daily visits to the post office, although she received no mail. Neighbors gossiped and tried to guess what had happened to William but Sara Lou always on the alert to shield him, would explain:

"Ah guess maybe my William done jes' gone to Atlanta and started in dat Atlanta Preaching school tryin' to 'sprise me wid de news when he's all straight an' everythin'."

Walking from her house they would discuss her excuse and shake their heads sadly over the deep silent sorrow that was eating at her vitals.

Long nights in December dragged on with just herself and Jim, who was always reading now. Sitting alone—waiting—always waiting to hear something from her beloved William.

The approaching holiday season held no joy for her but she prayed unceasingly that they would bring her boy home, and lived on her faith.

* * *

Monday morning, Christmas eve dawned bright and clear with a crispy chill in the air that sent one's blood coursing delightfully through his veins. A holiday spirit filled the otherwise dull village of Byron with excitement. Early shoppers idled around the general store discussing the topics that interested them most. In the tree lined streets children shouting with happiness ran beside their parents, who dragged large green Christmas trees from the surrounding woods.

At the little wooden railroad station the usual loafers lounged around, their jaws protruding with huge wads of tobacco. Long streams of brown spit spattered the tracks, as they diligently whittled slender wooden sticks and waited from force of habit, the incoming train. It's three short blasts were soon followed by a grinding stop. A single passenger alighted.

No one recognized in the pale, stooped emaciated man, as he walked slowly down the three wooden steps to the street, the straight handsome William Carter they had all known.

Early in December Daddy Jenks' brother had returned to the saw mill and been told about the stranger who had inquired for him, saying he had brought a letter from his brother. He had written at once to Daddy Jenks, telling him about William having been shot, and although he had recovered from the serious bullet wound, he was still in a Jacksonville hospital seriously ill with tuberculosis, and no one knew who his people were nor from where he had come.

Daddy Jenks had lost no time getting to Jacksonville, and William had awakened from an afternoon nap one day to find him and Ethel standing at his bedside. He had felt happy and relieved when Daddy explained Ethel's presence with: "Ethel's

my wife now, Carter.   Ah couldn't git rid uh de-
pest so Ah ups an' marries her."

Daddy had scolded him for not letting him know
he was sick but William like most tubercular
patients, had not considered his condition serious
and expected to be able to go home any day soon.

It had taken several weeks for him to get sufficient
strength to make the trip, but Daddy and Ethel
waited and brought him to Macon with them.   But
he had insisted on making the journey to Byron
alone and Daddy had reluctantly let him have his
way.

During the seventeen miles' ride, he sat motion-
less staring unseeingly at the fast moving scenery
from the window.   The months he had spent at the
mill, the weeks he had suffered in the hospital not
wanting to let his mother know because of the
anguish the knowledge of his illness and accident
would cause, the long, restless nights filled with
thoughts of Ruth whom he realized he could never
possess—passed through his mind in retrospect.

Stumbling feebly through the short streets of the
village, visions of his home with its green, cool, fer-
tile fields stretched inviting arms to him.   He would
be well and strong here in no time, he told himself
over and over.

An automobile came swiftly towards him.   He
raised his head as it came abreast.   Owen Gordon
at the steering wheel saw him and stopped the car
beside him, saying quietly: "Get in, William, I'll
take you to Sara."

Jim, mending a broken place in the front porch,
lay down his hammer and came quickly to the side
of the car when it stopped at the gate.   Owen Gor-

don assisted him in getting William into the house, leaving as soon as he finished getting a bed ready for him in the parlor downstairs, with an abrupt:

"I'll send Doctor Clarke right out, Jim."

Alone again in his car, his hand hastily brushed a moisture very much like a tear, from the corner of his eyes.

Sara Lou, who had been hastily summoned to the bedside of Aunt Salisbury whom old age was removing from her world of roots and herbs, had been mercifully spared the anguish of seeing William brought home dying with tuberculosis and took it better than anyone imagined she would when she came home and found him there.

Even Doctor Clarke, who told her in the kindest possible way that William would hardly live to see the New Year, was surprised that she did not break down entirely. But after her first uncontrollable burst of grief, her real characteristic ability of self control exerted itself as she, seated in her favorite rocker in the dining-room, swayed back and forth, moaning pitifully.

"Ah done ask God to send him home to me an' he did. Ah ain't tell him how. Ah jes' sayd please send him home. Ah al'lers loved him with all my heart. Maybe too much kaise God is uh jealous God an' ain't wanted me to worship no other God but him. Maybe dat's why he takin' him from me kaise Ah worshipped him. Oh Lawd, have mercy on my pore boy. Save his soul if yuh kaint save his body, Lawd?"

Prayers and tears mingled in a steady stream all day while the minister and church aid members grouped around trying to console the grief-stricken woman. Sissy for the first time since she ran away some years earlier, came from Macon to help and comfort her in her great sorrow. Ruth forgot the wall of misunderstanding that had grown between herself and Jim, and came as soon as she heard of William's illness, to help care for him. Neighbors overflowed the house, anxious to do what they could for the grief-stricken family to whom Christmas day seemed a hollow mockery.

Day by day William grew weaker, sometimes drifting into semi-consciousness, his eyes closed, his sunken features rigidly still between spells of spasmodic coughing that racked his frame. At other times he lay, his large, black eyes roving restlessly around the room.

Sara Lou stole noiselessly into the room from time to time and seated on the side of his bed, ran her fingers through his damp curly hair mumbling words of endearment into his ears, as her hot tears watered his face. William, aroused, would pat her hand affectionately, a twisted smile flitting over his waxen face.

Ruth and Jim would finally coax her away and lead her back to the dining-room, where she again took up her rocking back and forth, mumbling prayers to herself.

Saturday morning Doctor Clarke came again and told Jim what he had already seen since the first faint rays of sunshine had penetrated the room. William was dying. Gently he bathed his forehead and wiped the moisture from his lips. Ruth seated on the opposite side of the bed, watched him tenderly care for the brother, who had hated him and so cruelly wronged him. In her heart a strange calm pervaded. William had said little to anyone during the days he lay so near death. She wondered whether he had made his peace with God, and fervently prayed he had.

The day dragged slowly on. Midnight, dark and still, broken only by the howls of Jim's old dog Towser, enveloped them. William lay quiet and unseeing until a few hours before dawn when he opened his eyes and let them rest on his brother, Jim.

"I'm leaving you Jim for good," he whispered weakly.

"Yeah, William, is dere anythin' yuh want?" Jim asked, trying to hide the catch in his voice.

"I wants to tell Ma about me causing you to go to prison."

"Ah kaint let yuh, William. She don't know nothin' 'bout dat uh none uh de things youse done. De faith she's allers had in you is been her very life. Don't take it from her now when she ain't got nothin' to live for," Jim pleaded.

"All right, Jim. I guess you're right as you've always been," William acknowledged and after a moment's rest, said:

"Call Ruth over here. I want to ask her forgiveness and yours for the many things I've caused you to suffer."

Ruth, who was standing at the window, came to the side of the bed. William reached for her hand, lightly it rested in his. His voice a thin whisper, broke in places, as he spoke.

"I want to ask you and Jim to for-give me, Ruth, for all the trouble I've caused you. I lied to Jim and caused him to break you'alls engagement but I loved you, Ruth, I still loves you. It's been the only real thing in my life. But Jim loves you too and you love him. I know it now and I want him to know it too. You two must marry and be happy, after I'm gone. Promise me you will."

He closed his eyes, exhausted. A coughing spell racked his frame. Jim hastily raised him in his arms and placed a glass of water to his lips. Ruth looked at Jim timidly, as he rose to place the glass on the stand.

"Ah'll marry you, Jim if you still wants me," she whispered.

" 'Course Ah wants you, Ruth," he replied looking into her eyes, his heart beating suffocatingly.

William's eyes were again open. He smiled up at them. A single word fell from his lips.

"Brother."—His eyes closed again. He lay still. Jim looking down on him, wondered, why he should love him so much after all the wrongs he had heaped upon him. His heart seemed ready to burst with sorrow because he knew his brother would soon leave them forever.

Their mother came softly into the room and kneeling beside the bed, buried her face in the covers at his side. Tenderly Jim knelt beside her and assured her that William had not left them but was just resting quietly.

Outside the early dawn cast fitful shadows through the leafy boughs of the trees that grew near the house. Jim placed his arm around Ruth's waist, and led her over to the window to watch the sunrise painting the skies a rosy pink beyond the

Eastern horizon. Faint shafts of light like long pink fingers reached far into the room.

From the dining-room came the voices of the church aid sisters singing softly.

> "Ah'm gonna lay down my burden
> Down by de ribber side,
> Down by de ribber side."

Jim spoke to Ruth softly. "Ah feels lak de words uh dat song Ah'm layin' down my burden."

"To find happiness an' study war no more," Ruth added.

"Yes, you an' me honey and Ma," he ·held her close to him.

"Yes, Jim, we three."

Sara Lou kneeling beside William's bed, heard him whisper "Ma" and placed her ear to his lips to hear what he was saying.

"Take me in your arms," his words trailed off.

Protectingly she placed her arms around him and drew him to her breast.

"I-want-them-to-sing-in-here-for-me," came haltingly from his lips, as he smiled up into her face.

Ruth, turning from the window, pointed to the bed.

"Look Jim!" she whispered, "his eyes is open. He's smilin' and uh ray of sunlight is shining right aroun' his head. Ain't it purtty? Less go over dere wid An' Sara."

"William wants de church aid sisters to sing in heah for him," Sara Lou said, looking up at them.

Jim called them from the door. They entered the room singing softly through their tears.

"Ah'm gonna lay down my burden,
Down by de ribber side
Down by de ribber side
Down by de ribber side . . . "

William's eyes closed slowly. His hand rested upon his mother's bowed head. She gathered him closer into her arms. His smiling lips became still and set, his body stiffened. Ruth and Jim kneeling on the other side of the bed, hid their faces in the covers.

Sara Lou leaned down and kissed his pallid lips and straightened his body upon the narrow bed. Then burying her face on his breast, sobbed wildly.

Bravely the women sang on to the end of their song.

"Ah ain't gonna study war no more."

(THE END)

ABOUT THE EDITORS

Henry Louis Gates, Jr., is the W. E. B. Du Bois Professor of the Humanities, Chair of the Afro-American Studies Department, and Director of the W. E. B. Du Bois Institute for Afro-American Research at Harvard University. One of the leading scholars of African-American literature and culture, he is the author of *Words, Signs, and the Racial Self* (1987), *The Signifying Monkey: A Theory of Afro-American Literary Criticism* (1988), *Loose Canons: Notes on the Culture Wars* (1992), and the memoir *Colored People* (1994).

Jennifer Burton is in the Ph.D. program in English Language and Literature at Harvard University. She is the volume editor of *The Prize Plays and Other One-Acts* in this series. She is a contributor to *The Oxford Companion to African-American Literature* and *Great Lives from History: American Women*. With her mother and sister she coauthored two one-act plays, *Rita's Haircut* and *Litany of the Clothes*. Her fiction and personal essays have appeared in *Sun Dog, There and Back*, and *Buffalo*, the Sunday magazine of the *Buffalo News*.

Susanne B. Dietzel received her Ph.D. in American Studies in 1996 from the University of Minnesota, where she taught courses in American studies, women's studies, and composition. She has contributed to the forthcoming *Oxford Companion to African-American Literature* and to *The Complete Poems of Ellen Frances Watkins Harper*, edited by Maryemma Graham (1988).